# LIBRARY OF HEBREW BIBLE/
# OLD TESTAMENT STUDIES

# 425

*Formerly Journal for the Study of the Old Testament Supplement Series*

# CAN A CUSHITE CHANGE HIS SKIN?

An Examination of Race, Ethnicity,
and Othering in the Hebrew Bible

Rodney Steven Sadler Jr

t&t clark

NEW YORK • LONDON

T & T Clark International, Madison Square Park, 15 East 26th Street, New York, NY 10010

T & T Clark International, The Tower Building, 11 York Road, London SE1 7NX

T & T Clark International is a Continuum imprint.

**Library of Congress Cataloging-in-Publication Data**
Sadler, Rodney Steven, 1967–
    Can a Cushite Change His Skin? An Examination of Race, Ethnicity, and Othering in the Hebrew Bible / Rodney Steven Sadler, Jr
        p. cm. -- (Journal for the study of the Old Testament. Supplement Series, 425)
    Includes bibliographical references (p.      ) and index.
    ISBN 0-567-02960-3 (hardcover) — ISBN 0-567-02970-0 (pbk.)
        1. Cushites. 2. Blacks in the Bible. 3. Bible. O.T.—Criticism, interpretation,
        4. Race (criticism), etc. I. Title. II. Series.
    DT367.45.C86S23 2005
    221.8'3058965—dc22

Printed in the United States of America

ISBN 0-506-0708091-0      10 9 8 7 6 5 4 3 2 1

*I dedicate this book to my grandmothers, Pearl, Bobbie, and Dora, who love me unconditionally and pray for me daily; to my dads, Rodney and Stuart who gave me a strong sense of history; to my moms, Audrey and Anne who nurtured in me a love of learning; to my many aunts and uncles who expect only the best from me. They have given me a fine heritage and have been wonderful examples of faith, commitment, and achievement. Their love has sustained me, their support has encouraged me, and their prayers have kept me.*

*I also dedicate this book to my grandfathers, true gentlemen who exemplified spiritual commitment, dignity, and the pursuit of perfection. Though at home in more glorious estates, I know that they are rejoicing with me.*

# CONTENTS

ACKNOWLEDGMENTS

There are many to whom I am grateful for their support and encouragement.

I must first thank God without whom this research would have been impossible. I hope that it lays to rest the idea that racialist thought originates in the words that bear God's imprimatur. I also so wish to express my gratitude:

To the Sadler-Hollis-Powell-Graham-Kelch-Ryan-Mason-McClenney-Wood family, my family, whose constant support and encouragement have made me dream big dreams and have the faith that I could achieve them.

To my inspirational teachers Robert Didden, Mrs. Powell, Rose Ravitz, Tom Smith, Wade Boykin, Jules Harrell, Gene Rice, Kelly Brown Douglas, Alice Bellis, Michael Newheart, Cheryl Sanders, and Elias Farajaje-Jones.

To my mentors in ministry who have set high standards; Paul Sadler, Lawrence Jones, Cain Felder, Walter Fauntroy, James Wilson, Clarence Newsome, and Randall Bailey.

To my graduate advisor at Duke University, Eric M. Meyers, who has been a source of constant support and an excellent example of a dedicated researcher who has a passion for teaching. Also to my doctoral committee; Orval Wintermute, Carol Meyers, and Anne Allison for their guidance, support, and instructive criticism; and other faculty members including Willie Jennings, William Turner, and Melvin Peters for many acts of kindness.

To Gay Trotter for providing direction with a pleasant smile.

To Joanne Jennings and the many prayer-warriors who kept me lifted up.

To my colleagues at Union-PSCE at Charlotte who have made this publication possible and have helped me at every stage along the way; to Tom Currie, the most supportive and pastoral dean (and friend) for whom any professor could hope to work; to Louis Weeks, my president, a source of endless encouragement who has made my research a priority; to Susan Hickok who has worked tirelessly to find support for our school and Terry Johns who allotted no small amount for my research; to Susan Griner and Dorcas Leonhardt who administrative gifts have been a needed blessing; to Richard Boyce who worked twice as hard so I could write; to David Mayo who finds the books I need; to Pamela Mitchell-Legg who sets the bar high; to Jan Parler, Jill Duffield, Sue Setzer, and Bill White for their constant encouragement.

To David T. Adamo, Marta Hoyland-Lavik, and Knut Holter who share a love for the Cushites and who each have encouraged me with this project.

To David McCarthy, my friend and instructor in all things Presbyterian who translated key French texts at the 11th hour.

To Henry Carrigan, my editor, who partnered with me to publish my research; and to Duncan Burns, my copy-editor, who tirelessly and gently has labored to bring this book to fruition.

To Peggy Currie and Katie Cruz who lovingly guarded what is most precious to me while I worked.

To Ariyah McClenney Sadler my beloved daughter, the sweetest little girl in the world who gives meaning to all I do and always makes me smile.

Finally, to Madeline Gay McClenney-Sadler, PhD, my wife, partner, and friend with whom I have shared nearly every aspect my life for the past two decades. It is my greatest joy that our first books found a home in the same series!

# ABBREVIATIONS

| | |
|---|---|
| *ABD* | *The Anchor Bible Dictionary*. Edited by David N. Freedman. 6 vols. New York, 1992 |
| BDB | Francis Brown, S.R. Driver and Charles A. Briggs. *A Hebrew and English Lexicon of the Old Testament*. Oxford: Clarendon Press, 1907 |
| Dtr | Deuteronomistic Historian |
| *IB* | *The Interpreter's Bible*. Edited by G. A. Buttrick et al. 12 vols. New York, 1951–57 |
| *OEANE* | *The Oxford Encyclopedia of Archaeology in the Near East*. Edited by E. M. Meyers. New York, 1997 |
| *OTP* | *The Old Testament Pseudepigrapha*. Edited by James Charlesworth. 2 vols. New York, 1983 |

# Chapter 1

## RACE, ETHNICITY, OTHERING,
## AND THE FORMATION OF IDENTITY

### 1.1. *Establishing the Problem*

Who were the Cushites?[1] To what extent did the people of ancient Israel/Judah know them? On the surface, these appear to be rudimentary questions, which we could easily answer by reciting the longitude and latitude that defined Cush's national borders and rehearsing the customs and political relationships that defined its ethnic boundaries. Yet lurking beneath the surface lie a host of murkier issues often overlooked by contemporary scholars. Among these are: Why has the identity of the Cushites been the source of such controversy among modern exegetes?[2] Also, why has this group received less sustained attention than the other Others who have a history of political affiliations with Israel/Judah?

1.    The terms כּוּשׁ ("Cush") and כּוּשִׁי ("Cushi") are the principal foci of this study. The first term, כּוּשׁ, usually refers to the nation of Cush and the eponymous ancestor of that nation in the Hebrew Bible. Typically, I will translate this term "Cush." The term כּוּשִׁי is used in the Hebrew Bible both as a gentilic meaning "one from Cush" or as a personal name that became popular in Palestine during the mid-eighth century. When the term is used as a gentilic, I will translate it as the "Cushite" and when the term is used as a personal name, I will translate it "Cushi." We will, however, encounter instances where it will be difficult to discern with certainty whether the term כּוּשִׁי is intended as a gentilic or as a personal name (e.g. 2 Sam 18; Jer 36:14; Zeph 1:1).

2.    Modern exegetes seem to be uninformed about the identity of the people of Cush. Were the Cushites a despised and uncivilized people living on the fringes of the ancient world, or a wealthy and mighty nation known in Egyptian iconography that played a critical role in the unfolding Levantine history? Consider the words of Martin Noth who concluded that the Egyptians portrayed the Cushites in an "incorrect manner, with typical Negro faces…incorrectly classifying the Nubians as Negroes. The Nubians were at most very slightly related to the Negro tribes bordering them on the south" (Martin Noth, *The Old Testament World* [trans. Victor I. Gruhn; Philadelphia: Fortress, 1966], 236). We could also consider Gary V. Smith's opinion that the "reason for [Amos] choosing the sons of Cush [for comparison with Israel] is unclear; perhaps they were despised by some (Num 12:1), or maybe they were simply representatives of peoples far away who live in the God-forsaken fringes of the civilized world" (Gary V. Smith, *Amos: A Commentary* [Grand Rapids: Zondervan, 1989], 270). We should also consider James Luther Mays's comments that "the Cushites were a distant, different folk whom the Israelites knew mostly as slaves. 'You are to me,' says Yahweh, 'as these Cushites are to you.' What the comparison does is to humiliate Israel completely with respect to Yahweh, to reduce them to the role in Yahweh's order of things which the Cushites placed in their own society" (James Luther Mays, *Amos: A Commentary* [Philadelphia: Westminster, 1969], 157). As we will see in the course of this study, these perspectives are representative of the misconceptions that persist in the works of competent biblical scholars. I presume that such opinions are more likely the result of contemporary racialist biases than careful historical-critical analysis.

It is an altogether different issue, however, to ask who the Cushites were to the people of Israel/Judah? Contemporary scholars commonly perceive this group as "black" or "African."[3] Both of these terms imply a distinction from either a "white" or "European" norm. However, is this the way Cushites were perceived by the ancient authors of the Hebrew Bible? Were the people of Cush deemed essentially Other? Did the Judean biblical authors view distinctive Cushite phenotypical traits as indications of ontological distinctions between the Cushites and themselves? Was there a hierarchy of human types at play in these authors' minds? Were the Cushites othered by these ancient authors in any or all of the ways we think of as "racial" in our contemporary milieu, or were they viewed not unlike the other Others who found themselves in the pages of Hebrew literature?

In order to address these questions, we have to begin to understand what contemporary theorists have concluded about race. Though what modern theorists say about this topic would seem on the surface to be irrelevant to and anachronistic in a discussion about how Others are perceived by ancient Near Eastern authors, this modern discourse is important. As we seek to ascertain whether the Cushites were viewed by the Israelite/Judahites as an essentially distinct human type in a manner that approaches a racial category, the notions of racial and ethnic othering employed in this work need to be clearly distinguished and explained within the context of anthropological and sociological discourse. To this end, I will attempt to negotiate the murky waters that surround academic and popular notions of race and ethnicity to determine what experts would deem racial traits, elements indicative of racial thought. In subsequent chapters, I will endeavor to determine if these elements are present in passages that explicitly reference Cush in biblical literature. The results of this study regarding race will be two-fold: (1) it will ascertain whether racial categories that resemble modern ones were utilized in ancient Israel/Judah; and (2) it will ascertain if such notions of essential difference were used in the Bible—particularly as it regards the Cushites, a people who would be deemed "black" by modern standards.

Before I begin to determine what race is, there are a number of concerns to address. Again, when discussing the notions of race, ethnicity, and othering in this study, I use the terms as contemporary theorists have used them. Some readers might caution that modern understandings of race would be anachronistic inasmuch as this study focuses on ancient biblical texts. However, though it is likely these modern ways of subdividing the human species are relatively recent constructions, framed in post-enlightenment debates, we cannot, for instance, assume *a priori* that ancient authors were void of prejudices and ideology that resemble racial thought. Nor can we assume *a priori* that biblical authors did not resort to essentializing patterns of othering when describing Cushites, or that human hierarchies did not exist in the ancient Hebrew social milieu.

---

3.    Cf. J. Daniel Hays, "The Cushites: A Black Nation in the Bible," *Bibliotheca Sacra* 153 (Oct–Dec 1996): 396–409 (399); *idem*, "The Cushites: A Black Nation in Ancient History, *Bibliotheca Sacra* 153 (July–Sept 1996): 270–80. See also David T. Adamo, "The Place of Africa and Africans in the Old Testament and its Environment" (Ph.D. diss., Baylor University, 1986).

Also, inasmuch as this study is intended to be a contribution to the continuing dialogue about race, ethnicity, and othering, I need to use the terms in a manner that is consistent with the way other participants have used them. This will require an examination of the way these terms have been used in contemporary discourse. In this regard, readers will be able to discern what is intended by the use of these terms and the results of this study will be comprehensible to contemporary ethnographers and race theorists.

Another relevant issue concerns the application of ethnographic terms and theories intended to represent living societies to an ancient society known only by literary sources. This is further problematized by the fact that the biblical texts examined become the informants of this analysis, not actual Israelite/Judahites themselves. As a result, there is no way to ascertain that our assessment is valid by appealing to the objects of inquiry themselves. However, by employing historical-critical methods, by carefully exegeting the relevant biblical passages, and by examining pertinent extra-biblical texts and archaeological data, I hope to gain insight into the thinking of ancient Israelite/Judahite people.

A similar issue is whether the portrait we develop from texts written by biblical authors accurately represents the Israelite/Judean perceptions of Cushites. To this I offer two responses. First, the Hebrew Bible as an artifact provides the most comprehensive view of that ancient society. Although we cannot gain direct access to Judahites, we do have the testimony of numerous different authors writing over a period of several centuries to bear witness to their perspective of Cushites. Second, because the modern interest in Israel/Judah principally arises from the Bible and its continued influence on Western cultures, the biblical portrait of Judean thought is the most relevant portrayal for this particular study. Because of the nature of this study, to determine whether modes of distinguishing between and governing the treatment of differing human populations, which are similar to those used by contemporary people existed in ancient Israel/Judah, these terms are invaluable. Hence, in spite of the fact that there are problems associated with using modern ethnographic terms and theories in analyses of ancient societies, they are the best tools for a study such as this.

Race is a significant concern for anthropologists who continue to revise their views on the nature of the human species. As we will see below, there is a growing movement to eliminate the concept of "race" from the discourse on human difference. However, the term itself persists as a means of categorizing groups of humans.

Before we begin to explore race and ethnicity, a review of the noted psychologist Gordon Allport's theories on human group formation and alienation is needed to provide a context within which we can begin to understand human othering. In his *The Nature of Prejudice* (1979), Allport observes a universal learned tendency among human groups to develop overgeneralizations about Others in order to comprehend more simply the complexities of the world and human relations.[4] In his paradigm, Allport recognized a tendency among humans

---

4.   Gordon Allport, *The Nature of Prejudice* (Reading, Mass.: Addison-Wesley, 1979), 27.

to esteem the group to which they belong (in-group) above those of Other groups (out-group), who are deemed ethnically and socially different, and hence, not preferred.[5] The recognition of these differences leads to inter-group animosity and "group scorn" toward Othered out-groups.[6] According to Allport, this is a manifestation of "ethnic prejudice," which is defined as an

> antipathy based upon a faulty and inflexible generalization. It may be felt or expressed. It may be directed toward a group as a whole, or toward an individual because he is a member of that group.[7]

In order for a determination of ethnic prejudice, Allport concluded that the following elements must be present:
1. Definite hostility toward and rejection of the out-group.
2. Condemnation of the out-group based upon membership in another less-favored group, a "categorical rejection" for no other reason than the group membership.[8]

Ethnic prejudice is manifest in either or all of the five following ways:
1. Antilocution/talking about members of the disliked group;
2. Avoidance/refusal to engage in social intercourse with the othered group;
3. Discrimination/active negative treatment of othered group, that is, segregation, etc;
4. Physical attack/violent reaction to othered group members; or
5. Extermination/genocidal activity against othered group.[9]

Allport deemed ethnic prejudice a universal and pervasive phenomenon that was "a bona fide psychological problem."[10]

Allport's concept of ethnic prejudice as a psychological problem forms an adequate framework upon which to construct a dialogue about human othering in general, and in antiquity in the ancient Near East in particular. The human tendency to other is best described as both a universal and rational phenomena for differentiating between groups of people who share cultural traits and a legitimate psychological malady which leads people to isolate and alienate entire groups of people based upon perceived group differences. It is in the context of Allport's definition of ethnic prejudice and its constituent "faulty and inflexible generalizations" that the notion of "race" begins to take form.

### 1.1.1. *What Is Race?*
The concept of distinct races arises in part as the ultimate manifestation of human othering, for implicit in the notion of races are ontological differences between

---

5. Allport, *Nature of Prejudice*, 29–46.
6. Allport, *Nature of Prejudce*, 4.
7. Allport, *Nature of Prejudice*, 9.
8. Allport, *Nature of Prejudice*, 5.
9. Allport, *Nature of Prejudice*, 14–15.
10. Allport, *Nature of Prejudice*, 12.

types of human beings. These differences are inevitably associated with alienation, hostility, and condemnation of members of other races. The essence of "race" is on the surface clear. Based upon explicit differences in somatic type and phenotypical presentation, human beings can be subdivided into a relatively small number of discrete varieties. As the renowned physical anthropologist Ashley Montagu found:

> What "race" is everyone seems to know, and is only too eager to tell. All but a very few individuals take it completely for granted that scientists have established the "facts" about "race" and that they have long ago recognized and classified the "races" of mankind.[11]

In his influential *Man's Most Dangerous Myth* (1942), Montagu deconstructs the concept of race, deeming it a social construct undergirded by biased scholarship and political interests.[12] He illustrates the circular reasoning involved in scientific arguments for multiple races. He notes that authors who defend such views begin with the *a priori* assumption that racial categories and the essentialisms related to somatic type are both valid, then they subsequently tailor their research to support their suppositions.[13] On the genetic level Montagu concludes that what we call "race" is fundamentally the expression of

> [a] process of genetic change within a definite ecological area; that "race" is a dynamic, not a static, condition; and that it becomes static and classifiable only when a taxonomically minded anthropologist arbitrarily delimits the process of change at his own time level.[14]

Montagu's work marked a revolution in thought about race and significantly altered the use of the term by subsequent anthropologists.

### 1.1.2. *Definitions of Race*

Before I discuss the deconstruction of race in too much detail, we will first begin our study by reviewing several definitions of this term in order to set the context for our subsequent analysis. In this regard, I will not be exhaustive in my review but representative, seeking to present several key ideological positions. We will see immediately not only that the term "race" is defined differently, but also that scholars have emphasized various aspects of the concept. The notion of race that Montagu vigorously opposes was race as a "subdivision of a species, which inherits the physical characteristics serving to distinguish it from other populations of the species."[15]

Allport defines the notion of race in contrast to ethnicity, employing the traditional social-scientific categories of nature and nurture where race was a natural and ethnicity was a synthetic category. So, for Allport, race refers to "hereditary

---

11. Ashley Montagu, *Man's Most Dangerous Myth: The Fallacy of Race* (New York: Columbia University Press, 1945), 1.
12. Montagu, *Man's Most Dangerous Myth*, 154.
13. Montagu, *Man's Most Dangerous Myth*, 3–4.
14. Montagu, *Man's Most Dangerous Myth*, 40.
15. Montagu, *Man's Most Dangerous Myth*, 6.

ties" and inherent genetic behavioral "traits" that define human populations.[16] Whereas Montagu emphasizes phenotypical differences in his definition and opposed the linkage of heredity and behavior in his argument, Allport's definition assumes a relationship between heredity and behavior.

In a recent article in which he describes the lack of validity of racial categories based on genetic variation between human populations, Alan Templeton identifies a significant aspect of many definitions of the term: race is synonymous with subspecies. This goes beyond Montagu's definition, highlighting the perceived ontological distinctions inherent in racial othering. Templeton opposes the notion of "races" as "geographically circumscribed and genetically differentiated population[s]."[17] As such, he calls into question the traditional candelabra model of human development. That model, consistent with the traditional popular and "scientific" view of race, suggests that three sub-categories of humanity had an extended period of independent evolution. Upon analysis of human genetic data, he notes that genetic variance among human populations is remarkably low, implying genetic exchange among geographically circumscribed human populations has occurred throughout the evolution of our species. In its place he posits the trellis model of human development, indicating cross-population mating over the period of human existence as continual trans-geographic gene exchange is evidenced by modern genetic research.[18]

But race is not solely a matter of phenotypes, heredity, and genetics; race is also political. Thomas Gossett notes the political nature of the concept of race and the tendency of those who employ racial categories to do so for political reasons. According to Gossett, the concept often involves "the self-aggrandizement of one's own people and the denigration of others."[19] This subsequent hierarchy serves both ideological and practical ends. In his assessment of sociological definitions of race, anthropologist Marcus Banks notes that:

> dissimilar groups are in some sort of long-term unequal power and/or economic relationship where the dominant group justifies its position through some kind of legitimating ideology.[20]

Prominent public intellectual and Harvard literary critic Henry Gates considers race to be:

> a dangerous trope ... a trope of ultimate, irreducible difference between cultures, linguistic groups, or adherents of specific belief systems which—more often than not—also have fundamentally opposed economic interests.[21]

---

16. Allport, *Nature of Prejudice*, 107.

17. Alan Templeton, "Human Races: A Genetic and Evolutionary Perspective," *American Anthropologist* 100 (1998): 632–50 (632).

18. Templeton, "Evolutionary," 635–36.

19. Thomas Gossett, *Race: The History of an Idea in America* (New York: Oxford University Press, 1997), 411.

20. Marcus Banks, *Ethnicity: Anthropological Constructions* (London: Routledge, 1996), 54.

21. Henry Louis Gates, "Editor's Introduction: Writing 'Race' and the Difference it Makes," in *"Race," Writing, and Difference* (Chicago: University of Chicago Press, 1986), 1–20 (5).

Further, Ugandan anthropologist Peter Rigby suggests that race is a relatively recent phenomenon that was conceived to facilitate the formation of European identity and hence unity of disparate ethnic units in the development of Western capitalism and colonialism. In this regard, fundamental to the concept of race is the notion of hierarchical differences that place Europeans at the pinnacle of humanity and diminish the status of Africans.[22] In the opinion of these authors, race is more than a means of dividing human populations into biological categories; it is a tool employed for political and economic ends in order to insure the supremacy of a dominant group.

The essence of "race" presents a significant problem for modern social scientists and anthropologist. Inasmuch as this seemingly commonplace term is fraught with a surprising number of nuances and its history is one of oppression and alienation, it has become a major source of contention in recent ethnographic discourse. An increasing number of modern researchers more readily question the fundamental theory upon which the concept rested and its value as an anthropological tool, for, as Montagu determined,

> ["race"] should be dropped from the anthropological, as well as from the popular, vocabulary, for it is a tendentious term which has done an infinite amount of harm and no good at all.[23]

However, other scholars argue against the prevailing sentiments, suggesting, despite the abundance of evidence against their view, that racial categories are valid genetic subspecies designations. These are often not blanket acceptances of racial categories. For example, Allport views race as a legitimate means of grouping humans and sees many "racial" differences as authentic. Still, he has a difficult time clarifying what race is relying on an amorphous set "stocks, types, races or breeds," following the confusion extant in anthropological thought during the 1950s.[24]

The 1990s witnessed to a handful of new attempts to confer validity upon "race." In Glayed Whitney's article "On Possible Genetic Bases of Race Difference in Criminality," he posits the validity of racial subspecies, genetic differentiation paralleling popular perceptions, group differences, and racial causes of criminal behavior.[25] Hernstein and Murray's popular *The Bell Curve* (1989) is perhaps the best known work in this genre, followed by Rushton's infamous *Race, Evolution, and Behavior* (1994).[26] However, as the September 1998 edition of *American Anthropologist* claims, the aforementioned books represent the fringes of sociological, psychological, and anthropological work. This journal,

---

22. Peter Rigby, *African Images: Racism and the End of Anthropology* (Oxford: Berg, 1996), 1–5.

23. Montagu, *Man's Most Dangerous Myth*, 28.

24. Allport, *Nature of Prejudice*, 107–28.

25. Glayed Whitney, "On Possible Genetic Bases of Race Differences in Criminality," in *Crime in Biological, Social, and Moral Contests* (ed. Lee Ellis and Harry Hoffman; New York: Prager, 1990), 134–49 (135), as cited in Rigby, *African Images*, 27.

26. Richard J. Herrnstein and Charles A. Murray, *The Bell Curve: Intelligence and Class Structure in American Life* (New York: Free Press, 1989); J. Philippe Rushton, *Race, Evolution, and Behavior* (New Brunswick, N.J.: Transaction, 1994).

focused on the current status of the race debate in anthropological thought, describes the current tendency of those in the field to disregard racial categories.[27]

From this brief review it can be surmised that race is a multifaceted enigma, intended to delineate phenotypically and behaviorally distinct human populations that evolved in particular geographic regions, and circumscribed by political and ideological considerations. Yet the different emphases of the aforementioned scholars clearly indicate that in current anthropological thought, "race" is an increasingly contested term. As Faye Harrison, editor of the *American Anthropologist* issue on race concludes, in spite of the features common to many definitions of race,

> there is no theoretical, methodological, or political consensus shared across any of the subdisciplines on how to interpret and explicate the realities that constitute race.[28]

Hence, I will propose an admittedly synthetic set of criteria to assess the presence of racial thought below.

### 1.1.3. *What Is an Ethnic Group?*

In contrast to the notion of a race, I will employ the concept of an ethnic group. This, too, is a complex and multifaceted notion, as is evident with even a cursory examination of the works of prominent anthropologists and social scientists. It is fitting to begin by considering Montagu's contribution to this discourse. At the outset, it should be noted that Montagu has proposed the "ethnic group" as the unit of analysis for studying human populations as opposed to "race," a concept he deemed illegitimate. For Montagu:

> An ethnic group represents part of a species population in process of undergoing genetic differentiation… An ethnic group represents one of a number of populations comprising the single species Homo sapiens which individually maintain their differences, physical and cultural, by means of isolating mechanisms such as geographic and social barriers.[29]

An example of a social barrier would be American attitudes against "miscegenation." The emphasis on genetic differentiation and barriers to out-group intermixing recalls the definitions of race described above and is to be expected, inasmuch as Montagu's agenda calls for the elimination of that concept to account for biological and social criteria.

In contrast, Allport's decision to maintain race as a valid sub-division of humanity allows him to emphasize non-biological factors in his definition of

---

27. A significant exception to this trend would be Duke Professor, Lee D. Baker, *From Savage to Negro: Anthropology and the Construction of Race, 1896–1954* (Berkeley: University of California Press, 1998). Baker argues that race should be maintained as a tool to note the continuing unequal treatment of racially othered groups in American society. In his words, "(c)ritical cultural anthropologists are rarely called on to explain that even though a biological category of race is meaningless, the social category of race is very real, meaningful, and still dictates life chances and opportunities" (227).

28. Faye V. Harrison, "Introduction: Expanding the Discourse on 'Race,'" *American Anthropologist* 100 (1998): 609–31 (610).

29. Montagu, *Man's Most Dangerous Myth*, 43.

ethnicity. For Allport, ethnicity was an expression of social, cultural, and other learned traits. In this paradigm, ethnicity is not something one is born into but who one becomes based upon environmental influences.[30] He further distinguishes ethnicity from "national character," though he does suggest that there is a significant overlap in the meaning of these terms.[31]

Anthropologist Ronald Cohen provides a thorough survey of the term "ethnicity" in his article, "Ethnicity: Problem and Focus in Anthropology." Cohen begins his analysis of the meaning of the term "ethnicity" by reviewing the use of the term in the works of other prominent anthropologists and sociologists. For example, he noted Max Weber's perspective, wherein he views ethnicity as "a sense of common descent extending beyond kinship, political solidarity vis-à-vis other groups, and common customs, language, religion, values, morality, and etiquette."[32]

Cohen also reviewed Frederick Barth's works. Barth found that:

> anthropological definitions (of ethnicity)…(usually had) four elements: 1. a biological self-perpetuating population; 2. a sharing of culture values and forms; 3. a field of communication and interaction; 4. a grouping that identifies itself and is identified by others as constituting a category different from other categories of the same type.[33]

But Barth had a nuanced view of ethnicity whereby he separated culture from ethnicity, noting that the terms have distinct referents. Barth recognized that ethnicity was based not upon the behaviors and customs of a people, but upon the boundaries that a group uses to define itself and distinguish itself from others. Further, an ethnic group's culture can change over time though the boundaries defining the group persist.[34] This view of culture is not unlike that of Diana Edelman who asserts, following the Comaroffs, that "Ethnic consciousness involves both an assertion of a collective self and the negation of collective other/s, creating a world of asymmetrical 'we–them' relations."[35]

Cohen's own definition of ethnicity bears the influence of Weber and Barth. For Cohen, who wrote soon after the term became the common parlance of anthropology,[36] ethnicity attends to the unit or entity, which is the ethnic group.

---

30. Allport, *Nature of Prejudice*, 107.

31. Allport, *Nature of Prejudice*, 116–19.

32. Ronald Cohen, "Ethnicity: Problem and Focus in Anthropology," *Annual Review of Anthropology* 7 (1978): 379–403 (385); Max Weber, "Ethnic Groups," in *Theories of Society: Foundations of Modern Social Theory* (ed. Talcott Parsons, Edward Shils, K. D. Naegele, J. Pitts; New York: Free Press, 1961), 301–9.

33. Cohen, "Ethnicity," 385, cited in Frederick Barth, *Ethnic Groups and Boundaries: The Social Organization of Culture Difference* (London: Allen & Unwin, 1969).

34. Cohen, "Ethnicity," 383–87, citing Barth, *Ethnic Groups and Boundaries*, 38. Also see Werner Sollors, *Beyond Ethnicity: Consent and Descent in American Culture* (New York: Oxford University Press, 1986), 27, where he too points out that Barth suggests the boundary markers of an ethnic group mark their "ethnicity" not their culture, which is a temporal and evolving social feature.

35. Diana Edelman, "Ethnicity and Early Israel," in *Ethnicity and the Bible* (ed. Mark G. Brett; Leiden: E. J. Brill, 1996), 25–55 (25).

36. See Cohen, "Ethnicity," 380, where Cohen notes that the terms ethnic and ethnic group come into vogue in the early 1970s largely displacing culture and tribe as units of peoples. See also Sollors,

This group is composed of members with "cultural and social commonality," and the boundaries of this group are set by adherence to "similar and continuing rules."[37] He also notes that in-group and out-group definitions of an ethnic group may vary. Further, ethnicity is descent-based, flexible, and may include multiple identities.[38]

But this is far from the last word on ethnicity. In *Anthropology as Cultural Critique* (1986), George E. Marcus and Michael M. J. Fischer further complicate this concept by suggesting that it varies not just by groups, but also by its constituent members. They declare that ethnicity:

> cannot be encompassed by discussions of group solidarity, traditional values, family mobility, or other categories of sociological analysis applied to ethnicity… [It] is something reinvented and reinterpreted in every generation by each individual.[39]

Note the dynamic and individual quality of ethnicity in Marcus and Fischer's definition, which transcends its essentialist trappings and is intentionally more fluid than universal.

From the above survey, I surmise that there are several factors a general definition for ethnicity should consider: (1) that the term refers to a human population distinguished by delineated boundary markers; (2) that the particular group may be recognized by members of the group and by Others as distinct; (3) that said group may share certain social and cultural features at different times though may not be limited to them; and (4) that the group may be viewed as deriving from common biological origins. One caution, however, when considering terms denoting ethnicity: any of several factors could be missing when an ethnic term is applied. For example, in the New Testament when the term Ἑλληνίς is employed in Mark 7:26, it is not necessarily intended as a term describing a woman who had a Greek heritage and would have self-identified herself as such, for she is also designated a "Syrophoenician." It is likely that the usage of the ethnic designation "Greek" here and in other instances implied something about the perceived dominant cultural traits of the described Other.[40]

---

Beyond Ethnicity, 21, where he agrees with Cohen that ethnicity became a popular descriptive for human groups in the early 1970s and was early championed in the works of Andrew Greeley, Michael Novak, and Pierre van den Berghe.

37. Cohen, "Ethnicity," 386.

38. Cohen, "Ethnicity," 386–87.

39. George E. Marcus and Michael M. J. Fischer, *Anthropology as Cultural Critique: An Experiment in the Human Sciences* (Chicago: University of Chicago Press, 1986), 173.

40. There have been various interpretations of the term Ἑλληνίς in Mark 7:26. Some have understood the term to refer to the Syrophoenician woman's religious affiliation. Hence, by saying she was Greek, the author meant to express that she was "pagan." Cf. Hugh Anderson, *The Gospel of Mark* (London: Oliphants, 1976), 190; Donald English, *The Message of Mark: The Mystery of Faith* (Leicester: Inter-Varsity Press, 1992), 142. Others have suggested that Ἑλληνίς referred to this woman's larger cultural identity inasmuch as she was a product of a Greek city. Cf. C. E. B. Cranfield, *The Gospel according to Saint Mark* (Cambridge, England: Cambridge University Press, 1985), 247; John Painter, *Mark's Gospel: Worlds in Conflict* (London: Routledge, 1997), 115. It is clear that being identified as Greek in no way diminished her Syrophoenician heritage.

This may also be true for biblical Cushites, who ruled Egypt from the mid-eighth to the mid-seventh centuries B.C.E. When Hezekiah relied on "Egypt" for support in his rebellion against Sennacherib in 2 Kgs 18:21, it is likely that "Egyptian" is used as the national and cultural term for armies that were likely an ethnic mix of Cushites, Egyptians, and other allies. The term is similarly employed in Exod 2:19 in reference to Moses, a man clearly perceived as an ethnic Hebrew by the biblical redactors.

One other author, the literary critic Werner Sollors, should be considered for his understanding of ethnicity. Though the focus of Sollors' work is the United States, his insight into the term "ethnicity" has merit for our particular discussion. Sollors notes the peculiarity of the term "ethnicity" when employed in biblical literature. In Greek translations of Hebrew literature, the term *goy* is represented by *ethnikos*. Noting that the term *goy* is generally reserved by Israelite/Judahite authors for Others and not themselves, Sollors recognizes the tendency by dominant groups to impose ethnicity on Others while denying their own. This practice, he suggests, should be challenged, for every group is subject to its own ethnicity. Also, since Western culture was built upon Christian biblical interpretation, where *goy* and *ethnikos* developed a negative connotation as "heathen," the term "ethnic" often carries with it a pejorative sense.[41]

Sollors' definition of ethnicity will prove significant for the purposes of this definition, for it resonates with the biblical notion of Others. Israel was a distinct socio-political and cultural entity with an identity based upon its unique status. It is likely that if Cush was not racially othered, it was ethnically othered in a manner similar to the host of populations bordering Israel: In this vein, we may discern instances where Cushites are disparaged not because they are racially Other, but simply because they are Other. In this study, the term "ethnic group" will be used to denote a human population distinguished by delineated boundary markers that are recognized by members of the group and by Others as distinct, that generally share certain social and cultural features that change over time, and that are generally viewed as deriving from common biological origins. Further, inasmuch as the definitions of ethnic groups described in this section emphasized biology only in regard to descent and were silent about phenotypic differences and power relationships, we will also use these factors to distinguish between racial or ethnic systems of othering.

### 1.1.4. *Toward a Model of Racial Thought*

That race is an increasingly problematic notion is the result of modern theory. The ancient world, often thought to be the source of modern prejudices,[42]

---

41. Sollors, *Beyond Ethnicity*, 24–26.

42. See Robert E. Hood, *Begrimed and Black: Christian Traditions on Blacks and Blackness* (Minneapolis: Fortress, 1994). Hood suggests that the roots of modern racial thought and racism can be traced to the evolving Christianity in the midst of the Greco-Roman world. Still, he would identify negative views of blacks and blackness in a variety of ethno-cultural groups throughout history. See also Lloyd A. Thompson, *Romans and Blacks* (London: Routledge/Oklahoma University Press, 1989). Though Thompson would suggest that racial thought could not have existed in the ancient

however, did not have the benefit of these recent ideas. For the sake of this study, we will focus our attention not on whether a coherent and complete racial paradigm existed in ancient Israel/Judah, but rather if these ancient people employed "constituent elements"[43] of racial paradigms when they described the Cushite Other. Once we conclude our investigation, we will be able to determine if we have found these constituent elements, whether they express the genesis of racial thought.

In the absence of a consensus about what race is,[44] I will offer a set of criteria that indicates the presence of constituent elements of racial thought to be employed in this study.

In his noticeably anachronistic work, *Race, Evolution, and Behavior*, Canadian psychologist J. Philippe Rushton rehashes some of the most inflammatory racial arguments of the seventh to the early twentieth centuries. Arguing against the best scholarship in sociology, anthropology, and psychology, and following in the traditions of *The Bell Curve*, Rushton sets out to prove that racial categories are valid and that heredity is the principal factor determining human outcomes along the simplest understanding of the three race model.

Consistent with his argument, founded on the pseudo-scientific racial studies of the late nineteenth and early twentieth centuries, Rushton maintains that human beings can be arranged hierarchically from Africans, possessors of the worst of human qualities, to Asians, the dominant sub-species of human beings. Though his arguments are too seriously flawed to merit rehearsal,[45] they are invaluable inasmuch as they explicitly illustrate the traditional behavioral assumptions made about African peoples by proponents of racial thought that will prove useful for any analysis of race.

---

world because the constituent sociological factors were not present in Roman society, he does locate a number of instances where Greco-Roman authors and artists explicitly disparaged "blacks."

43.   Audrey Smedley, *Race in North America: Origin and Evolution of a Worldview* (Boulder: Westview, 1993), 26–27. Smedley defines this term as the collection of "ideological ingredients" that when perceived in concert form "a singular paradigm constituting the racial worldview."

44.   Harrison, "Introduction," 609–31.

45.   J. Phillipe Rushton, *Race, Evolution, and Behaviour* (Special Abridged ed.; New Brunswick, N.J.: Transaction, 1999). Rushton's work is fraught with unwarranted statements regarding the connection between size of head and intelligence (pp. 47–58) without noting known differences in density of human neurons; linking criminality and race (pp. 27–38) without regard to the social implications of illicit behavior; associating behavioral traits with genetic factors (pp. 59–72) in the absence of any genetic data; explaining the nature of the sexual behaviors of the three "races" (pp. 39–46) omitting discussion of social policies, sociological factors, and cultural practices which govern these behaviors. For example, in his assessment of hypersexuality of racially "black" peoples, he highlights the higher birthrate for this group contrasted with the lower birthrate of whites and Asians. However, he does not take into account the significant impact social policies have on the number of offspring produced by a union. For example, many "white" Catholics have families significantly larger than the mean due to religious factors. Further the low birthrates among Chinese people can be traced directly to government mandates to curtail the excessive population growth related principally to abnormally high birthrates. Stated succinctly, his conclusions are far too simplistic for the complex phenomena he proposed to assess critically and his ideological biases have obscured the assumed "objectivity" of his "scientific" search for "truth" (pp. 9–10).

Even though we are considering an ancient civilization that precedes the existence of African Americans by millennia, many would argue that "racially" the Cushites should be categorized, like African Americans, as Negroes. In this regard, it will be interesting to determine whether ancient writers noted any of the same "racial" traits mentioned by Rushton and others. According to Rushton, the African race is characterized by criminal behavior, hypersexuality, immaturity, low intelligence, and poor levels of cultural achievement.[46] Allport notes a similar set of traits frequently associated with African Americans mental inferiority,[47] and superstitious, immoral, or lazy behavior.[48]

Montagu provides a general set of phenotypical descriptions of African Americans that seem representative. Montagu notes that Negroes have greater skin pigmentation, wavy-curly-frizzly-wooly hair, less bodily hair, more sweat glands, distinctively flatter noses and larger lips.[49] Words like "greater," "more," and "less" necessarily imply an unstated but assumed norm that is obviously non-"black." Such notions of deviance from the unstated norm subtly undergird notions of racial hierarchy in what Banks calls a "legitimating ideology,"[50] hence are relevant for understanding the political and ideological import given to such differences in somatic type. This is reminiscent of what Cornel West calls the "normative gaze," a component of notions of racial superiority often manifest in the aesthetic valuations of the racial Other.[51]

The aforementioned issue of the *American Anthropologist* contains two statements on race issued by reputed national anthropological organizations. Both of these provide data suitable for our purposes of developing criteria for characterizing racial thought. One represents the determined efforts of the American Association of Physical Anthropologists (AAPA) to develop an official statement on the dubious nature of the concept of "race." In its eleven-point statement, published in 1996, the guild of "scientists who study human evolution and variation" offered their definitive opinion to explicitly thwart the use of "popular conceptualizations of race" that had been used for the furthering of "institutional discrimination."[52] The eleven points are summarized as follows:

1.    All humans belong to the same, undifferentiated species and maintain minimal biological variation.

2.    Biological differences can be traced to the interaction between hereditary and environmental factors.

---

46.  Rushton, *Race*, 19.

47.  Gates discusses this perspective in his assessment of the correlation between African illiteracy and ignorance in Western literature. He cites such renowned philosophers as Hegel, Hume and Kant as proponents of this position. Gates, "Introduction," 9–11.

48.  Allport, *Nature of Prejudice*, 196–99.

49.  Montagu, *Man's Most Dangerous Myth*, 193–94. See also Frank M. Snowden, Jr., *Before Color Prejudice* (Cambridge, Mass.: Harvard University Press, 1983), 5, 10–17.

50.  Banks, *Ethnicity*, 54.

51.  Cornel West, *Prophesy Deliverance: Afro-American Revolutionary Christianity* (Philadelphia: Westminster, 1982) 54–56.

52.  "AAPA Statement on Biological Aspects of Race," *American Journal of Physical Anthropology* 101 (1996): 569–70, as reprinted in *American Anthropologist* 100 (3 September, 1998): 714–15.

3.    Pure races do not exist as all human groups reflect significant genetic diversity.
4.    There are clear physical differences between populations in geographically distinct regions due to an interaction of a variety of genetic and environmental factors.
5.    The traits traditionally used to define different groups are transferred independently, hence are not collective traits stereotypic of any group.
6.    There are neither superior or inferior races.
7.    There are no biological barriers to cross "racial" mating, and humans are not adapted exclusively to any environment.
8.    The genetic composition of human populations changes continually.
9.    There are no biological reasons for restricting intermarriage.
10.   There is no relationship between physical and behavioral traits nor between genetic background and cultural traits.
11.   People, though influenced by heredity, are individuals and as such differ intellectually and behaviorally. Such differences cannot be traced to "racial" traits.[53]

The second statement was composed by the American Anthropological Association (AAA), the organization that publishes the *American Anthropologist*. It represents not a consensus of AAA members, but the best assessment of the current state of thought about race by leading practitioners in the field. This statement largely reiterates the sentiments of the earlier AAPA statement, though often more emphatically. There are several nuances in the AAA statement that are noteworthy. For instance, the AAA statement emphasizes that more genetic variation exists within each "race" than between any two; that "race" has always been an ideology-laden social construct; that "race" was a colonialist instrument used for political ends; and that the way a given society relates to a "race" also affects the performance of people from that race in that given society.[54]

Based upon the aforementioned elements, we can derive a set of criteria useful for our analysis. In our analysis, if we discern a pattern whereby the following (or similar) constituent elements of racial thought are employed in a systematic pattern in passages in the Hebrew Bible, we will conclude that a racial ideology exists:

Behavior:
- tendency to criminal or violent behavior;
- childishness-immaturity;
- inferior cultural development;
- sexual perversion-hypersexuality;
- laziness;
- immorality;
- peculiar behavioral stereotypes.

53.  "AAPA Statement," 714–15.
54.  "AAA Statement on Race," *American Anthropologist* 100 (1999): 712–13.

Somatic Type:
- distinctive hair (curly, frizzled, wavy, etc.);
- distinctive dark pigmentation;
- distinctive-flat noses;
- distinctive-full lips;
- aesthetic valuations of distinctive phenotypical traits;
- peculiar descriptions of phenotypical traits.

Other aspects of racial thought:
- group essentialisms/stereotypes-phenotype connected to behavior;
- group ontological differences/groups of differing types;
- group superiority or inferiority;
- barriers to inter-group mating;
- ideologically marked differences for political ends;
- legitimating ideology/peculiar manner of justifying the othering of Cushites.

In addition to these criteria for racial thought, we will also want to consider more generally how Cushites are portrayed:
- positive, negative, or neutral representation;
- similar to or distinct from other ethnic groups;
- in an informed or ignorant manner;
- in a manner consistent with what is known from other sources.

In the following sections I will employ these criteria to determine whether Hebrew literary notions of Cush tend toward essentializations, which, though distinct from modern ideas, represent othering based on constituent elements of a racial paradigm. I will search for instances where the description of distinctive phenotypical or behavioral traits of Cushites occur and assess whether Cushites are represented in a manner inconsistent with references to other Others.

But lest I be misunderstood, the issue under contention is "racialism,"[55] not "racism." Kwame Anthony Appiah makes the clear distinction between these two notions, noting that they are, however, related. For "racism" is impossible without some notion of "racialism." I am concerned not with whether systemic racism existed in ancient Israel/Judah; though this is a matter worthy of future

---

55. Kwame Appiah, former Duke professor and current Harvard social critic, defines "racialism" as the acceptance of the proposition "that there are heritable characteristics, possessed by members of our species, that allow us to divide them into a small set of races, in such a way that all the members of these races share certain traits and tendencies with each other that they do not share with members of any other race. These traits and tendencies characteristic of a race constitute, on the racialist view, a sort of racial essence" (Kwame Anthony Appiah, "Racisms," in *Anatomy of Racism* [ed. David Theo Goldberg; Minneapolis: University of Minnesota Press, 1990], 3–17 [4–5]). Appiah would argue that a racialist view is not intrinsically immoral, like a racist posture. However, I would argue that racialism is a necessary, though not a sufficient precondition for racism. Also see Appiah's article "Race: An Interpretation," in *African: The Encyclopedia of the African and African American Experience* (ed. Kwame Anthony Appiah and Henry Louis Gates, Jr.; New York: Civitas Books, 1999), 1575–80 (1576). I will employ the term racialism throughout this study in the following chapters.

investigation, it is a distinctly different issue. What I am concerned with investigating at this time is whether the Israelite/Judahites did or even could have conceived of this particular people as essentially distinct in a "racialist" manner. Because of differences in phenotypical presentation and cultural customs, were the Cushites racially othered by the Hebrews, or were such differences viewed with less significance than they have been in a contemporary milieu?

I will also consider other practical concerns, such as: Are there adequate data to suggest that there was a well developed picture of Cush that existed outside of general stereotypes? Is there adequate material in Hebrew literature to develop a comprehensive portrait of Cushite society (religion, politics, economic policies, family life) or only to make general statements about Cush known to ancient Hebrew authors? Perhaps the most significant question for biblical scholarship is: Is there a need to reassess contemporary understandings of Cush in the Hebrew Bible as a result of this study?

### 1.2. Why Study Cush?

For several reasons, Cush is worthy of attention for a discussion about Israelite/Judahite understanding of Others. First, Cush stands out from the other North African "sons of Ham" as a decidedly racially charged term. Cushites[56] were known through Egyptian[57] and Assyrian[58] epigraphy as a dark skinned people with features consistent with modern notions of "negroes." Whereas the "racial" identity of Egyptians, Libyans, and Canaanites has been posited with less certainty, Cushites generally have been viewed as "racially black."[59]

Further, Cush is a term often racialized by modern exegetes (see 1.3 below). In this regard, the term "Cushi," a singular gentilic used to describe people from Cush, has become a translational equivalent for the racial term "Negro" in modern Hebrew.[60] Also, throughout the history of biblical translation, the term

---

56.  Or "Kushites" as the term is transcribed in the literature of Egyptologists.

57.  For example, see Snowden, *Color*, Plates 4, 6, 7a-b, 8a-b, 9, and 10.

58.  For example, see Snowden, *Color*, Plate 13.

59.  I would ask the reader to consider the works of Hays and Adamo who define the Cushites as "black" and "African" respectively; see Hays, "Cushites: Bible"; *idem*, "Cushites: History"; and Adamo, "Africa." A notable exception would be the widely respected biblical scholar, Martin Noth, who held what can best be described as an illogical bias that caused him to question Egyptian eyewitness' representations of Cushites. For example, consider this quotation: "The Egyptians also portrayed the people living along the Nile south of Egypt in a generalized and certainly incorrect manner, with typical Negro faces, beardless, and with large earrings especially in the stereotypic lists of conquests in foreign lands, by incorrectly classifying the Nubians as Negroes. The Nubians were at most very slightly related to the Negro tribes bordering them on the south" (*The Old Testament World*, 236).

60.  See "kooshee/-m," in *Webster's New World Hebrew Dictionary* (ed. Hayim Baltsam; New York: Prentice Hall, 1992), 188, where the term is defined as "Negro; Blackman"; "כּוּשִׁי," in Reuben Sivan and Edward A. Levenston, eds., *The Megiddo Modern Dictionary Hebrew–English* (Tel Aviv: Megiddo, 1965), 326, where the term is defined as "Ethiopian; negro, 'darky' (not insulting)"; or "Negro, negro (n; adj)," in Ben-Ami Scharfstein, Raphael Sappan, and Zevi Scharfstein, *English–Hebrew Dictionary* (Tel Aviv: Dvir Publishing Company, 1961), 439, where the terms are translated "כּוּשִׁי."

Cush found its way into Greek in the LXX as "Ethiopian,"[61] a word whose denotation implicitly has potentially racialist implications since it means "burnt face." Hence, the people known to the Hebrew Bible's authors as Cushites were known by those author's Greek-speaking descendants not by their place of origin or ethnicity (Cush), but by an essentialist assessment of their phenotypical presentation, "burnt face."

Hence, whereas other "Hamitic" nations generally have not been racialized to the same extent, Cush has an extensive history of racial prescription. The current analysis pertains to the potential origin of such racialization: Did it occur in the Hebrew Bible?

### 1.3. *Brief Literature Review of the Topic*

There have been several monographs that have sought to fill the general void of knowledge about the Cushites that appear in the Hebrew Bible. Among the recent studies that have begun to address the biblical Cushites, the following merit attention in any attempt to understand the relationship between Cushites and Israelite/Judahites.

Perhaps the first significant recent articles on the issue were those of Charles B. Copher and Gene Rice. Copher, Professor Emeritus at the Interdenominational Theological Center, a scholar often revered as the father of Afrocentric biblical scholarship, began chronicling the history of "blacks" in the Bible in a series of articles and papers in the early 1970s.[62] Because of his work, many scholars and clergy began to revisit the issue of "black presence" in the Bible and to identify both "African" peoples in Bible and the extra-biblical sources, and to argue for a "black presence" in these texts.

Copher's dialogue partner, Gene Rice, also was an early proponent of Afrocentric biblical interpretation, as evident from his paper "The African Roots of the Prophet Zephaniah," published in the late 1970s. In this article, Rice builds on the framework laid by Copher and argues for a Cushite faction in the Judean royal administration.[63] Though the works of these two pioneers piqued interest of subsequent generations of scholars, the nature of their projects generally did not require them to systematically delineate notions of race and ethnicity, nor the manner in which biblical authors othered the Cushites.

---

61. This association between Cush and Ethiopia has further complicated matters inasmuch as there is a modern African nation that bears this name. This conflation of ancient Cush and contemporary Ethiopia clouds the already murky waters, as do the Ethiopian traditions suggesting extensive contact between Ethiopia and Israel in biblical times. Consider the confusion evident in Benjamin Braude, "The Sons of Noah and the Construction of Ethnic and Geographical Identities in the Medieval and Early Modern Periods," *William and Mary Quarterly* 54 (1997): 103–42.

62. Charles B. Copher, *Black Biblical Studies: An Anthology of Charles B. Copher* (Chicago: Black Light Fellowship, 1993). This anthology represents twenty years of evolution in Copher's thoughts regarding biblical interpretation of text significant to ancient and contemporary "black" peoples.

63. Gene Rice, "The African Roots of the Prophet Zephaniah," *JRT* 36 (1979): 21–31.

Sten Hidal's 1977 article, "The Land of Cush in the Old Testament," is a brief but insightful review of many of the biblical texts that refer to Cush. In his work he concludes that there were three principal regions identified as "Cush" in the Hebrew Bible. The first is the region south of the first cataract of the Nile, up-river from the Egyptian Empire. The vast majority of times when a Cush-related term is used in the Hebrew Bible, it is used in reference to this land or its people. The region identified by a Cush-related term in the Hebrew Bible with the second greatest frequency is not the land of the Kassites, as many scholars have proposed, but the region located on the southern border of Judah. This land extended south along the eastern coast of the Red Sea, adjacent to Edom and perhaps overlapping with the land of the Midianites (cf. Amos 9:7; Hab 3:7; possibly Num 12:1). The land of the Kassites, Hidal concedes, should only be identified with כוש in Gen 2:13 and 10:7. Having identified the three regions represented by Cush-related terms, Hidal proceeds to group references to Cush-related terms with the regions they represent. In spite of its obvious merit, Hidal's article avoids any discussion of race or ethnicity and also is silent regarding the Hebrew authors' perspective of the enigmatic Cushites.[64]

Roger W. Anderson began to investigate biblical Cush while a professor in Mozambique. In response to numerous requests form his students that he discuss the presence of "Africans" in the Bible, he began to research the Cushites and the role they played in the biblical texts. His article, "Zephaniah ben Cushi and Cush of Benjamin," takes seriously the issue of the relationship between Cush and Judah, suggesting that there was a significant Cushite presence in and around Syro-Palestine throughout the biblical period but particularly after the eighth century. Anderson even broaches the question of the "ethnic and racial composition of the various population groups in the ancient Near East."[65] However, he employs such terms as "ethnic" and "racial" without careful consideration of their meanings, and often seems to assume the utility of these categories in the ancient world.[66]

Similar conclusions can be drawn about the detailed work of David Tuesday Adamo. Though Adamo examines the literary history of Cushites in the Hebrew Bible in his 1986 dissertation, there is a fundamental difference in the work that Adamo did and the analysis that I am undertaking. Adamo, a Nigerian scholar who gained an appreciation for Afrocentric research during his training in America, sought to demonstrate that there were "Africans," people who could be defined as racially "black," who played a significant role in the unfolding story of the Bible. His contributions to the understanding of the relationship between Cush and Israel have proven invaluable, as has his challenge to traditional biblical scholarship in its approach to the nations of continental Africa inscribed

---

64. Sten Hidal, "The Land of Cush in the Old Testament," *SEÅ* 41 (1977): 97–106.

65. Roger W. Anderson, "Zephaniah ben Cushi and Cush of Benjamin: Traces of Cushite Presence in Syria–Palestine," in *The Pitcher is Broken: Memorial Essays for Gosta W. Ahlström* (ed. Steven W. Holloway and Lowell K. Handy; Sheffield: JSOTSup 190; Sheffield Academic Press, 1995): 45–70 (65); Hidal, "Cush," 97–106.

66. R. W. Anderson, "Zephaniah," 69.

in the pages of the Hebrew Bible. Yet, by nature of the question Adamo has addressed, he has assumed that the term "Cush" has a racial and, hence, an "African" connotation.[67]

This is also true for Daniel Hays, who even goes so far as to make the following comment about Num 12, the incident about Moses' Cushite wife: "Apparently the family objected to this interracial marriage, but God approved."[68] Both this quote and the title of the article elucidate Hays' racialist presumptions. Both Adamo and Hays' works have been significant additions to the growing dialogue, confirming that people who would be deemed "African" in a modern context were significant actors in the ancient biblical world. Yet they do not address the concern of whether Cushites were racially othered by the biblical authors themselves.

Though each of these works represent significant recent attempts to reclaim the often overlooked history of the relationship between Cushites and ancient Israel/Judah, each of them worked to different ends than those I propose. Further, each of them is lacking in one or more of the following elements: (1) concern for the change in understandings of Cush(ites) in Hebrew literature over time; (2) necessary depth to produce a complete portrait of Cush from the perspective of biblical authors/audiences; (3) a systematic analysis of whether constituent elements of racialist thought were employed in biblical representations of Cushites. In fact, as we have seen, many of them refer to Cush as a "black" nation, adding the modern racial description to this ancient ethnic term.

In this regard, I offer the present study to fill in the gaps in the larger discourse about race, ethnicity, and othering in the Hebrew Bible, concentrating primarily on the biblical authors' perspectives of Cushites. By focusing on explicit references to Cush-related terms, we will likely overlook other implicit references to Cush and Cushites as well as other peoples whom many contemporary scholars would identify as "African" or "Negro." However, we should gain valuable insight into how the Judean authors of the Hebrew Bible perceived human difference by assessing the manner by which they represented Cush and Cushites in their literature.

In the next three chapters I will examine biblical representation of Cush and Cushites in literature that dates to three periods. Chapter 2 will focus on reference to Cush-related terms in tenth- to eighth-century biblical literature. Chapter 3 will examine Cush-related terms in literature composed between the seventh century and the Babylonian Exile. Chapter 4 will consider Cush-related terms in post-exilic biblical literature. Each of these chapters will be subdivided into

67. Adamo, "Africa." In this vein, also see St. Clair Drake, *Black Folk Here and There: An Essay in History and Anthropology*, vol. 2 (Los Angeles: Center for Afro-American Studies, University of California, 1990), 3–17. In this section Drake briefly assesses the biblical view of "blacks" in the Hebrew Bible and provides a valuable contribution to the discourse regarding Jewish views of "African" peoples. Similarly, Knut Holter, *Yahweh in Africa: Essays on Africa and the Old Testament* (New York: Peter Lang, 2000) is a recent contribution to the discussion of the role "Africa" plays in the Hebrew Bible. Though he questions Adamo's use of "Africa" as a translation of Cush, he suggests that "the quest for an analysis of the Old Testament portrayal of Africa has been, and still is, regarded as a priority within traditional western Old Testament scholarship" (p. 95).

68. Hays, "Bible," 399. Also see Hays, "History," 270–80.

sections in which I will discuss these terms in specific biblical passages; and these chapters will contain summaries describing the use of Cush-related terms in literature composed during the relevant historical period. Finally, in Chapter 5 I will present my conclusions about how Judeans viewed the Cushite Other as evidenced in the Hebrew Bible, present a brief ethnography of Cush through Judean lenses, and discuss the larger implications of this project for biblical studies.

# Chapter 2

## A Word Study of the Hebrew Root "Cush" in Tenth- to Eighth-Century Hebrew Literature

### 2.1. Introduction to the Exegesis of Tenth- to Eighth-Century Hebrew Literature

In what are thought to be the some of the earliest traditions in the Hebrew Bible, we find references to Cush and the Cushites. In fact, we even find Cush employed as a geographical marker in the Garden of Eden narrative found in Gen 2. Though the details in that account are scanty, the initial presentation of Cush indicates that the people of Israel/Judah were essentially familiar with the geography of this distant riparian land. Genesis 10 also indicates familiarity with the political and diplomatic alliances that existed between the Cushites and other ancient nations.

In this chapter I will begin to explore the way the Israelite/Judahite authors of tenth to eighth centuries B.C.E. viewed the land of Cush and its people. The texts we will encounter herein are from the Pentateuch (Gen 2; 10; Num 12), and the Prophets (Amos and Isaiah). Among these texts are some of the most significant for our research, including the narrative about Moses' Cushite wife (Num 12), the prophetic comparison of the people of Israel to the Cushites (Amos 9), and the best ethnography of the Cushites in the Hebrew Bible (Isa 18).

Though the aim of my research is to understand the nature of Israelite/Judahite representation of Cushites, this endeavor would be impossible without a thorough exegetical analysis of the literature, history, and social context of the biblical world. I will dedicate considerable attention to exegesis of the relevant biblical texts in order to comprehend as much as possible the way that the intended audience would have understood these texts. Because we will not always be able to ascertain the best interpretation of the text, I will on occasion present a variety of plausible options. In these instances, I will consider the implications of the most plausible options for understanding how the Israelite/Judahite authors represented the Cushites.

My analysis of each passage will typically contain the following elements: (1) a presentation of the Cush-related terms in the passage and the number of occurrences; (2) an historical-critical analysis of the passage; (3) an assessment of the most plausible understanding(s) of the passage; and (4) the implications of this passage for our research. In some instances I will propose new readings of the passage, challenging the traditional interpretations of previous exegetes. It is hoped that these readings will also be valuable for subsequent exegetical analysis of these passages and that they will facilitate a better understanding of the Cushites known to the Israelite/Judean authors of the Hebrew Bible. We should add one note of caution. In light of the present lack of consensus in biblical studies in regard to historical sources, my perception of the actual historical merit of references to Cush will be tempered. Thus, I will at the outset concede that the conclusions of this study are based on literary materials that can accurately describe what the Judean authors and audience of these texts would have considered historically plausible. Whether or not the texts accurately reflect the actual history or Israel/Judah will be left to biblical historians.[1]

The list of racialist traits described in the previous chapter will guide my discussion of the nature of Judean representation of Cushites. I will examine the data gleaned from exegetical analysis through the lens provided by this list to determine whether the Judean othering of the Cushites approaches what we would deem racialist thought. In addition, I will also note the commonplace significance of Cush and Cushites to the Israelite/Judahite authors, grouping the various passages based upon the type of Cush reference in each source. For example, I will encounter a number of instances where Cushites are described as warriors; these references exploit the commonplace understanding of the "mighty" Cushites and will hence be deemed "mighty" Cushite types of usages.

At the end of this and subsequent chapters, I will review the portraits of Cush and Cushites that have been identified in Hebrew literature compiled during the period under examination. Further, I will consider what each representation of Cush says about the extent of contact between it and Israel/Judah, the perception of this Other, and the image of Israel/Judah that is implied in the biblical presentation of Cushites.

A final comment about translations is needed. Unless noted, all translations are my own. In other instances, the appropriate citation or biblical version will be included.

---

1.   The idea of biblical history has been transformed in recent years, resulting in a range of varying positions on the historicity of the Hebrew Bible. Of late the debate has motivated biblical historians and archaeologists to form synthetic ideological coalitions. One camp, identified as biblical minimalists or revisionists, posits that there is little relevant historical information included in the Hebrew Bible and that archaeological data should be interpreted without reference to these historically unreliable texts. Scholars such as Philip R. Davies, Niels Peter Lemche, and Thomas L. Thompson are associated with this camp. Cf. Philip Davies, *In Search of "Ancient Israel"* (JSOTSup 148; Sheffield: JSOT Press, 1992); Niels Peter Lemche, *The Israelites in History and Tradition* (Louisville, Ky.: Westminster John Knox, 1998); and Thomas L. Thompson, *The Mythic Past: Biblical Archeology and the Myth of Israel* (New York: Basic Books, 1999). Their ideological opponents, often called biblical maximalists, hold the mainstream position that the Hebrew Bible is itself an artifact that provides valuable, though not totally reliable, historical information to biblical scholars and archaeologists. Cf. John Bright, *A History of Israel* (Philadelphia: Westminster, 1981); William G. Dever, "Archaeology, Ideology, and the Quest for 'Ancient' or 'Biblical Israel'," *Near Eastern Archaeology* 61 (1998): 39–52; *idem*, "Histories and Non-histories of Ancient Israel," *BASOR* 316 (1999): 89–105.

## 2.2. *Analysis of the Term "Cush"*
### *in Tenth- to Eighth-Century Hebrew Literature*

### 2.2.1. *Cush in the Pentateuch*

Because the Pentateuchal narratives that mention Cush are complex combinations of traditions and documentary material, some likely dating to various moments in the Iron II period, we will consider them together. The terms "Cush" and "Cushite" (f.) occur in Gen 2; 10; and Num 12. In addition, we will consider Gen 9. Though this chapter does not contain a Cush-related term, Gen 9 is relevant to our discussion since the narrative often described as the "Curse of Ham" occurs in its latter verses. Because this narrative resurfaces in rabbinic literature and influences our interpretation of Gen 10, it seems appropriate to exegete it carefully here, thereby facilitating subsequent conversations about the use of Cush in biblical and rabbinic literature.

### 2.2.1.1. *Genesis 2: A Tale of Two Rivers.*

The term כּוּשׁ ("Cush") occurs once in Gen 2, in v. 13. Cush occurs here not as a reference to a person or a nation, but as a geographical region. The apparent purpose of this chapter is to establish the importance of Eden as a source of life for much of the known world.[2] Yet it is interesting to note that Cush figures prominently in this list of the four rivers thought to encompass the breadth of the world.[3] The second river mentioned is the Gihon, said to surround all the land of Cush. Though the name Gihon recurs in the Hebrew Bible as a spring located on the western side of the Kidron Valley, just east of the City of David, it is designated a river only in Gen 2:13.

Some scholars have speculated that only the Tigris and Euphrates can be identified with any degree of certainty from this account. In this regard, Driver proposed that those who wish to identify these four rivers must start with the two certain ones and then look for the two enigmatic ones in their proximity. Following this reasoning Driver concluded that the Gihon and the Pishon could probably never be identified, but may have been northern tributaries of the Tigris and Euphrates. Hence, the birthplace of civilization would be located in the Mesopotamian region northeast of Palestine.[4]

Could the Gihon be a river that flowed around the land of the Kassites? Could the biblical authors have mistaken the Kassites for the Cushites as many suspect has occurred in Gen 10:8–14? This is unlikely for two reasons. First, this passage

---

2. Claus Westermann, *Genesis 1–11: A Commentary* (Minneapolis: Augsburg, 1984), 216. Westermann challenges the traditional understanding of the four rivers to identify the region where the mythical Eden lay, suggesting that this passage implies that Eden is the source of these four great rivers, hence, the source of life for the world.

3. Gerhard von Rad notes the symbolism of the number "four" for the rivers in light of other instances where it is intended to "circumscribe the entire world," citing Zech 2:1–4 (EVV 1:18–21) where the number is employed similarly. Gerhard von Rad, *Genesis: A Commentary* (Philadelphia: Westminster, 1961), 77. See also, Westermann, *Genesis 1–11*, 217.

4. Samuel R. Driver, *The Book of Genesis* (London: Methuen, 1907), 59–60. His view is also inconsistent with his earlier conclusion on p. 29 that Havilah was "[m]ost probably a region in the NE. of Arabia, on the W. coast of the Persian Gulf."

implies that the rivers flow around major regions of the world. The boundaries of Kassite territory are too limited to fit this criterion.[5] Also, it would be a glaring oversight for a description of the source of life for the entire world to omit any reference to the politically and economically significant lands south of Judah.

The river Gihon has been assumed by many to be the Nile or the "Nubian Nile" south of the first Cataract.[6] In this regard the name "Gihon" may find meaning as the source of the Egyptian Nile, whence it "bursts forth."[7] This is consistent with what is known of Cush, a nation built upon the banks of and sustained by the Nile. Indeed, since the Nile is the only river frequently associated with Cush, the Gihon could represent a southern branch of the Nile with which the Yahwist, the author of this account, was only vaguely familiar.[8]

The first river mentioned is the Pishon[9] (*hapax legomena*), which is said to surround the land of Havilah. This unknown river is also associated with Cush. Of the seven times the name Havilah occurs in the Hebrew Bible, it is mentioned on three occasions in association with Cush (here and as a descendant of Cush in the genealogical lists in Gen 10:7 and 1 Chr 1:9; hence, it could be assumed to be in Cushite territory). Twice it is used as a marker of distance associated with Shur (Gen 25:18—"And they settled from Havilah unto Shur near Egypt in the direction of Assyria"; 1 Sam 15:7—"Saul smote Amelek from Havilah [until] Shur which is near Egypt"). In both the latter instances Havilah is used as a reference marker for a geographic distance. These connections to Cush and Cush's neighbor, Egypt, are not insignificant.

What is more significant is the description of Havilah as a source of gold and precious stones. Müller identifies Havilah as two distinct regions in the southern portion of the Arabian Peninsula in what is modern Yemen. These regions are inhabited by two groups of people called the Haulan who share a common ancestry, but who have been separated by ancient political and military factors. These regions are also rich in gold, precious stones, and aromatic resins.[10] Though Müller was able to locate several rivers in the General Haulan, he was unable to

---

5.    Westermann, *Genesis 1–11*, 218. The Kassites were a people from the mountains of what is now Kurdistan who were sovereign over Babylon from the latter part of the seventeenth to the late twelfth century B.C.E. Cf. Herbert G. May, *Oxford Bible Atlas* (New York: Oxford University Press, 1989), 133.

6.    See von Rad, *Genesis*, 77. This is also supported by the LXX version of Jer 2:18 which has Γηων for the MT's שׁחוֹר, probably meaning the "black waters," referring to the Nile and Josephus's *Antiquities* I.1.3.

7.    According to BDB, 161, the Hebrew root גיח means "burst forth."

8.    Cf. Manfred Gorg, "Gihon," in *ABD* 2:1018–19. Gorg provides an alternative perspective. He suggests that the Gihon is the Jordan River, here taking its name from the spring in Jerusalem. In his argument Cush represents Egypt under the aegis of the XXVth Cushite Dynasty and that the Jordan was imagined to flow around Egypt. His argument is implausible since the Yahwist's audience would have known that (1) the Jordan ends in the Dead Sea, (2) that Egypt was associated with the Nile, not the Jordan, and (3) that the "land of Cush" was distinct from the Cushite administered "land of Egypt." His argument rests solely on philological grounds, yet does not take into consideration that the root גיח, meaning "burst forth," may imply any number of different rivers.

9.    Cf. Gorg, "Gihon," 1018. He specualates that the Pishon may actually be the Nile.

10.    Walter W. Müller, "Havilah," in *ABD* 3: 82–83. S. R. Driver (*Genesis*, 39) also notes that Arabia was noted for its gold.

identify one that he could ascertain linguistically. He even cites a linguistic argument, attributed to Gorg,[11] that more satisfactorily derives the word from the Egyptian article, *pi*, which would make the word *Pishon* simply "the river," hence the Nile.[12] This conclusion is consistent with several ancient sources[13] and suggests that we should look for Havilah further to the west.

The region near Cush is perhaps a better place to look for Havilah. To the Egyptians Cush was a source of fine gold,[14] and to the Hebrews it was a region known for its precious stones (Job 28:19). Driver proposes that part of the tribe called Havilah lived on the western coast of the Red Sea near Cush, opposite their kin group on the Arabian Peninsula.[15] In this regard, a branch of the Nile is likely what is intended by this reference to the Pishon.

Further, if the four rivers are meant to encompass the scope of the entire known world, it would be peculiar if the author of this narrative gave no attention to the great kingdoms of the south, which were known to be riparian nations. In any regard, it seems as though two of the great rivers flowed through the region south of Israel, one clearly running through the region of Cush, the other loosely associated with Cush and forming either a tributary to the Nile or flowing through the southeastern portion of Arabia.

The author of this passage viewed Cush as one of the regions watered by the Garden. That the Yahwist saw the region of Cush as a land that merited mention in the story of the world's origins is significant. Though there is no mention of people, there is also clearly no attempt to defame the region[16] or disparage the people in this chapter. To the contrary, the Yahwist thought it necessary to include Cush in the origin story of the people of Israel.

In fact, as regards this type of Cush reference, in Gen 2 Cush is used as a geographic or boundary marker.[17] We can understand from this chapter that YHWH's concern for the world extended to the furthest points of the globe. The concern was expressed by the watering of the land of Cush by the great rivers that flowed forth from YHWH's choice Garden even unto the ends of the earth.

11. Cf. n. 8 above.

12. Walter W. Müller, "Pishon," in *ABD* 5:374.

13. Samuel D. Luzzatto notes that the Samaritan Pentateuch, Rashi, Saadiah Gaon, and Nachmanides had each supported the view that the Pishon was the Nile; see Luzzatto's *The Book of Genesis: A Commentary by ShaDaL* (Northvale, N.J.: Jason Aronson, 1998), 37.

14. See, for example, Peter L. Shinnie, "Trade Routes of the Ancient Sudan 3,000 BC–AD 350," in *Egypt and Africa: Nubia from Prehistory to Islam* (ed. Winifred V. Davies; London: British Museum Press, 1993), 49–53 (49).

15. S. R. Driver, *Genesis*, 119.

16. Often, we will note, racialist ideology has influenced Western perceptions of Africa and, hence, Africans. Katherine George, "The Civilized West Looks at Primitive Africa, 1400–1800," *Isis* 49 (1958): 56–72, notes that accounts written from the time of Herodotus until 1700 demonstrate a bias against Africa. Patrick Brantlinger, "Victorians and Africans: The Genealogy of the Myth of the Dark Continent," in *"Race," Writing, and Difference* (ed. Henry Louis Gates, Jr.; Chicago: University of Chicago Press, 1986), 185–222, traces the evolution of the "myth of the Dark Continent" in Western literature and how racial perspectives influenced European and American perspectives of the African continent. Such biases are absent from the Gen 2 reference to the region of Cush.

17. Cf. Esth 1:1 and 8:9 (Section 4.2.4 below) for similar usage.

*2.2.1.2. Excursus on Genesis 9: The "Curse of Ham."* Though Gen 9 does not
include an occurrence of the term Cush, it cannot be ignored in any discussion
about race in the Hebrew Bible. This chapter contains the enigmatic "Curse of
Ham/Canaan" that has been employed at various times to validate racial divisions
and justify the hypothesis that African peoples were cursed.[18] This argument
never occurs in the Hebrew Bible; but it does surface in the Talmud,[19] hence it is
appropriate that we preface that discussion here in our analysis of the Pentateuch.

The curse itself is enigmatic for a number of reasons: (1) the actual offense
that Ham committed is unclear—וַיַּרְא חָם אֲבִי כְנַעַן אֵת עֶרְוַת אָבִיו ("And Ham the
father of Canaan saw the nakedness of his father", 9:22); (2) the offending party
is not the one cursed—though Ham sees his father's nakedness, Canaan is
cursed; (3) there is a discrepancy regarding the relationship of the cursed party to
Noah —was he Noah's youngest son as v. 25 suggests, or his grandson, the son
of Ham as vv. 18 and 22 suggest?

One means of solving the second and third of these dilemmas has been proposed by Driver and followed by von Rad, who both argue that the original
narrative had a Palestinian emphasis, presenting a situation where Shem, Japheth,
and Canaan, respectively, were the sons of Noah. Evidence for this view is found
in vv. 24–27, where the "youngest son" is accused of committing the offense and
Ham disappears from the familial formula. Based upon 9:18 as well as 5:32,
6:10, 7:13, and 10:1, Ham is the second son. As mentioned above, 9:18 and 22
also suggest that Canaan was Ham's son, not Noah's.[20] Hence, the extant text
represents the later redaction of two sources, a narrative focused on Palestinian
elements (Shem, Japheth, and Canaan), and another that was more universal in its
scope. These sources were woven together with minimal attention given to the
internal inconsistencies produced in the extant text.

As a result, the redactor transformed this legitimating ideology justifying the
subjugation of Canaanites into a text that impugned Ham. This was likely not the
intention of the redactor who composed the extant version of Gen 9; his or her
desire to create a generally inclusive narrative in Gen 10 apparently forced him
or her to modify Gen 9 to less favorable ends. Following this reasoning, the curse
fell on Ham and was later ascribed to the sons of Ham depicted in Gen 10. The
subsequent "Curse of Ham" was an unfortunate, unintended by-product of a

18. For a thorough discussion of the use of this passage in racialist discourse, see Charles B.
Copher, "The Black Presence in the Old Testament," in *Stony the Road We Trod: African American
Biblical Interpretation* (ed. Cain Hope Felder; Minneapolis: Fortress, 1991), 146–65 (147–48); Cain
Hope Felder, "Race, Racism, and the Biblical Narratives," in *Stony the Road We Trod: African
American Biblical Interpretation* (ed. Cain Hope Felder; Minneapolis: Fortress, 1991), 127–45 (129–
32); and Clarice Martin, "The *Haustafeln* (Household Codes) in African American Biblical Inter-
pretation: 'Free Slaves' and 'Subordinate Women,'" *Stony the Road We Trod: African American
Biblical Interpretation* (ed. Cain Hope Felder; Minneapolis: Fortress, 1991), 206–31 (215); Thomas
Peterson, *Ham and Jepheth: The Mythic World of Whites in the Antebellum South* (Metuchen, N.J.:
Scarecrow, 1978); Shelton H. Smith, *In His Image, But...* (Durham, N.C.: Duke University Press,
1972).

19. Cf. *b. Sanh.* 70a, 108b.

20. See S. R. Driver, *Genesis*, 109–112; von Rad, *Genesis*, 131–32.

theologically motivated textual emendation meant to demonstrate YHWH's sovereignty over the entire world.

Had the redactor intended to denigrate Ham or his descendants, other than the Canaanites, he of she could have simply removed all trace of Canaan from this passage and hence established a clear legitimating ideology justifying Ham's subjugation and any subsequent disenfranchisement of Hamites' rights to autonomy. However, such a legitimating ideology was not evoked for Ham; it functions only for Canaan in the extant narrative. Though this passage has become fodder for racist discourse, "race" was not the interest of the redactor, as will be discussed below. Regarding Cush and his sons, the redactor's intent in this passage and in the subsequent Table of Nations (Gen 10) was to maintain a consistent portrayal of Noah's family and to represent it as the source of all humankind. Narratives that described the origin of Palestinian populations thus evolve into global origin narratives and Israel/Judah's God, YHWH, becomes the Creator of the entire world.

2.2.1.3. *Genesis 10: Cush and his Sons.* The term כּוּשׁ occurs three times in the Table of Nations of Gen 10, in vv. 6, 7, and 8. The author of this patronymic, often thought to belong to the Yahwist school, has been characterized by some as an ancient ethnographer developing a genealogy of peoples familiar to the Judean community. Further, the categories defined by this "ethnographer" have also influenced linguistic categories, giving rise to such terms as "Semitic" and "Hamitic" languages.[21] Hence, Gen 10 has become one of the passages most frequently referenced in discussions of human difference.

In this chapter, the sons of Ham seem to be the eponymous ancestors of four North African nations: Cush, Egypt, Put, and Canaan. The name חָם ("Ham") was probably derived from the Egyptians' name for their country *Kmt*,[22] an Egyptian term meaning "black land,"[23] most likely referring to the color of the rich arable soil deposited along the banks of the Nile. In support of this contention, there are several instances in Late Biblical Hebrew where the term Ham appears to be used to describe Egypt: Pss 78:51 (where it could be Egypt or the alliance of Egypt and Cush); 105:23, 27; 106:22.[24] Ham could be an ancient transliteration of *Kmt* arising in Israel/Judah's preliterate phase before phonetic sounds were linked to specific letters. As such, *Kmt* may be regarded as a term for Egypt no longer *en vogue* during the period when the Table was composed, yet still familiar enough to represent the historic alliance of Cush, Egypt, Put, and Canaan.

This pericope is a literary complex consisting of the work of more than one author. Most scholars have noticed telltale variants in the genealogical formulas

21. Cf. Moshe Greenberg, *Introduction to Hebrew* (Englewood Cliffs, N.J.: Prentice–Hall, 1965), 1–3. In his discussion of the origin of Semitic languages, we can see how readily ethnic origin and language types have been conflated.

22. This line of reasoning was also followed by S. R. Driver, *Genesis*, 117.

23. Cf. Raymond O. Faulkner, *A Concise Dictionary of Middle Egyptian* (Oxford: Griffith Institute, 1981), 286.

24. Cf. BDB, 326.

that suggest an original composition with later authorial and editorial emenda-tions. For example, the formula in the sixth verse begins, וּבְנֵי חָם כּוּשׁ ("And the sons of Ham are Cush") while v. 8 follows another genealogical formula, יָלַד אֶת־נִמְרֹד וְכוּשׁ ("And Cush fathered Nimrod"). In general, scholars have accepted the following division for this pericope: vv. 8–12 belong to the Yahwist and vv. 6–7 were composed by the Priestly writer (P) centuries later.[25]

If we accept this reconstruction, the Yahwist knew Cush as the father of Nimrod and the Mesopotamian peoples and also knew Mitzraim, Canaan, and Shem. Japheth, Ham, and Cush, father of the Afro-Arabian league, are found only in the Priestly writer's material. What we are left with, then, is a Yahwist's presentation that is largely Palestinian and seemingly inaccurate with regard to the some of the non-Palestinian nations. It is only centuries later, with the addition of the Priestly material, that the local list becomes the ecumenical Table of Nations familiar to modern exegetes.[26]

There is further evidence of redaction in the Yahwistic account (J). Genesis 10:8–12 has the mark of a composite text because vv. 9–12 has the distinctive form of a narrative rather than a patronymic like the rest of the J material. Further, it lacks the "rhyming" pattern found in the rest of the J account of Ham's sons (plural gentilic endings for Mitzraim's sons in vv. 13–14 and singular gentilic endings for Canaan's sons in vv. 15–18) that is clearly echoed in the Priestly writer's account of Cush's sons.

We should also consider the significance of the birth-order of Ham's sons. The Priestly writer lists Cush as the first son of Ham. Several scholars have specu-lated that this is simply a south-to-north arrangement of the nations.[27] However, this arrangement would prove generally problematic for two reasons. First, Put, often thought to have been Libya, was not to the north of Egypt. From the perspective of the Israelites, it would be to the southwest and should fall between Cush and Egypt. Westermann notes that Meyer, Gunkel, and Procksch proposed another possible identification for Put—the Egyptian Punt, or Somaliland. In this regard, the south-to-north arrangement would be further complicated since Put should then be mentioned first as the southernmost region.[28] Second, following Gen 9:24, the position of Canaan as the youngest son (whether of Ham or of Noah) has already been given ideological significance. It is unlikely that this arrangement is to be read solely geographically, omitting the political import of Canaan's filial position.

---

25. For the sum of ch. 10, S. R. Driver (*Genesis*, 113–14) attributes vv. 1–7, 20, 22–24, 31–32 to P and the rest to J save vv. 16–18a, which he considers a later gloss. Von Rad (*Genesis*, 135–43) offers a slightly different assessment with vv. 1a, 2–7, 20, 22–23, 31–32 assigned to P and all the rest to J. More recently, John J. Scullion, "The Narrative of Genesis," in *ABD* 2: 948, and Richard Elliott Friedman, *Who Wrote the Bible?* (New York: Harper & Row, 1989), 247, have generally followed suit, though Scullion questions whether J is responsible for the basic genealogical framework.

26. George W. Coats, *Genesis: With an Introduction to Narrative Literature* (Grand Rapids: Eerdmans, 1983), 91–93.

27. See Horst Seebass, *Genesis I: Urgeschichte (1,1–11, 26)* (Neukirchen–Vluyn: Neukirchener Ver-lag, 1996), 257–58; Westermann, *Genesis*, 510–11.

28. Cf. Westermann, *Genesis*, 511.

In a ranking such as this, where order has been ideologically valued, the priority of the first party mentioned is implied.[29] That this list occurring in v. 6 is thought to be a later Priestly addition to the Yahwist's earlier patronymic is supported by the notion that the text was composed during or after the period when the XXVth Cushite Dynasty ruled Egypt (mid-eighth to mid-seventh centuries).

Subsequent to the advent of this historical period, Cush could have been seen as the most potent of these nations, that is, the eldest of Ham's sons. Also historically significant is that this arrangement of nations reflects the Priestly writer's knowledge of the political exigencies during (and likely after) the XXIInd Dynasty. Such a familiarity with historical detail is illustrated in 2 Chr 12; 14; and 16 where elements of Shishak (Sheshonq I) and Orsokon I's armies are described. There they are said to have consisted of Cushites, Libyans, Philistines, and other ethnic groups, reflecting the arrangement of Ham's sons presented in Gen 10:6. Hence, it is unlikely that the text could have been composed prior to the early eighth century nor long after the mid-seventh century B.C.E., based upon the historical alliances implied in this chapter. Von Rad concurs, suggesting that a period near the seventh century is further affirmed by the absence of the Persians, who played a key role in Judahite history after the Exile.[30]

If we accept that Cush as the firstborn son of Ham represented the author's perception of the recent political primacy of Cush over the other nations in the Hamitic League, then the presentation of Canaan as the youngest son may be important.[31] It could reflect the efforts of the author to diminish the status of the Canaanite peoples or to depict their status as the nation that was most dependent in this configuration. This would be a fair assessment of the remnant Canaanite population. Though the Israelite/Judahite population would have remembered that Canaanites were once members of the Egyptian Empire[32] and likely associated them with this league, they would have viewed them as lesser members of the "family" defined by this later military alliance.

Cush is listed as the progenitor of an extensive list of descendants (vv. 7–12). This list probably represents political alliances known historically prior to or during the period when these texts were composed. Among these nations are Seba, Havilah, and Sheba in vv. 7–8. Seba and Sheba, often thought to refer to the same people with the difference in the pronunciation of the initial radical reflecting dialectical differences,[33] are paired in Ps 72:10, suggesting that they may have been associated in the minds of members of the Judahite community. Also paired in the Hebrew Bible, in Gen 10:7, are Sheba and Dedan, a pairing which recurs in tandem in Gen 25:3, in another genealogy, and in Ezek 38:13, which describes an invasion by Gog and earlier refers to Cush and Put.

29. Robert R. Wilson, "Genealogy, Genealogies," in *ABD* 2: 929–32.

30. Von Rad, *Genesis*, 140.

31. Again, note the ideological significance of 9:24 in the larger context of 9:18–29.

32. Cf. Bright, *A History of Israel*, 108–20; Donald B. Redford, *Egypt, Canaan and Israel in Ancient Times* (Princeton, N.J.: Princeton University Press, 1992), 125–237.

33. Walter W. Müller, "Seba," in *ABD* 5: 1064.

Cush is further associated with Seba twice in Isaiah (43:3; 45:14) and with Havilah in Gen 2 in the description of the rivers flowing from Eden. The verses from Isaiah also include Cush's most common partner, Egypt. Cush and Egypt are frequently paired in the Hebrew Bible and in subsequent literature, likely due to the Israelites'/Judahites' knowledge of the strong political, economic, and social ties between these two southern nations. The repetitious connection of these various groups demonstrates that the Israelite/Judahite authors of the biblical texts conceived of them as allied groups.

Several of the ancestors mentioned in Gen 10 appear in more than one genealogical list. For example, Cush is said to be the father of Havilah and the grandfather of Sheba through his son Raamah in v. 7. However, both these characters recur in Shem's genealogy. In vv. 28–29, Sheba and Havilah are said to be brothers, sons of Joktan and great-, great-, great-grandsons of Shem. In like manner, Meshech appears in two genealogies. He is a son of Japheth in v. 2 and a grandson of Shem in v. 23. Similarly, in v. 13, Ludim (which sounds like a plural gentilic related to the name Lud) is a son of Mitzraim and grandson of Ham, while Lud occurs in v. 22 as a son of Shem.[34]

The differences in the construction of the names Lud and Ludim may be the result of a curious feature of the genealogies for the sons of Ham—namely, the names follow a general pattern. The offspring of Cush tend to have names that have *–ah* endings (an "a" vowel before a *heh* or an *'aleph*), while the offspring of Mitzraim have names with *–îm* endings (ם') and the offspring of Canaan have names with *–iy* endings ('). In light of this, the *–îm* ending on the root "Lud" in v. 13 may be a stylistic feature of the Yahwistic writer, not an indication of a different people.

So, what does that mean for our study? Simply, the presence of names representing the same peoples in different lineages emphasizes that the author did not intend to present the Table of Nations as ethnically pure human strains.[35] The narrative evidences ethnic mixing and diversity, not exclusivity. Whether due to conflicting data among his or her sources, or a lack of certainty on his behalf, the author presented a model that implied genetic exchange between the lineages of Noah's three sons. In spite of the logical implausibility of comprehending the manner in which the mixture of lineages could have occurred, based on the internal logic of these genealogies,[36] that many of the people's represented owed their lineage to more than one of Noah's sons is implicit.

---

34. There is also another possible repetition of the Dodanim in v. 4, a son of Japheth and Dedan in v. 7, a grandson of Cush. Both names appear to be derived from the same root and may well represent the same people. This issue is, however, complicated by the LXX, which reads Rodanim for the MT's Dodanim.

35. Japhet suggests that the inclusion of "identical names, in different genealogical contexts, is characteristic of these lists, and probably reflects ethnic circumstances and developments"; see Sara Japhet, *I & II Chronicles: A Commentary* (Louisville, Ky.: Westminster John Knox, 1993), 58.

36. It is difficult to imagine how the author and later redactors could have accepted a genealogical table that traced the same person to different patrilineal groups. In these instances, the same eponymous ancestor is called the son of two individuals in different lineages, both portrayed as "fathers" and often occurring in different generations. Yet the duplicate references evidently represent the same characters, eponymous ancestors of known ethnic groups. These logical oversights demonstrate the

Accepting this, the Table of Nations cannot be understood as a presentation of genetically discrete and genealogically distinct ethnic development. In this way it is inconsistent with the classical candelabra model for human evolution espoused in racialist circles. In such a racialist model, representatives of *homo erectus* began their migration from Africa several hundreds of thousands of years ago, evolved independently into three distinct "sub-species" and have since had limited genetic exchange.[37] However, the evidence gleaned from the Table of Nations suggests genetic exchange was likely.

The model of human evolution that most closely resembles that expressed in the Table of Nations is the trellis theory of human development. In this paradigm, groups of geographically circumscribed human beings develop specific somatic characteristics based upon factors in their environment, but they are subject to periodic genetic exchanges that ensure the common evolution of the species. Genetic exchange is limited primarily by the significant, though not insurmountable barrier posed by geographic distance. In this paradigm, somatic type is not perceived as a racial characteristic, but an environmentally conditioned adaptation. This is confirmed genetically by the fact that people from different geographic regions in similar climes may have similar features, yet be more genetically divergent than people with markedly different phenotypes.[38] Just as the trellis theory is predicated on the implausibility of genetic purity in the human race, similarly the Table of Nations demonstrates that there were no ideological barriers to ethnic mixing influencing these genealogical narratives.

In sum, we can discern four reasons why the Table of Nations could not represent distinct races as perceived by modern thinkers. First, there appear to be several instances of admixture suggested by the appearance of the names of the same eponymous ancestors of several groups in distinct patronymics. Second, there is historical evidence to suggest that the principal considerations for the author were the political, linguistic, and trade relationships between members of the patronymics (i.e. the known political alliances between the Cushites, Egyptians, and the Putim in subsequent biblical texts). Third, there are instances where a "racial" categorization based upon phenotypes and somatic types contradicts what is known about particular groups (i.e. we would have to assume that the Cushites were of the same "racial type" as the Lydians-Lud,[39] the Cretans-Caphtor, and the Philistines). (4) Fourth, general geographic continuity and political alliances based on proximity (Hamites primarily north African; Jephathites primarily European) could also be plausible reasons why these genealogies were employed, but not the anachronistic concept of "race."

---

speculative quality of these genealogies while illustrating the complex political web of relationships indicated by the Table of Nations.

37. Templeton, "Evolutionary," 635–36.

38. Templeton, "Evolutionary," 636.

39. Unless we assume Lud is a North African nation and not Lydia, as suggested by the evidence of a relationship between Gyges of Lydia and Pharoah Neco of Egypt. See the section below on Ezek 38 (3.2.6.3) for a more detailed discussion of Gyges' role in Egyptian politics.

As a result, the Table of Nations should not be viewed as an ontologically distinct division of the "human race" into three sub-set "races,"[40] particularly not with the ideological baggage traditionally associated with this social construct. What the Table does represent is a collection of the nations known to the Yahwistic and Priestly authors, a collection which a subsequent redactor arranged primarily by geography. This view accounts for the complex web of relationships between and among the nations. What should also not be lost on the exegete is that the author conceived of the narrative as the story of a single family, indicating that he or she perceived all humanity as ultimately related, not as distinct subspecies. This view is further reinforced by the perceived inter-lineal origins of some of the ethnic groups. An author wishing to maintain pure "racial" stocks could easily have eliminated such overlapping patronymics.

2.2.1.4. *Addendum to Genesis 10.* There seems to be an addition to the genealogy of Cush. Verses 8–12 discuss Nimrod, a mighty hunter and the "beginning" of Babel, Erech, and Accad. This narrative section does not seem to be a component of the genealogical account. Without this section, Cush's lineage is a succinct two verses of characters with names which end in an –*ah* sound. This would make it a close parallel to Mitzraim's lineage in vv. 13–14, as it is both succinct and consists of character names ending in –*îm*. Though the subsequent Genealogy of Canaan is much longer, this is to be expected due to the proximity of the Canaanites to the Israelites. Still, the descendants have names with consistent –*iy* endings.

The addition of vv. 8–12 to Cush's lineage appears to be a conflation of Cush with a northern group (Kassites) whose name employs the same unpointed root consonants. Confusion with this known northern group would account for the introduction of peoples native to lands non-contiguous with those of other Hamites.[41]

There are also other hints that this portion of the text may not be original. None of the names mentioned in Nimrod's lineage has the characteristic –*ah* endings of Cush's descendants. Further, the introduction of Nimrod as a son of Cush contradicts v. 6, which lists Cush's sons. Without this departure, the narrative seems more consistent. Though it is unlikely that this pericope is a part of the original tradition, it is significant that these groups are ascribed to Cush's lineage. Nimrod and his descendants have a glorious history that is in part recorded in this pericope. Had the Yahwist considered Cush worthy of derision or pejoration, he would not have listed them among the glories of Cush.

2.2.1.5. *Numbers 12: Moses' Cushite Wife.* The term כֻּשִׁית ("Cushite" [f.]) occurs twice in this chapter, both instances in v. 1. Numbers 12 is a chapter requiring careful attention since it is enigmatic for a variety of reasons. It is immediately

---

40. Other scholars have noted this as well. S. R. Driver, *Genesis*, 114, stated that, "It will be evident that the Table of Nations contains no scientific classification of the races of mankind. Not only this, however; it also offers no historically true account of the origins of the races of mankind." Von Rad (*Genesis*, 136) noted that race or language was not a factor governing the construction of this list.

41. Cf. Hidal, "Land," 104–6.

evident that the cause of the conflict in this chapter is not apparent. Why do Miriam[42] and Aaron complain against Moses? Considering v. 1, the reason seems to be Moses' marriage to a Cushite woman.

Evidence from Jewish literature composed during the latter centuries B.C.E. illustrates how much of a problem this woman caused hermeneuts.[43] Exodus 2:15–22 describes Moses' union with Zipporah, identified as a daughter of Midianite priest Reuel,[44] while Judg 1:16 and 4:11 imply that Moses married a Kenite woman, daughter of Hobab. Though the question about whether Zipporah was a Midianite or a Kenite was seldom the cause of much contention,[45] whether Moses married a Cushite woman was a matter of significant interest. Did this mean that Moses had married a second wife? Or was this label, Cushite, consistent with her identity as a Midianite? These two questions point to the two principal solutions early Jewish authors offered to this dilemma.

Demetrius the Chronographer and Ezekiel the Tragedian, both favoring the first solution, determined that Moses had only one wife and offered explanations of how Zipporah could properly be deemed Cushite.[46] Artapanus and Josephus chose the second solution, introducing legends of a military campaign into Ethiopia to the Moses narratives.[47] Though Artapanus makes no explicit reference to the wife of Num 12, the Ethiopian campaign seems to provide a context for a resolution of the dilemma raised by this passage, as is expressed explicitly in Josephus's use of the campaign legend (*Ant.* 2.252). The introduction of this Cushite woman was apparently a reason for concern.

However, suggesting that the cause of contention was the Cushite wife raises another equally potent question: What was it about this wife that provoked Miriam (and Aaron), causing her (them) to complain? In theory, there are a number of compelling motivations for the complaint, not the least among these being the issue of race. Cain Felder, in *Troubling Biblical Waters* (1989), concluded that despite the "extraordinarily progressive racial values of the Bible," the complaint was based upon Miriam's assessment of Moses' wife's racial identity. Hence, in

---

42. Actually it looks like the text has been edited by a redactor who included Aaron at a later time, perhaps to vilify this leader and elevate the status of Moses (12:6–8). Note that the initial verb employed in this chapter (12:1) is feminine singular though the extant text would seemingly call for a plural verb since the subjects are Miriam and Aaron. Also note that Miriam is the only recipient of YHWH's wrath (12:10). Also see Adamo, *Africa*, 111.

43. See, e.g., Ezekiel the Tragedian, Demetrius the Chronographer, Artapanus, and Josephus.

44. Cf. Exod 3:1, where the priest father-in-law of Moses is identified as Jethro. This narrative clearly contains strains of numerous traditions.

45. This is due largely to the conflation of the stories about the Kenites and Midianites, both thought to be populations dwelling south of Judah and connected with Moses traditions. Cf. Baruch Halpern, "Kenites," in *ABD* 4:17–22. Here Halpern notes that the differences in the use of ethnic terms Kenite and Midianite relate to differences in the literary sources and political interests of Mushite and Aaronid schools. In this regard, it is most significant that the many sources that mention Moses' wife and in-laws agree on two principal points: that he married a non-Israelite woman from the region south of Judah.

46. Cf. Robert G. Robertson, "Ezekiel the Tragedian," in *OTP* 2: 803–20; James Hanson, "Demetrius the Chronographer," in *OTP* 2: 843–54.

47. Cf. John J. Collins, "Artapanus," in *OTP* 2: 889–904; Louis H. Feldman, "Josephus' Portrait of Moses," *JQR* 83 (1993): 301–30.

this paradigm, we should contrast Miriam's visceral reaction against this Cushite woman in v. 1 with the nature of YHWH's punishment of Miriam in v. 12.[48] I will say more about this below.

Felder, however, uncomfortable with the implication that "race" could cause such contention in Israelite/Judahite society, only hesitantly contended that the Hebrew Bible could contain racialist thought and was later pleased to recant this initial assessment in his 1991 article, "Race, Racism and the Biblical Narratives."[49] In this article he, accepting Randall Bailey's hypothesis,[50] revised his earlier conclusions, suggesting that the complaint was not based upon the perceived racial inferiority of the Cushite wife, but upon the perceived social valuation of the Cushite wife. Hence, for Felder, what seemed to be a conflict stemming from a matter of racialist denigration of the Cushite Other is actually a matter of conflict over the elite social status associated with the Cushite Other.[51]

Alice Bellis notes that there may be reasons for the objection beyond the racial and social status issues. Following Drorah Setel, she suggests that the issue of the Cushite wife may have been cultic. If this wife is indeed Zipporah, as Bellis contends,[52] the conflict may have to do with her status as a priestess (cf. Exod 4:24–26). Moses' union with a priestess, then, may have bestowed upon him a particular prophetic authority over that of Miriam (and Aaron), hence producing the tension between Moses and his siblings.[53]

Bellis has also hypothesized that the reason the author introduced the conflict over the Cushite wife into the context of the Pentateuch may stem from an issue of contemporary relevance for the author. The purpose of the narrative may be to resolve the issue of Moses' marriage to a foreign wife when this issue was becoming a problem in Israelite society.[54] It is beyond contention that Moses married a foreign woman from the south,[55] and the redactor of Numbers to his or her

48. Felder, *Troubling*, 42. Cf. John Waters, "Who was Hagar," in *Stony the Road We Trod: African American Biblical Interpretation* (ed. Cain Hope Felder; Minneapolis: Fortress, 1991), 187–205 (204). Though Felder thinks the Num 12 passage is an anomily, Waters thinks it represents a "growing dislike for Africans."

49. Felder, "Race," 127–45.

50. Cf. Randall Bailey, "Beyond Identification: The Use of Africans in Old Testament Poetry and Narratives," in *Stony the Road We Trod: African American Biblical Interpretation* (ed. Cain Hope Felder; Minneapolis: Fortress, 1991), 165–86 (179). This article is discussed in greater detail below.

51. Felder, "Race," 135–36.

52. Alice Ogden Bellis, *Helpmates, Harlots, Heroes: Women's Stories in the Hebrew Bible* (Louisville, Ky.: Westminster John Knox, 1994), 103.

53. Bellis, *Helpmates*, 104–5.

54. Bellis, *Helpmates*, 104. Bellis also rehearses a number of other raisons d'être for this complex passage, including that it was an attempt do deal with Moses' adultery as he had married a second wife; the objection about the wife was a "pretext" for the actual dilemma, prophetic authority; or the matter was one of cultic purity (*Helpmates*, pp. 255–56 n. 27).

55. He married either a Midianite (Exod 2:11–22; 3:1; Num 10:29), a Kenite (Judg 1:16; 4:11), or a Cushite (Num 12:1). However we understand these various passages, it is clear that Moses had married a foreign woman from the south. It is possible to conflate each of these peoples. For example, Judg 1:16 would allow us to conclude that Midians and Kushites could be the same peoples. Hab 3:7 would suggest that Midian and Cushan could be conflated. Hence, we could determine that the Cushite wife is actually Cush(an)ite, from the region to the south of Edom.

specific ends employed this fact to achieve the purpose of the present passage.[56] Technically, each of the designations[57] may overlap in the minds of Israel. The actual reason for the objection to the Cushite wife occurring in 12:1 may continue to be a matter of contention for exegetes; however, the lack of clarity regarding why the issue was raised in the first place should not distract us from the fact that it was. For the sake of this discussion, I will primarily address the existence of the complaint and not the reason for it.

Exegetes have not always perceived this chapter as a single coherent textual unit. In fact, Martin Noth saw two distinct literary strands interwoven in this complex which could no longer be "disentangled."[58] Eryl W. Davies, who attempted to sort the two narratives, later championed Noth's position. He did so as follows:

1. Cushite wife controversy—vv. 1, 9a, 10ab, 13–16.
2. Authority controversy—vv. 2–5a, 6–8, 9b, 10aα.

Davies' hypothesis posits that Miriam alone was the antagonist in the first story, while Miriam and Aaron act cooperatively in the second.[59] In regard to the odd construction of the feminine singular verb ascribed to both Miriam and Aaron in v. 1, the anomaly is explained: it was never intended to have Aaron as its subject. Davies' interpretation runs contrary to that of Noth who sees the construction simply as another example of the predicate in first position assuming the form of the initial subject in a series.[60] Davies takes this as evidence that Aaron was not a character in the first narrative. Were he included, then he probably would have been mentioned first as the most recognizable character.[61]

Davies' "two narratives" explanation clarifies a number of the problems in this chapter since it provides a clear cycle of problem, confrontation, and resolution for both narratives. Further, his solution allows us to address the matter of the Cushite wife on its own grounds: it is a specific complaint raised by Miriam, then resolved by the punishment of YHWH. The inclusion of the material from a subsequent intervening Aaron and Miriam story only serves to complicate matters.

However, one cannot easily overlook the contributions of Gordon Wenham for understanding the structure of this chapter. Wenham has found in the extant passage evidence of a pattern also repeated in Num 11, 14, 16 (twice), 17 and 21, which is as follows:

> a) the people complain; b) the Lord appears/hears; c) the Lord is angry and punishes; d) the people appeal to Moses; e) Moses prays for people; f) the judgment ceases.[62]

In this regard, the two narratives in ch. 12 fulfill the pattern found in the literary context only in their present intertwined state, suggesting that the redactor may

56. Bellis, *Helpmates*, 255 n. 21.
57. Midianite, Kenite, or Cushite, though we are by no means definitively arguing that Zipporah was the wife of Num 12:1.
58. Martin Noth, *Numbers: A Commentary* (Philadelphia: Westminster, 1968), 93.
59. Eryl W. Davies, *Numbers* (Grand Rapids: Eerdmans, 1995), 114.
60. Noth, *Numbers*, 93.
61. E. W. Davies, *Numbers*, 117.
62. Gordon J. Wenham, *Numbers* (OTG 5; Sheffield: Sheffield Academic Press, 1997), 51–52.

not have intended them as independent units. Thus, while employing Davies' notion that two distinct complaints have been combined for analytical purposes, we should be careful not to disregard the symmetry of the complete extant passage.

These structural insights help to clarify the confusion most scholars have when confronting this passage. There are two distinct concerns or two distinct narratives conflated into one composite narrative. The Cushite wife was evidently a concern for Miriam that was resolved when YHWH punished her with a temporary case of skin disease and a period of banishment from the community. More will be said about this below.

This text contains the only explicit reference to a Cushite woman in the Hebrew Bible.[63] That fact alone makes Num 12 significant, for the portrayal here of Moses' wife provides the limited information we have about how Cushite women were viewed by Hebrew authors. Among the information that can be gleaned from this passage is the fact that the Cushite woman, whose identity is emphasized by repetition of the fact that אִשָּׁה כֻשִׁית לָקָח ("he had taken [married] a Cushite woman"), is refused agency and voice. She neither speaks nor acts and is a flat character whose role in the narrative is limited inasmuch as she serves only as a cause for Miriam's complaint. Following v. 1 she disappears.

Because the text does not provide adequate detail, we cannot be sure what it was about this woman's identity that offended Miriam, provoking her objection. Whether the objection was due to aesthetics or cultural otherness is unclear. One could argue that the principal objection was to the union of this prominent Levite with a non-Hebrew woman.[64] This would be true whether the Cushite woman was Zipporah or a subsequent bride (though if we identity her with Zipporah, she can then be associated with a priestly lineage, hence perhaps assuaging the problem). Had Moses married any other non-Levite woman, it could have produced this reaction by the prophetic matriarch, Miriam.

Still, the repetition in v. 1 of the MT confirming the Cushite identity of Moses' wife emphasizes that she is Other, significantly unlike Moses. If we choose to read the complete chapter as a single story, we note from the contextual clues the ambiguity with which the difference is valued. What is clear is that Miriam

---

63. There may also be others in the Bible, including the Queen of Sheba in 1 Kgs 10, following Charles Copher and the suggestion by Edward Ullendorff, who, based upon his reading of Josephus (*Ant.* 8.6.5–6), would look for Sheba in South Arabia or in Cush–Egypt, or would connect her with Queen Candace in the New Testament (Acts 8:27). But the former is not an explicit reference to a Cushite woman and the latter is not in the Hebrew Bible. Cf. Copher, *Black*, 62; Edward Ullendorff, *Ethiopia and the Bible* (London: Oxford University Press, 1968), 131–45; Cain Hope Felder, *Troubling Biblical Waters: Race, Class, and Family* (Maryknoll, N.Y.: Orbis, 1989), 141. Also, if this woman is identified with Zipporah and deemed of Midianite/Kenite–Cushan heritage (cf. Hab 3:7), then other women (and men) so identified may merit our attention.

64. Cf. Exod 34:16; Deut 7:1–4; 23:1–7. However, we should note that Hamilton found that prohibitions of exogamous marriages are limited to few Others in the pre-exilic period and only are universal in the post-exilic writings of Ezra (9–10) and Nehemiah (9:2; 10:30; 13:3, 23–28); see Victor P. Hamilton, "Marriage (Old Testament and ANE)," in *ABD* 4: 559–68. Also see Bellis, *Helpmates*, 255 n. 21.

implies the Cushite woman was Other, and the difference mattered; Moses has somehow by this marriage elevated himself above his siblings. Hence, it is not likely that the Cushite wife was denigrated because of her Cushite identity, perhaps just the opposite, she stood as a symbol of Moses' status and authority.[65]

However, according to Davies' hypothesis, the Cushite wife narrative is also paradoxical. Even though it cannot be said to prohibit Moses' union with this Cushite woman, the fact that it posits the partnering as a matter of contention implies that it raised a red flag for Miriam. In this regard the passage is a double-edged sword: it both indicates by Miriam's complaint that the marriage challenged normative assumptions of who is marriageable, demonstrating that this union could be seen as unacceptable by certain members of the Hebrew community; and it affirms by YHWH's silence in response to Miriam's complaint that such unions could not be categorically proscribed.

This narrative is further complicated by the way YHWH punished Miriam. The introduction of the phrase מְצֹרַעַת כַּשָּׁלֶג, meaning "leprous as snow," in v. 10 adds to the text another layer of complexity. According to the narrative, after the cloud containing the presence of an angry YHWH departed from the tent, "Miriam had become leprous, as white as snow" (v. 10 NRSV). Note the additional aspect of color present in the NRSV translation. Whether or not the notion of color is germane to מְצֹרַעַת כַּשָּׁלֶג is a matter of significance for our study; but the text is by no means unambiguous on this point. No explicit color terms (i.e. לבן) are used in this chapter. However, מְצֹרַעַת כַּשָּׁלֶג cannot be deemed void of all color content. Athalaya Brenner classified the root of the latter word in this construction, שֶׁלֶג, as a secondary color term, or a term that functions in certain contexts "as specifications of לבן."[66] In this manner, מְצֹרַעַת כַּשָּׁלֶג has often been understood as a simile for "whiteness" in Num 12:10, as well as in Exod 4:6 and 2 Kgs 5:27, as is apparent in the NRSV.

This being said, some scholars have argued against connoting color in these three aforementioned verses. Most notably, Brenner herself has suggested that the term as it is employed here should not be understood as a simile for "whiteness" but for flakiness, reflecting the texture of snow.[67] Though the notion of

65. Bailey, "Africans," 179. Here Bailey argues that Miriam's complaint is not racist but a matter of status. Moses' marriage to an African woman bestows a higher status on him than on his siblings (his elevated status is implied in vv. 3–4 and marriage to an African was also a symbol of status for Solomon in 1 Kgs 3:1). Bailey's reading is significant because he argues against conventional wisdom, that association with an "African" would serve to diminish one's status, and is consistent with the arrogance Miriam appears to oppose. He concludes by noting the irony associated with the contrast between a Cushite woman in 12:1 (black) and Miriam's punishment (being "white as snow") further stating that being "white as snow" is a matter of punishment, citing Isa 1:18, which he analyzes grammatically as a curse (cf. 2 Kgs 5:27).

66. Athalya Brenner, *Colour Terms in the Old Testament* (JSOTSup 21; Sheffield: JSOT Press, 1982), 42.

67. Brenner, *Colour Terms*, 82, 90, 168. Brenner follows E.V. Hulse, "The Nature of Biblical 'Leprosy' and the Use of Alternative Medical Terms in Modern Translations of the Bible," *Palestine Exploration Quarterly* 107 (1975): 87–105. Also see Gordon J. Wenham, *Numbers: An Introduction and Commentary* (Leicester: Inter-Varsity, 1981), 113.

considering the term a reference to the flaking associated with a psoriasis-like condition is entirely plausible, we should realize that it would be arbitrary to preclude its connotation as a color term[68] in Num 12:10. This is also true for Exod 4:6 and 2 Kgs 5:27, each of which address similar stories of a skin disorder brought on by YHWH's activity. In fact, Brenner herself recognizes the clear use of כַּשֶּׁלֶג as a simile for "whiteness" in Isa 1:18; Ps 51:9; and Dan 7:9; and more directly she states "that 'white' can be signified by a comparison to snow."[69] In addition, a psoriasis-like condition can be described as "shiny-silvery scales"[70] which by no means makes the simile "white as snow" implausible. Further, following Brenner's conclusion that כּוּשִׁי can have a connotation of "dark-skinned person," particularly in reference to Jer 13:23, it seems likely that the author of Num 12 intentionally employed two secondary color terms, כֻּשִׁית in 12:1 and כַּשֶּׁלֶג in 12:10, knowing that the irony of the consequence of Miriam's complaint against Moses' marriage to the Cushite woman being a sickness that made her "as snow" would not be lost on his audience.[71]

Bellis has also offered a challenge to interpretations of this passage that presume that the author employs color connotation in this narrative. Bellis suggests that the image of מֵת אֲשֶׁר בְּצֵאתוֹ מֵרֶחֶם אִמּוֹ, or the "stillborn infant" in 12:12, should govern our interpretation of this passage. In her estimation, it is not color that is being emphasized in this simile, but the leprosy-like condition of the corpse where its skin has been eaten away. She further argues that the color of the corpse would not be "white" but "gray and mottled."[72] Though this perspective does emphasize the debilitating effect of the leprous condition, I do not see where this changes the "color" aspect of this verse. If anything, it strengthens the notion of the contrast between the "pale" complexion of the infant and the "dark" complexion of the Cushite woman. Further, since the contrast is not between the distinct opposites, "black" and "white," but between generally tanned to dark-brown Mediterranean complexions, "dark" and "pale," the potency of Miriam's punishment remains intact. She has forfeited whatever natural skin-coloration she had, and became like a corpse, not "white" as we think of it with its constituent ideological baggage, but a blotchy vitiligo-like[73] "whiteness" perceived as the absence of color.

---

68. Particularly so for another reason. These texts were likely composed in Judah, a region not known for an excessive amounts of snow. Though snow does fall occasionally in Judah, the intended audience would perhaps be most familiar with snow seen from a distance, that is, upon Mt Hermon or other high mountains. Hence, I would suggest that the most likely metaphorical value of snow would be to evoke images of "whiteness," not the other proximately relevant qualities like "flakiness" or "wetness." See E. W. Davies, *Numbers*, 124.

69. Brenner, *Colour Terms*, 82.

70. Brenner, *Colour Terms*, 90.

71. Felder, *Troubling*, 42; Bailey, "Africans," 180.

72. Alice Ogden Bellis, "Zipporah: Issues of Race, Religion, Gender and Power" (an unpublished paper presented at the Duke Hebrew Bible Fall Seminar. Durham, N.C., 12 October 2000).

73. *Webster's New Universal Unabridged Dictionary* (ed. Noah Webster and Jean L. McKechnie; New York: Dorset & Baber, 1983), 2045, defines vitiligo as "a disease characterized by the formation of smooth, white pigmentless patches on various parts of the body."

The introduction of a color-laden concept into Miriam's punishment at the end of this pericope suggests another reason for the emphasis on the Cushite wife. There is a strange irony to the story of a woman who complains against a woman identified as Cushite, implicitly dark-skinned, whose skin is then transformed, as a result of YHWH's punishment, to be void of color.[74] The author of the Hebrew text exploited the obvious contrast between the Cushite woman's skin and Miriam's leprous skin. But instead of explicitly stating that YHWH punished Miriam for her prejudice against this female Other by "whitening" her skin, she or he employed the power of the commonplace terms כְּשֶׁית and כַּשֶּׁלֶג, knowing that the ironic contrast between these terms would have an impact on her or his audience.

Despite her inactive and mute role, the Cushite wife remains a significant character because her presence in this chapter clarifies a number of issues. First, her presence in this narrative implies that Hebrew authors presumed a Cushite element in the initial migration from Egypt to Israel. Second, as the narrative affirms, a Cushite woman's connection with so significant a character in the unfolding historical narrative in no way diminished his stature and standing in subsequent generations. Third, the lack of a negative response from YHWH to Miriam's complaint about Moses' marriage precludes the existence of a narrative prohibiting such unions. Fourth, following Bailey and reading the combined extant passage, it seems that Moses' association with this Cushite woman elevated not diminished his social standing, since the affirmation of Moses' humility in v. 3 would be irrelevant were the marriage perceived as demeaning.

So, what is the conclusion of the matter of the Cushite wife? We are far from any permanent solution to the issues raised by this chapter, but on the matter under investigation—whether the Israelites/Judahites viewed Cushites through a racialist lens—we can come to certain qualified conclusions. If we accept the contention that the author intended to contrast the color of the Cushite woman's skin with Miriam's after YHWH's punishment, then we also have to accept that the color of a Cushite's skin was a prevalent feature in the mind of the audience. In this regard, to say "Cushite" could invoke images of dark skin (cf. Jer 13:23) in a manner similar to the way saying "snow" conjured images of "whiteness." Based upon this, we should categorize this story as a "phenotypical" passage, for the aspect of Cushite identity emphasized in this text is the distinctive Cushite physical appearance.

Though the association of an ethnic group with a prominent phenotypical trait is a constituent element of racialist thought, we cannot readily conclude that the author had a racialist mindset. As we have determined above, the *Tendenz* of the author definitively opposed Miriam's disdain for the union of Moses and his Cushite wife. We may even conclude that the chapter is anti-racialist in its orientation, seeking to combat the notion that Cushites were ontologically different from Hebrews, symbolically transcending perceived otherness by placing

---

74. Cf. Timothy R. Ashley, *The Book of Numbers* (Grand Rapids: Eerdmans, 1993), 227; Felder, *Troubling*, 42; Waters, "Who was Hagar?," 204.

YHWH's seal of approval on Moses' union with a Cushite woman. Hence, what we have in this narrative is an early biblical author's strategy for addressing a color prejudice by highlighting YHWH's ironic response to Miriam's complaint.

### 2.2.2. *Amos 9: Offspring of the Cushites*

The phrase כִּבְנֵי כֻשִׁיִּים ("as sons of [the] Cushiyim") occurs once in this chapter in v. 7. We find in this chapter the fifth of Amos' visions about the fate of Israel.[75] In these visions, the prophet has provided progressively worse news to the "elect" community. As Peter Craigie has suggested, the fifth vision confirmed Israel's imminent destruction and demonstrated that its citizens had compromised the benefit of their election by persistent evil and injustice.[76] In fact, Mays has identified it as a text unique "in the entire Old Testament" since it stands in clear contrast to others emphasizing Israel's favor with YHWH.[77] Formally, v. 7 consists of two rhetorical questions that YHWH, through Amos, posed to his northern audience to arouse tension preceding the prophetic announcement of judgment on Israel.

The text is also a singularly important reference since it is perhaps the only occurrence of the term Cush in a book composed for a northern, Israelite audience. The text demonstrates that at the point of the fall of Israel in the latter part of the eighth century, YHWH compared the Cushites, for whatever reason, to Israel. Because this rhetorical question occurs amid an oracle of destruction, we can reasonably conclude that YHWH intended Israel to perceive a negative aspect of Cushite identity as the crux of the simile. Whether this reference contains implicit denigration of the Cushites or of the people of Israel, as some have suggested, has yet to be determined; what is apparent is that Amos utilized the Cushites to reassess YHWH's relationship with Israel. But what precisely is his message?

Though not explicitly stated, the premise of this chapter is that YHWH was responsible for the unfolding histories of other nations; "Israel's God" had founded and cared for other nations besides Israel.[78] With this revelation, the prophet sought to prepare a "sinful" people to accept that the favor of YHWH had passed from them. No longer would their election be enough to save them from the impending destruction coming at the hands of the same God who had previously protected them, for they are to YHWH like their neighbors. There is a particular reason that Amos decided to focus on the Exodus in v. 7b. It was the founding event of the nation of Israel that was deemed similar to the founding events of the Philistines and the Arameans, whom Wolff calls Israel's "two great

---

75. For discussion of the visions see Peter C. Craigie, *Twelve Prophets*, vol. 1, *Hosea, Joel, Amos, Obadiah, and Jonah* (Philadelphia: Westminster, 1984), 188–89; G. V. Smith, *Amos*, 260.

76. Bright, *History*, 262–63; Craigie, *Twelve*, 189–90; Mays, *Amos*, 157; J. A. Soggin, *Introduction to the Old Testament: From its Origins to the Closing of the Alexandrian Canon* (trans. John Bowden; Louisville, Ky.: Westminster John Knox, 1989), 286.

77. Mays, *Amos*, 156.

78. Bright, *History*, 442.

arch-enemies."[79] YHWH takes responsibility for the exodus of the Philistines מִכַּפְתּוֹר ("from Caphtor" [likely Crete])[80] and the Arameans מִקִּיר ("from Kir").[81] Further, we learn in v. 7a that the Israelites are כִּבְנֵי כֻשִׁיִּים ("as the sons of the Cushites") to YHWH, their own deity.

Biblical scholars have not unanimously agreed on the prophet's perspective of Cushites in this passage.[82] Over the course of the twentieth century, many scholars have perceived that the comparison was predicated on denigration of the Cushites. For instance, Horton reads this passage in light of the "Curse of Ham" in Gen 9,[83] deeming the Cushites, "the descendants of Ham, the despised and accursed branch of Noah's family."[84] Edghill, another early twentieth century exegete whose views demonstrate how modern racial biases influenced analysis, determined that the passage disparaged Israel by comparing it with Cush, a nation that Amos would have viewed with condescension.[85] As far as Edghill was concerned, the Cushites of Amos' time were "uncivilized" and "despised blacks."[86] In like fashion, Ullendorff suggested that this verse could only be "fully appreciated if the [Cushites] serve, in the present context, as the epitome of a far-distant, uncivilized, and despised black race."[87] Mays continues this reasoning, suggesting that the comparison was intended to "humiliate Israel completely with respect to Yahweh, to reduce them to the role in Yahweh's order of things which the Cushites played in their own society."[88]

But these views were not limited to the early or middle periods of the twentieth century. In a similar vein, André Neher has concluded that the prophet used the Cushites because they were a primitive and inconsequential people in the Bible. They could thus serve as an acceptable commonplace for the belittling of Israel in YHWH's eyes. Robert Martin-Achard summarizes Neher's position as follows:

79. Hans Walter Wolff, *Joel and Amos: A Commentary on the Books of the Prophets Joel and Amos* (Philadelphia: Fortress, 1977), 347.

80. Cf. J. Alberto Soggin, *The Prophet Amos: A Translation and Commentary* (trans. John Bowden; London: SCM Press, 1987), 142; Wolff, *Joel*, 347.

81. Cf. Henry O. Thompson, "Kir, 2," in *ABD* 4:83–84.

82. Mays (*Amos*, 157) concedes that the actual reason Amos employed the Cushites in this passage "must unfortunately remain somewhat obscure," though he does offer an unsatisfactory explanation, discussed below.

83. The actual recipient of the Curse was not Ham, but Canaan; yet misinterpretations of that passage have influenced exegesis of Amos 9 as well. See the discussion of this complex passage in the Excursus on Gen 9 above (Section 2.2.1.2).

84. Robert F. Horton, *The Minor Prophets*, vol. 1 (Edinburgh: Oxford University Press, 1904), 172.

85. This perspective ignores the historical exigencies of Amos' period when the Cushites were gaining sway in Egypt. More will be said about this below.

86. Ernest Arthur Edghill, *The Book of Amos* (London: Methuen, 1926), 90.

87. Ullendorff, *Ethiopia*, 9.

88. Mays, *Amos*, 157. It is apparent that Mays has a very limited understanding of the role the Cushites played in the Hebrew Bible. See also G.V. Smith, *Amos*, 270.

A. Neher points out that the word Cush is never used in the Hebrew Bible as a synonym for slave or inferior creature; Cushites would be the example of a people left at a natural level, not included in history unlike Israel, Aram, and the Philistines.[89]

In fact, the perception that this passage has racial overtones and that it assumed a demeaning connotation of the term Cushites has been held by many modern exegetes over the course of the entire twentieth century.[90]

Each of these exegetes predicates his interpretation on his perception that the Cushites were a "primitive" people who were disdained by the ancient Near Eastern world. Hence, their reading of v. 7 would suggest that YHWH has rejected Israel, allowing it to condescend to the level of the vilified people of Cush. Were we to accept Edghill, Ullendorff, Mays, Horton, and Neher's analyses, we would have interesting fodder for our discussion of racialist traits. Yet, we should note that their assumptions about the Cushites during the period when Amos prophesied are historically inaccurate.[91] As Rice has suggested, "there are no grounds

89. Robert Martin-Achard, *Amos: L'homme, le Message, l'influence* (Geneva: Labor et Fides, 1984), 124 (translation by Professor David B. McCarthy). Martin-Achard summarized the view of André Neher in *Amos: Contribution à l'etude du Prophetisme* (Paris: J. Vrin, 1981), 140.

90. To understand how pervasive this perception has been, see Gene Rice, "Was Amos a Racist?," *JRT* 35 (1978): 35–44 (35–36 n. 1). Rice believes that the various scholars who held this view were influenced by the bellicose history Israel shared with Aram and Philistia. Based on this history, they determined that v. 7 must be viewed in toto as having a negative bias. Such a view coupled with a predisposition to think of the color of the Cushites as cause for offense played a role in their exegesis. We should also note that the *a priori* assumption that the color of the Cushites was cause for offense or that the Cushites were uncivilized is rooted in modern racial assumptions. Nowhere is this more evident than in the following quotation from Desnoyers: "They are the sons of Israel, become unfaithful to the terms of the covenant, who are lowered to the rank of Cushites, those African and Arabian Negroes, nearly as scorned by the Semitic world of that time as people of color are by Yankees of our times" (translation by Professor David B. McCarthy); Louis Desnoyers, "Le prophète Amos," *RB* 26 (1917): 218–46 (230). Other post-civil rights era exegetes that have perceived that the author understood Cushite color, exotic alien nature, or another "racial" trait to be at issue in this passage include: Ullendorff, *Ethiopia*, 8–9; Erling Hammershaimb, *The Book of Amos: A Commentary* (Oxford: Basil Blackwell, 1970), 134; Hyman J. Routtenberg, *Amos of Tekoa: A Study in Interpretation* (New York: Vantage, 1971), 123–24; Bruce C. Birch, *Hosea, Joel, and Amos* (Louisville, Ky.: Westminster John Knox, 1997), 253.

91. Against these positions we should note that the Cushites of Amos' time were clearly neither uncivilized nor isolated in their own territory. According to Willoughby, Amos began his prophetic activity ca. 760 BCE; see Bruce E. Willoughby, "Amos, Book of," in *ABD* 1:203–12. Smith puts the time of his prophecy between 560–740 BCE. Regina Smith, "A New Perspective on Amos 9.7a 'To Me, O Israel, You are Just like the Kushites,'" *The Journal of the Interdenominational Theological Center* 22 (1994): 36–47. The circumstances surrounding this prophecy in ch. 9 indicate that his prior four visions were not heeded and that time has past in the interim. This would mean that by the time Amos uttered the oracle in ch. 9, he would likely be familiar with the Cushites who were active in the Levant for centuries (see Sections 3.2.7.2 and 4.2.1). Further, the news of the increasing hegemony of Cushites in Egypt would have likely reached Judah too since the advent of Amos' prophetic activity was contemporary with the advent of the XXVth Cushite Dynasty under Kashta in 760 BCE. Cf. Timothy Kendall, "Kings of the Sacred Mountain: Napata and the Kushite Twenty-Fifth Dynasty of Egypt," in *Sudan: Ancient Kingdoms of the Nile* (ed. Dietrich Wildung; Paris: Flammarion, 1997), 160–204, who, again, citing Regina Smith, stated that she "found no evidence that the Kushites were despised, heathen, backward, strange, or any of the other frequent disparaging and pejorative

whatsoever for Amos' audience to take the comparison with the [Cushites] as demeaning."[92]

However, this is not the end of the matter. For instance, Wolff has taken a more moderate position, recognizing that to

> compare the Israelites with the Cushites probably does not in itself mean to say anything disdainful, much less anything reprehensible, about them. They are mentioned simply as representative of foreign and remote peoples who live on the outermost periphery of the known world. If Israel is the same as they in the sight of Yahweh, then it cannot claim any kind of privileged position.[93]

For Wolff, it was the *remoteness* of Cush that motivated the prophet to compare Israel to it. Rice follows suit, determining that Amos used the Cushites in this simile because they "were remote and different."[94] Similarly, Andersen and Freedman rehearse the image of Cush as a distant nation and determine that Cush in this prophecy symbolized all the nations of the world who would receive equal attention from YHWH.[95] Hence, based upon this hypothesis, we could determine that the basis of the comparison between Cush and Israel was that Israel was not more important to YHWH than the most distant nation located at the end of the known world.

Though the propositions of Wolff, Rice, Andersen, and Freedman have merit, we should also consider the unusual construction בְנֵי כֻשִׁיִּים ("sons of the Cushites") before we make any firm conclusions about the view of Cush implied in this comparison. This construction is unique in the Hebrew Bible. Typically the plural terms used for Cushites are כּוּשִׁים ("Cushites"), הַכּוּשִׁים ("the Cushites"), or once כֻּשִׁים ("Cushites") in Dan 11:43. Though the phrase בְנֵי כֻשִׁיִּים does not recur in the Hebrew Bible, we do see similar constructions. A like construction בֶּן־כּוּשִׁי ("son of Cushi"), occurs twice, in Jer 36:14 and Zeph 1:1. In each instance, this construction refers to a single son of a man either named Cushi or of Cushite origin.[96] Yet we can hardly compare the meaning of this personal genealogical phrase, בֶּן־כּוּשִׁי, to בְנֵי כֻשִׁיִּים, a phrase with a plural corporate meaning. When discussing the people of Cush, they are twice deemed בְּנֵי כוּשׁ ("sons of Cush") in Gen 10:7 and 1 Chr 1:9, both in the genealogical lists of the Table of Nations. The phrase is only employed here for the fictive direct descendants of the eponymous ancestor, Cush. Though this is the most likely parallel to

---

metaphors and adjectives that some contemporary biblical scholars utilize to describe Kush…the historical information does not substantiate it" (p. 44).

92. Rice, "Amos," 42.

93. Wolff, *Joel*, 347.

94. Rice, "Amos," 43. Though Rice's argument is plausible, we must qualify what he suggests since there is no clear evidence that the "different" nature of the Cushites was anything emphasized by the people of Israel/Judah. As will become increasingly apparent, those Cushite traits that are emphasized by modern exegetes with contemporary understandings of race, were largely ignored by Israelite/Judahite authors.

95. Francis I. Andersen and David Noel Freedman, *Amos: A New Translation with Introduction and Commentary* (AB 24A; Garden City, N.Y.: Doubleday, 1989), 903.

96. See the Sections 3.2.5.2 and 3.2.2.1 below on Jer 36:14 and Zeph 1:1 for a more detailed analysis.

the phrase בְּנֵי יִשְׂרָאֵל ("children of Israel"), where Israel is singular, it is only used in the context of the Table of Nations. Hence, we should be aware that we are dealing with an anomaly in Amos 9:7; it is unusual for a plural meaning "Cushites," and it is unusual in its plural form.

We should say more about the fact that the term used for "Cushites" is plural. This is the only instance in the Hebrew Bible where the formula X-בְּנֵי is used where the gentilic "X" is a plural. The closest parallels come in Deut 1:28 and 9:2, where we find the phrase בְּנֵי עֲנָקִים ("offspring of the Anakim").[97] However, we could argue that Anakim was less a gentilic than it was a phenotypical description of a group of people. Coming from the root עֲנָק meaning "neck," hence the connotation "long-necked" or "tall" people, it is most plausible that we should consider Anakim an identification only of a group's somatic type.[98] We can conclude from the rarely used X-בְּנֵי where "X" is plural that the Hebrew authors would have noted the redundancy of this construction to describe an ethnic group. Either the construction X-בְּנֵי where "X" is singular or the plural of "X" alone would have sufficed to denote a group of people like the Cushites. This unusual construction may signal an unusual meaning.

But the unique construction alone is not enough to support modifying our understanding of this passage. We should also consider other factors, such as the context. As mentioned above, v. 7 consists of two rhetorical questions, both of which the author expects the audience to answer in the affirmative. The phrase under consideration, בְּנֵי כֻשִׁיִּים appears in v. 7a and here the meaning of the phrase is contested. However, v. 7b explicitly focuses on YHWH's role in bringing Israel, Philistia, and Aram from foreign lands and settling them about the land of Palestine. Scholars have often taken v. 7a and v. 7b to be completely independent questions.[99] However, their independence is not certain.

Biblical authors often incorporated thematic parallels in consecutive lines of Hebrew poetry. In this regard, it would not be unexpected for Amos 9:7b to repeat the theme of v. 7a. There are other instances where rhetorical questions are similarly employed. The best example of this would be Jer 13:23, where the prophet uses two rhetorical questions with the same theme and answer to show his audience with crystal clarity the impending fate of YHWH's people. Perhaps in light of the context of the latter part of this verse, we should understand that the phrase בְּנֵי כֻשִׁיִּים in v. 7a is not just a plural gentilic meaning Cushites, but a phrase intended to specifically refer to the "*offspring of Cushites*," namely, those who have migrated from Cush to regions in the Levant. In this regard, we understand the two rhetorical questions in v. 7 as thematic parallels. Amos intends to remind the Israelites that as YHWH brought them out of bondage and gave them a

97. This phrase is also translated "offspring of the Anakim" in the NRSV. Consistency should have led the translators of Amos 9:7 to consider a similar translation.

98. Though likely insignificant, we should note that the Cushites (Isa 18:1 and 7) and the Sabeans (45:14), a group associated with the Cushites (in Isa 45:14 as well as in Gen 10:7 and 1 Chr 1:9), are also characterized as "tall." In fact, the Cushites, the Sabeans, and these mythical giants, the Anakim, are the only groups characterized as "tall" in the Hebrew Bible.

99. For instance, Martin-Achard, *Amos*, 125–26.

home, Israel's God also "brought out" the Philistines, the Arameans and, yes, the local Cushites from their homelands and settled them in portions of the Holy Land.

But do we know of any likely Cushites to whom v. 7a would apply? Actually we will encounter several candidates for Levantine Cushite offspring in our present study. There were groups such as the people of Cushan in the region of Edom referred to in Judg 3 (see Section 3.2.7.1) and Hab 3 (see Section 3.2.3). There were Cushites thought to have been involved in the Hebrew exodus from Egypt according to Num 12 (see Section 2.2.1.5). There were hosts of Cushites stationed by the Egyptians in southern Palestine according to 2 Chr 12, 14, 16, and 21 (see Sections 4.2.1.2–5). We even know of Cushite courtiers in Judah from explicit references in 2 Sam 18 (see Section 3.2.7.2) and Jer 38–39 (see Section 3.2.5.3–4). Based upon the contextual clues in this passage and the evidence for Cushites in the Levant,[100] we should adopt our special interpretation for the phrase בְּנֵי כֻשִׁיִּים in Amos 9:7, where the phrase refers to a group(s) of *offspring of the Cushites* who have settled in the immediate environs of Judah. As with Israel, Philistia, and Aram, they were known to have come from another region, Cush; but their presence in the vicinity of Judah evidenced YHWH's hand in their own exodus narrative.

In this regard, we should reconsider the positions of Wolff and Rice. The prophet may not have used the comparison to Cush to suggest that YHWH's concern for Israel is no greater than that of the most remote nation known to his audience at all. Instead, Amos suggested that these *offspring of the Cushites* who have also found a home in southern Palestine were of no less concern to YHWH. YHWH had a hand in their origin; Israel's God "brought them out" and settled them in a portion of the Holy Land as well. Hence, there is no reason for Israel to feel that it would not suffer the brunt of YHWH's wrath because of its malevolence. In fact, this passage displays a general sense of justice that extends beyond perceived election, for YHWH will judge those who have perpetuated injustice with equal ferocity, whether it be Israel or one of the gentile nations.[101]

I should emphasize my particular understanding of the "offspring of the Cushites," because my understanding of this group's position with YHWH is contrary to what I would expect based upon the work of Deutero-Isaiah. In that corpus, Israel's ego is boosted by YHWH's promise to give Egypt, Cush, and Seba as ransom for Israel.[102] However, that authors employed Cush to different ends supports my contention that "Cush" was a malleable trope in biblical literature. Here, when the prophet confronts Israel's arrogant posture, the Cushites are employed as a people for whom YHWH also cares in order to demonstrate that Israel is like other nations. It was YHWH that called all nations into being, and it is the same YHWH that can hold each of them accountable for their acts of injustice.

100.    R. W. Anderson, "Zephaniah," 45–70.

101.    James Montgomery Boice, *The Minor Prophets: An Expositonal Commentary Volume 1 Hosea–Jonah* (Grand Rapids: Zondervan, 1983), 178; Martin-Achard, *Amos*, 126.

102.    See the discussions on Isa 43 and 45 (Sections 3.2.4.1–2).

Such emphasis changes in Isa 43 (see Section 3.2.4.1). There, the anonymous prophet's purpose was to restore the esteem of a broken Israel/Judah that had endured the indignity of the Exile, showing them that they were again important to their God and that YHWH would forfeit stable, wealthy, and mighty nations to free them. In Isa 43 Cush is debased in order to achieve Deutero-Isaiah's purpose, while in Amos 9:7 Cush is set on common ground with Israel to express YHWH's contempt for Israel's hubris and to reify the notion of YHWH's justice.

Hence, the overall purpose of Amos' words in 9:7 was to emphasize the integral role YHWH plays in the unfolding of the history of various nations and, thus, to curtail his audience's arrogant sense of election. Amos knew that they had to be reminded that YHWH held them as accountable for their acts of injustice and immoral deeds as the Cushites, Philistines, and Arameans were for their own. YHWH's actions on their behalf were not unique, nor was the level to which he held them accountable for their transgressions of their deity's laws.

In spite of the host of hypotheses predicated on modern racial biases forwarded by many biblical exegetes to explain Amos 9:7, the Cushites are not debased explicitly or implicitly in this passage. There are no hints of racialist traits or attempts by the author to draw attention to Cushite phenotypes, though he could easily have done so were that his intention. Further, there was no attempt of any kind to associate Cushites with cultural deficiencies or stereotypic behavior in spite of modern exegetes' attempts to eisegete them into the text. In Amos 9:7, the prophet othered the Cushites in a manner consistent with his depiction of Israel and the other nations in v. 7. In fact, this passage demonstrates that Rice's question in his 1978 article, "Was Amos a Racist?," should be answered in the negative.

The use of the "offspring of the Cushites" in this passage is unique in the Hebrew Bible, as it is the only direct comparison between a Cush-related people and Israel. Yet the purpose of the passage is not unlike the many other instances where Cush was used to say something about Israel. The message here, election and the act of "bringing out," did not increase Israel's status before YHWH; both Israel and the "offspring of the Cushites" could be viewed as equal before YHWH's moral lens.

### 2.2.3. *Cush in First Isaiah*
Cush-related terms occur in the work of Isaiah of Jerusalem in Isa 11, 18, 20, and 37. The texts that we will encounter in these sections are some of the most significant for our purposes and demonstrate a variety of the ways Judean authors viewed the Cushites.

### 2.2.3.1. *Isaiah 11: Israel in Cush.* The term כּוּשׁ occurs once in this chapter in v. 11. Upon initial examination this chapter presents numerous problems to the exegete. For example, the text evidences multiple editorial layers that have been redacted into a single chapter,[103] united by the metaphor of the שֹׁרֶשׁ ("root"), or

---

103.    Otto Kaiser, *Isaiah 1–12: A Commentary* (trans. John Bowden; Philadelphia: Westminster, 1983), 262.

"shoot," of Jesse, an image found in both Isa 11:1 and 11:10. We also note ambiguity about the period addressed in this prophecy since it seems unlikely that Isaiah would have known of exiles in regions as far afield as Cush in his day. Further, the mixed assortment of names used to identify the regions where the "remnant" will be assembled are problematic. We will address the latter concern first.

The reference to Cush in this chapter occurs amid a larger list of nations among whom the people of Israel (here identified as Ephraim) and Judah have been dispersed. This reference to a significant Diaspora has been thought by many to hint at the late date for vv. 11–16.[104] If any portion of the prophecy could belong to Isaiah ben Amoz, it is the portion that suggests a return from Assyria and Egypt resulting from the deportations of 733–31 and 722–20 B.C.E.[105]

This prophecy implies that we should look for a Diaspora community in Cush, though the period of composition may not be that of the surrounding material in Isaiah. Perhaps it is best to date it to the post-exilic period.[106] However, this community may well be affiliated with the Jewish community at Elephantine, whose border fortress guarded Egypt's southern border near the first Cataract of the Nile. This Jewish community had its genesis in the pre-Persian period and later served as a significant Persian outpost in Egypt.[107] It almost certainly predates 623 B.C.E., when the "Book of the Law" was "discovered" during Josiah's reign, precipitating his reforms due to the prohibition against sending Judeans to Egypt in Deut 17:16; and it may be from the period of Psammetichus I, even predating 656.[108] This would support the hypothesis that Judean forces participated in the battles that ended the XXVth Cushite Dynasty's sovereignty in Upper Egypt, though this is inconclusive.[109] A colony such as this one, situated on the northern border of Cush, likely served as the point of origin for Jewish settlements in Cush proper in later periods. We will return to this issue below.

The names used to identify the nations are also rather unusual. They are an interesting mix of nation and city names that are further complicated by a redundancy: Egypt and פַּתְרוֹס (Pathros) would both suggest that the prophet intended the larger region of Egypt. Perhaps the redundancy is due to the fact that the

---

104.  On this point, see George W. Wade (*The Book of the Prophet Isaiah: With Introduction and Notes* [London: Methuen, 1929], 32), who determined that the term for "stump" of Jesse implies the independent Judean monarchy was no longer in existence. See below for a discussion of those who hold similar opinions.

105.  For another opinion, namely that this is an authentic Isaianic reference, see Edward J. Kissane, *The Book of Isaiah*, vol. 1 (Dublin: Browne & Nolan, 1960), 138.

106.  See Wade, *Isaiah*, 86; Edward J. Young, *The Book of Isaiah: The English Text, with Introduction, Exposition and Notes* (Grand Rapids: Eerdmans, 1965). Childs suggests the prophecy is late post-exilic due to the perception of a worldwide Diaspora and hints of Deutero-Isaian hope for Israelite and Judahite reconciliation; see Brevard S. Childs, *Isaiah* (Louisville, Ky.: Westminster John Knox, 2001), 104.

107.  Werner Kaiser, "Elephantine," in *OEANE* 2: 234–36.

108.  Redford, *Egypt*, 444.

109.  J. Maxwell Miller and John H. Hayes, *A History of Ancient Israel and Judah* (Philadelphia: Westminster, 1986), 370.

author meant by Egypt the northern or Lower region and by Pathros, the southern or Upper region.[110] Yet this understanding is by no means certain. The חֲמָת ("Hamath") reference is puzzling since חֲמָת is not a capital city, but an unremarkable city in the region of Syria. Reference to חֲמָת may have been due to a large Diaspora community in that city,[111] and it is likely that the author intended it as a synecdoche or *pars pro toto* for Syria.[112]

Because of the unusual assortment of cities and nations in this Isaian account, many scholars think the most plausible scenario is that the passage initially limited the return, making it only from Assyria and Egypt. Subsequent redactors employed Cush along with פַּתְרוֹס (Pathros), עֵילָם (Elam), שִׁנְעָר (Shinar), חֲמָת Hamath), and the אִיֵּי הַיָּם ("Coastlands") to represent the great scope of YHWH's efforts to bring the people of Israel/Judah back home.[113] A vast portion of the world known to Hebrew authors is represented by these different states. The resulting picture is one of an ecumenical return, demonstrating the authority of YHWH over the nations of the world. In this regard, the in-gathering from Cush reflects YHWH's reach to the southernmost portions of the then known world.

However, we should be careful not to too quickly preclude references to an Israelite/Judahite presence in Cush in the time of Isaiah since this is not the only theoretically pre-exilic text to imply a return of Diaspora Israel/Judah from Cush.[114] Though we do not have the obvious historical motivating factor like Babylon to explain the migration of remnants of Judah to this distant land, we should not be surprised to find remnants of the defunct Northern Kingdom of Israel settled far from their Assyrian persecutors. Perhaps this was the meaning of the promise in v. 12: וְאָסֵף נִדְחֵי יִשְׂרָאֵל ("and he will gather those driven out of Israel"). Evidence from Elephantine about Jewish worship further evidences that the reclaimed remnant may be northern Israelite. YHWH was not the only deity worshipped by this colony of displaced Hebrews; they also worshipped Anat-bethel, Asham-bethel, Harambethel, and Bethel. Each of these deity names suggest that the community venerated Bethel, a cultic center of the Northern Kingdom, suggesting that the people of Elephantine may have come from Israel and not Judah.[115] Though we cannot definitively place this community in Egypt prior to the mid-seventh century, leaving us to wonder where they were from the late eighth century until that period, elements of this community would best satisfy the requisite criteria for the remnant in this prophecy: they were displaced

---

110. For a thorough explanation, see Hans Wildberger, *Isaiah 1–12: A Commentary* (trans. Thomas H. Trapp; Minneapolis: Fortress, 1991), 492.

111. O. Kaiser, *Isaiah*, 265.

112. See Wildberger, *Isaiah*, 487.

113. Wildberger, *Isaiah*, 488–90. Wildberger suggests the text may date to the Persian period. This correlates with this hypothesis that the Judean presence in Cush dates to the first campaign of Cambyses ca. 525 B.C.E. (p. 492). See also Ronald E. Clements, *Isaiah 1–39* (Grand Rapids: Eerdmans, 1987), 126; Arthur S. Herbert, *The Book of the Prophet Isaiah Chapters 1–39* (Cambridge: Cambridge University Press, 1973), 92; O. Kaiser, *Isaiah*, 262–67.

114. For example, Isa 18:7 (Section 2.2.3.2); Zeph 3:10 (Section 3.2.2.3).

115. Soggin, *Introduction*, 565–66; Miller and Hayes, *History*, 435–36.

Israelites dwelling on the borders of Cush near the time when Isaiah of Jerusalem composed his oracles. Perhaps it was from this community that settlements of Israelites migrated south into Cush. Though this is a plausible solution to the problems posed by this passage, it is at best speculative.[116]

The prophecy gives us little insight into how Cush was perceived except that it was not impossible to think of Israelites in that nation far to the south of Judah. Just as all the other nations housed Israelites in pre-exilic times or served as places of refuge for displaced Jewish people during and after the Exile, so did Cush; and as such it was not singled out for special attention or disparagement. It was just another nation that "welcomed" either Israelite settlers or an exiled community.

We can classify this text as being of the "return-from-Cush" type. As in Isa 18:7 and Zeph 3:10, a future day of in-gathering is prophesied where adherents to Yahwism will make their trek north to their home in the Promised Land. This type varies only slightly from the "gifts-from-Cush" or "proselytes-from-Cush" types that we will see in Isa 18 and Ps 68.

### 2.2.3.2. Isaiah 18: An Ethnography of the Cushites.

The term כוּשׁ occurs once in Isa 18, in v. 1. Unlike many other passages discussed above wherein the term כּוּשׁ occurs more frequently and the focus is on Israel/Judah, this oracle has Cush as its subject. In fact, this is perhaps the best ethnography of the Cushites in the Hebrew Bible. That being said, Isa 18 is a problematic text because its author

---

116.    However, we do have evidence that Jewish groups ventured into the regions south of Egypt thousands of years ago. A recent "Nova" program exploring the fate of the "Lost Tribes of Israel" found genetic evidence that definitively linked the distant Lemba people of South Africa to other Diaspora Jewish communities. Researchers even noted data suggesting the Buba tribe of the Lemba had a high instance of Cohen modal haplotypes. This suggests that the Buba may be remnants of a priestly community. Cf. <http://www.pbs.org/wgbh/nova/israel/familylemba.html>. Further, the instances of Cohen modal haplotypes occur with greater frequency among the Buba than among other Jewish Diaspora communities, demonstrating the strength of their connection with the ancestors of other Diaspora communities. Perhaps most significantly, their adherence to the cultic practices of the pre-rabbinic periods, such as cult sacrifice, in addition to other Jewish practices like strict endogamy and a kosher-like diet, suggest they are not only Jewish, but may trace their ancestry to the period prior to the destruction of Jerusalem in 70 CE though they remained isolated from other Jewish commuties. Cf. <http://www.pbs.org/wgbh/nova/israel/parfitt.html> and <http://www.pbs.org/wgbh/nova/israel/parfitt2.html>. We should also note the now well-known Beta Israelite community that until the past three decades were largely isolated in regions of Ethiopia and who also maintained a distinctive mix of ancient cultic practices, including open-air sacrifices, with their other Jewish customs. This group maintains origin myths that associate them with the "lost" northern tribe of Danites. See Steven Kaplan, *The Beta Israel (Falasha) in Ethiopia: From Earliest Times to the Twentieth Century* (New York: New York University Press, 1992); David Kessler, *The Falashas: A Short History of the Ethiopian Jews* (London: Frank Cass, 1996). Though their ambiguous origins obscure the time of migration, both the Lemba and the Beta Israelites demonstrate that Jewish groups penetrated into the heart of Africa, and perhaps did so prior to the advent of the Common Era. In light of these two groups, which ventured deep into Africa, and the known Jewish outpost on Egypt's southern border in the mid-seventh century, we should not think it implausible that Israelites settled in Cush during the late eighth or early seventh centuries.

employs a number of rarely used Hebrew terms,[117] and because the author's tenor is obscure.

As we begin our analysis, we must concede that the precise purpose of this prophecy is unclear. Was it meant to be an oracle of woe against Cush intended to send a message to Judah during a particular historical moment as Clements suggests, or an eschatological reflection on the breaking of Cush prior to their future trust in YHWH as Kaiser concludes?[118] Young even suggests that the text is not an oracle against Cush, but a message meant to inspire relief among anxious Judean citizens, letting them know that YHWH will address the Assyrian menace.[119]

Dating this prophecy has proven difficult. It is possible that it was inspired by events in the late eighth century (714–705 B.C.E.) when Cush, the Philistines, and several other Levantine powers, including Judah, planned a revolt against Assyria.[120] However, many scholars agree that elements in the passage (i.e. v. 7) are likely later glosses.[121]

If we accept that v. 7 is a later addition, then the form of the extant passage poses an additional problem. Most exegetes would consider this a wonderful example of eloquent Hebrew poetry, for, in addition to the author's use of a carefully chosen vocabulary, not an undesirable feature for poetry, he also crafted an *inclusio*. Because it is an *inclusio*, the audience is brought full circle by the end of the prophecy (v. 7) and is soothed by an optimistic portrait of the future artistically interlaced with a rehearsal of the eloquent introductory phrase previewed in v. 2:

מְמֻשָּׁךְ וּמוֹרָט אֶל־עַם וּמֵעַם נוֹרָא מִן־הוּא וָהָלְאָה גּוֹי קַו־קָו וּמְבוּסָה אֲשֶׁר בָּזְאוּ
נְהָרִים אַרְצוֹ

Those who argue for v. 7 being a gloss do so in part because they consider it the product of post-exilic redaction due to its "day of YHWH" eschatological content.[122] Yet, the prediction of a day when the nations of the world will come and

---

117. Since many of the terms in vv. 1–2 are *hapax legomena* and those that have multiple occurrences are rare, the meaning of the Hebrew is somewhat ambiguous, and translators depend largely on contextual clues to interpret this passage. The effect of this ambiguity is evident in the interpretation of this enigmatic text; consider, for example, the LXX translation and the distinctly different tenor of that version.

118. Consider Clements and Kaiser's varying interpretations of this passage. Clements is convinced that this is an oracle of "woe" uttered "against" the Cushites for particular historical reasons, while Kaiser sees this chapter as a generally ambiguous apocalyptic vision of the future. See Clements, *Isaiah*, 163–66; see Otto Kaiser, *Isaiah 13–39: A Commentary* (Philadelphia: Westminster, 1974), 89–104.

119. The strongest aspect of Young's argument (*Isaiah*, 478) is the ironic twist in v. 7. Here the people preparing to help defend Judah will later be found coming to worship YHWH, the Judean deity that rescued them.

120. For a view of scholarship on this chapter, see O. Kaiser, *Isaiah 13–39*, 90–91; Young, *Isaiah*, 475 n. 46.

121. However, it must have been composed prior to Ezekiel and circulated in its present form, since the author of Ezekiel, writing in the early sixth century, alludes to this passage in 30:9.

122. We must consider, however, that the whole passage could be late because eschatological imagery is employed elsewhere in the chapter. Both the universal scope and the image of the rallying

pay homage to YHWH as the one true deity does not have to be understood as the production of a post-exilic redactor (see Isa 2:2–5; Zeph 3:10). Based upon these other theoretically pre-exilic accounts of the nations recognizing the sovereignty of YHWH and on what we know historically about Cush in the late eighth century, we can reasonably conclude that v. 7 was part of an eschatological prophecy born of particular political events. Images of the fall of a mighty Cush would have been less poignant in post-exilic Palestine once the Cushite sphere of influence was limited to Cush proper. Though we will encounter images of "mighty-Cush" in post-exilic contexts, it is unlikely that this passage describing the Cushites as a people "feared near and far" or that images of Cushite diplomats in Jerusalem would have been as significant after the fall of the XXVth Dynasty. We will see that later prophecies that we will also classify as "mighty-Cush" references recall the tragic defeat of Cush at Thebes (i.e. Nah 3:8–9) or Cushite expeditionary forces in the wake of a subsequent battle (i.e. Zeph 2:12). This prophecy, particularly the verses that clearly address Cush (vv. 1–2, 7), would have been most effective in the mouth of Isaiah in the late eighth century B.C.E.

This passage provides considerable information about the land and people of Cush as understood by Isaiah, who perceived Cush as a distant land a sea voyage away. He also gives us insight into their mode of travel with his description of the כְלֵי־גֹמֶא ("vessels of papyrus"), whereby they made the voyage to Judah. Such vessels were the standard mode of Nile travel. Some consider this aspect of the passage fanciful because they deem it improbable that such crafts could withstand a Mediterranean voyage.[123] However, these seemingly fragile crafts were able to make voyages of considerable distances across the Mediterranean, though they risked becoming waterlogged if the sailors did not haul them out of the water occasionally and allow them time to dry.[124]

We can also glean information about the author's perspective of the land of Cush. The author describes the land as אֶרֶץ צִלְצַל כְּנָפָיִם ("a land of whirring wings"). This phrase has led some to conclude that Cush was perceived as a land plagued with flies[125] or swarming with swift and devastating armies.[126] Others have posited that this was a reference to boats with sails.[127] The latter seems more probable, for it provides insight into the mode of transport for rigorous Cushite trade and provides continuity for the subsequent imagery: אֲשֶׁר מֵעֵבֶר לְנַהֲרֵי־כוּשׁ ("that are beyond the rivers of Cush"). These statements indicate that Cush was known to be a riparian nation aflutter with sailing craft traversing its rivers.

---

shofar (cf. Joel 2:1, 2:15; Zeph 1:16) found in v. 3 suggest that v. 7 is an integral part of this eschatological oracle. Also note the eschatological tone of Isa 19. For a similar perspective, see O. Kaiser, *Isaiah 13–39*, 89–104.

123.  See O. Kaiser, *Isaiah 13–39*, 93; Young, *Isaiah*, 475.

124.  For example, Clements, *Isaiah*, 164; Herbert, *Isaiah 1–39*, 118.

125.  For example, O. Kaiser, *Isaiah 13–39*, 93; Childs, *Isaiah*, 138.

126.  For example, Young, *Isaiah*, 474.

127.  See Godfrey R. Driver, "Isaiah 1–39: Textual and Linguistic Problems," *JSS* 13 (1968): 36–57 (45). Driver argues that the Hebrew צִלְצַל could derive from the Arabic *zulzul*, meaning a "winged boat." Also see Clements, *Isaiah*, 164; John Oswalt, *The Book of Isaiah: Chapters 1–39* (Grand Rapids: Eerdmans, 1986), 359–60.

When we consider this section with the latter portion of v. 2—אֲשֶׁר־בָּזְאוּ נְהָרִים
אַרְצוֹ ("which the rivers divide its land")—we can understand that Cush was
thought to be a fertile land, unlike the largely arid land of Judah.[128]

The information that Isaiah of Jerusalem provides about the people is what is
most useful for our purposes. Perhaps the first essentialization in this passage, is
the reference to the מַלְאָכִים קַלִּים ("swift messengers"). This essentialization
may be of Cushites in general, or it may refer specifically to Cushite messengers[129] (cf. 2 Sam 18, where notion of a swift Cushite runner is assumed). This
allusion to athletic prowess is not unlike an aspect of racialist images of Africans
as fast runners and gifted athletes today.[130] The enduring legacy of this stereotype
merits mention.

Phenotypically the people are described as מְמֻשָּׁךְ וּמוֹרָט ("tall and smooth").
This information is valuable for a number of reasons. First, it suggests that there
was an implied norm in the mind of the audience that would note the distinct
presentation of the Cushites as taller than expected and without facial hair. In this
way, Cushite somatic type is distinguished as non-normal or different.[131]

However, it is not enough to assert that the author recognizes phenotypical
distinctions between the Judean community and the Cushites; it is also important
to discern how these differences were valued. The Cushite phenotype clearly
differed from the Judean norm, but the differences are not valued negatively nor
are the Cushites disparaged for their appearance. These Cushite phenotypical
traits generally appear to have been perceived positively, if not neutrally, based
upon the reverent nature of vv. 1–2 and 7 and their incorporation in the refrain
repeated in vv. 2 and 7.

Finally, it is important to note what the Isaianic author chose to emphasize
about the appearance of the Cushites in light of all the possible phenotypes he
could have highlighted. He made no reference to skin-color, to facial features
(besides lack of facial hair), to hair texture, or any of the features that are commonly elements of racialist thought. Further, he does not elaborate on the
aesthetic merits or demerits of Cushite presentation. He simply states that they
are מְמֻשָּׁךְ וּמוֹרָט ("tall and smooth"). Again, if we were to assume any valuation,
it would appear that Isaiah viewed their somatic type favorably.

In addition to their phenotypical presentation, Isaiah calls the Cushites עַם
נוֹרָא מִן־הוּא וָהָלְאָה גּוֹי קַו־קָו וּמְבוּסָה ("a people feared here and there, a nation

---

128. Wade, *Isaiah*, 123.

129. That the "swift messengers" In this passage are Cushites has not been universally excepted.
For example, Childs (*Isaiah*, 138) suggests that the "swift messengers" are actually Judean messengers to Cush; hence, the prophetic oracle is not targeted against Cush, but against Judah because if
has participated in a foreign alliance.

130. For example, consider the recent controversial text by Entine that suggests that blacks are
"biologically determined" to be better athletes than members of other groups; see Jon Entine, *Taboo:
Why Black Athletes Dominate Sports and Why we are Afraid to Talk about It* (New York: Public
Affairs, 2000).

131. Wade (*Isaiah*, 122) notes that Herodotus similarly described the Ethiopians (read Cushites)
as ανδρας μεγιστους και καλλιστους ("men tall and beautiful/honorable," III.114).

mighty and subjugating").[132] At the time Isaiah wrote, in the eighth century, the Cushite royal family had expanded its sphere of influence to include direct rule of Egypt and indirect sway over much of the Levant. For Isaiah, the Cushites were an imposing military power with a reputation that was well known in the ancient world. Perhaps Toivanen sums up the intent of this ancient ethnography best in a 1998 article:

> The purpose of this detailed and colourful description is not only to inform but also to create the impression of an exotic though obviously powerful and skilful people. The text is formulated in poetic form, but clearly has an operative function to the reader... It attempts to arouse the reader's curiosity and respect mingled with fear.[133]

The overall portrait of Cush in First Isaiah is of a mighty and feared nation that was esteemed by the Judeans for their prosperity, the fertility of their land, the appearance of their people, and their athletic prowess. Precisely because of this esteem, the Cushites are employed in this chapter to represent the great nation that may fall but that will regain its stature and come before YHWH assuming a reverent posture. And, as in Zeph 3:10 and Ps 68:31, we are left with the Judean expectation that at the eschaton, Cushites will be devout Yahwists.[134]

As regards the type of Cushite reference in Isa 18, we should recognize aspects of four categories. The former portion (vv. 1–2) of the passage could lead us to associate the text with "phenotypical" and "mighty-Cush" types. However, the ultimate verse (v. 7), is more appropriately categorized as both "gifts-from-Cush" and "Cushite-proselyte" types. This chapter contains the best Judean ethnography of this distant Other, as well as the most comprehensive collage of ways that Judean authors used the images of Cush in Hebrew literature.

2.2.3.3. *Isaiah 20: An Incident at Ashdod.* The term כוש occurs three times in this chapter, in vv. 3, 4, and 5. This brief chapter pertains to a discrete historical event: the planned rebellion of Ashdod and its Philistine allies against the Assyrians, ca. 712–711 B.C.E. The event was intended to spark an uprising of Palestinian and other North African nations a little more than a decade into the reign of Sargon II of Assyria (722–705).

As traditionally understood, this chapter posits that the conspiracy was planned in part as a result of the political ambitions of the XXVth Cushite Dynasty of Egypt following Pharaoh Piye's pacification of the entirety of Egypt. After ensuring internal stability Piye and his brother and successor, Shabako, turned their

---

132.    Clements concludes that the subject of the reference to the feared nation was Assyria. This, however, is improbable since the reference fits the larger context, a description of the people of Cush. Further, why would people plotting a rebellion against Assyria send advance word of their intentions? This would be militarily imprudent. Also, there is no explicit or implicit reference to Assyria in the entire chapter. We should understand that this passage demonstrates how mighty Cush is, hence, making the contrast feel all the more great. See Clements, *Isaiah*, 164–65.

133.    Aarne Toivanen, "A Bible Translation as the Communicator of Alien Culture," *Temenos: Studies in Comparative Religion* 26 (1990): 129–37 (132).

134.    Also interesting in this regard is Jer 39:15–18, where Ebed-melech, a Cushite court official, is promised favor for his service to YHWH.

attention to the former Egyptian vassals in the Levant. Finding them squarely under the thumb of the Assyrians and desperate for relief the Cushite king, Shabako, apparently pledged his support to his northern neighbors.[135] Isaiah, learning of this subversive alliance, warns his compatriots not to participate in this precarious plot by performing a prophetic drama.[136] Though this chapter is brief, the few verses pertaining to that performance are some of those most disparaging of the Cushites in the Hebrew Bible.

We cannot help but be moved by the artistic description of Isaiah's prophetic activity in ch. 20. In an elaborate performance, Isaiah strips his loincloth from his body and removes his sandals from his feet; he then walks about barefoot and naked, prophesying the doom that would come upon the participants in the Ash-dod rebellion. In this way the prophet graphically illustrates the folly of depend-ing on human strength, no matter how great it may be, over and above YHWH.

According to the prophecy in v. 4, the king of Assyria would lead away אֶת־שְׁבִי מִצְרַיִם וְאֶת־גָּלוּת כּוּשׁ ("the Egyptians captives and the Cushites exiles"). We must assume this prophecy never came to fruition[137] because there is no evidence that Shabako sent an expeditionary force to Ashdod, nor evidence that a fate similar to Isaiah's prediction befell the populace of Egypt or Cush.[138] In fact, Kitchen suggests that there were fair diplomatic relations between Shabako and his Assyrian counterpart.[139] Isaiah's prediction must hence be interpreted as pro-phetic hyperbole or as temporally displaced, belonging to a period between 701 B.C.E. and the mid-seventh century.[140]

---

135. This is the traditional interpretation; so George Adam Smith, *The Book of Isaiah*, vol. 1, *Isaiah 1–39* (New York: Armstrong & Son, 1890), 197–98; Oswalt, *Isaiah*, 381–86. It was perhaps based on A. Leo Oppenheim, "Sargon II (721–705): The Fall of Samaria," in *The Ancient Near East*, vol. 1, *An Anthology of Texts and Pictures* (ed. James B. Pritchard; Princeton, N.J.: Princeton Univer-sity Press, 1973), 195–98 (198). Here the outline of a rebellion is clear. The leader of Ashdod, Iamani, is said to have solicited the support of the Philistines, Judah, Edom, Moab, and several islanders to join him in revolt against Assyria. Further, the text contains a reference to Iamani sending "bribes to Pir'u, king of Musru [Egypt]—a potentate incapable to save them—and asked him to be an ally." But there is no reference to any Assyrian aggression against the Cushites or Egyptians.

136. See Clements, *Isaiah*, 173; Wade, *Isaiah*, 133.

137. See O. Kaiser, *Isaiah 13–39*, 113; Wade, *Isaiah*, 134.

138. Oppenheim, "Sargon II," 196. This section of the Sargon II materials, subtitled "According to the Annals of the Room XIV," also leaves out any reference to a battle against Cushite or Egyptian forces. The translated document only states the following in regard to the Cushite involvement in this incident: "The terror (-inspiring) glamor of Ashur, my lord, overpowered (however) the king of Meluhha and he threw him (i.e. Iamani [leader of the Ashdod rebellion]) in fetters on hands and feet, and sent him to me, to Assyria." Note that Meluhha was the Assyrian term for Cush.

139. Kitchen, *The Third Intermediate Period in Egypt (1100–650 B.C.)* (Warminster: Aris & Phillips, 1973), 143–44, 380. Kitchen argues that, based upon bullae bearing Shabako's insignia found at Nineveh and historical data revealing that Shabako extradited the the leader of the Ashdod revolt to Assyria, there were normal diplomatic relations between Egypt and Assyria during Shabako's reign.

140. Unless we can somehow associate it with the latter conflict between Egypt under the reign of Shebitku and Sennacherib's Assyria at Eltekeh in 701. Here there is evidence of a more extensive, but not "disastrous" Egyptian–Cushite defeat. Cf. 2 Kgs 18–19; Isa 36–37, and the discussion of these chapters below (Section 3.2.7.3). Also see Kitchen, *Third Intermediate Period*, 164, 383–86; Clements, *Isaiah*, 175; Herbert, *Isaiah 1–39*, 128.

The most derisive portion of the prophecy is when Egypt and Cush are to be led away עֵרוֹם וְיָחֵף וַחֲשׂוּפַי שֵׁת עֶרְוַת מִצְרָיִם ("naked, barefoot, and stripped [to the] bare buttocks [to the] shame of Egypt"). These images of nakedness associate shame[141] with the Cushite/Egyptian forces, emphasizing scandalous imagery and depicting their status as prisoners.[142]

This is a stark contrast from the glorious and mighty imagery typically associated with these nations.[143] This reversal of the paradigm is present in many of the passages mentioning Cushites. Isaiah later emphasizes this contrast in v. 5, when he recounts the sentiments of those who placed their trust in Egypt and Cush. According to the prophet Isaiah, anyone who chose to trust in this potent alliance will be both וְחַתּוּ וָבֹשׁוּ מִכּוּשׁ מַבָּטָם וּמִן־מִצְרַיִם תִּפְאַרְתָּם ("broken and ashamed from Cush their trust and from Egypt their glory"). Hence, Assyria will debase Cush and Egypt, two nations that represent strength and glory in Judean literature.[144]

Though there is certainly no way to deny the magnitude of Isaiah's disparagement of Cush in this passage, its racial implications are not certain. Though Cush is derided as a source of reliance for the people of the Levant in their rebellion against their Assyrian overlords, there is no indication that the defeat could be ascribed to negative Cushite behavioral traits. Further, there is no reference to distinctive Cushite somatic traits despite the fact that their "nakedness" afforded Isaiah the opportunity to chide them. In fact, the text is silent about racial qualities even when Isaiah most wants to portray them in a negative light.

The prophet's purpose is not to disparage Cush; his goal in this prophecy is to dissuade his people from forming a questionable alliance with nations doomed to fail in their efforts to defeat Assyria. Since YHWH has spoken against the rebellion, such an alliance could bring the venom of Assyria to bear on Jerusalem and this was to be avoided at all costs. The demands of Yahwism required that Judah remember that trust in human strength, even in the significant might of the Cushites, was misplaced trust.[145] Here the price of this reminder was the dignity of Egypt and Cush.

We are left with a prophecy that clearly demeans the Cushites with explicitly graphic depictions, yet does not do so in a manner that is markedly different from other Others. In fact, it is probable that an historical event formed the basis of this narrative, namely, the Cushite defeat at Eltekeh in 701 B.C.E. It is likely more descriptive than prescriptive, though the prophet seems to have exaggerated some

141. Cf. Gen 2:25; 3:7–11; Amos 2:16; Nah 3:5.
142. O. Kaiser, *Isaiah 13–39*, 114.
143. It is markedly different than that of Isa 18 (see Section 2.2.3.2).
144. Clements (*Isaiah*, 174) suggests that the prophecy was originally directed against Ashdod and the Philistines and that it was only after the fall of Ashdod, ca. 711 B.C.E., that the prophet shifted his attention to Egypt and Cush, to prevent Judah from relying upon them. The probable reason for the change in focus of the prophecy was the Egyptian–Cushite conspiracy of 705 B.C.E. O. Kaiser (*Isaiah 13–39*, 117–18) suggests it may have pertained to events as late as the mid-seventh century, when Egypt was actually invaded by Assyrians. But even at that time Cush was not conquered, and its leaders relocated their base of operations in their homeland.
145. O. Kaiser, *Isaiah 13–39*, 118.

of the details. Hence, in spite of the generally negative tenor of the overall passage toward the Cushites, there is no apparent racial quality to the text. Further, Isaiah presumes the notion of the "mighty-Cushites" to lend weight to the contrast he established between the commonplace image his audience would have had of the Cushites and the debased captives he foreshadows in his prophetic performance. This is the first of many instances of the "mighty-Cush" usage where the author will use the audience's knowledge of the legendary military might of this Other to reassert the vanity of relying on human strength. The image is effective precisely because of the irony of the fall of a contemporary superpower.

2.2.3.4. *Isaiah 37: Tirhakah Revisited.* Isaiah 37 contains a single reference to one מֶלֶךְ־כּוּשׁ תִּרְהָקָה ("Tirhakah, king of Cush"), in v. 9. It is nearly identical to the 2 Kgs 18–19 account of Sennacherib's assault on Judah (cf. Section 3.2.7.3). Because we will examine the account in the section on 2 Kgs 19 and because there is ambiguity regarding the original source of this account, [146] I refer the reader to that section for greater detail. I will assume here that Isa 37 rehearses a narrative known from 2 Kgs 19; it was probably redacted into Isaiah's prophecies because it explicitly mentions this prophet. This, too, is a "mighty-Cush"-type usage, as is its 2 Kgs 19 parallel account.

Considering that material within the larger Isaianic context does provide a clue for understanding the curtailed reference to the Cushite involvement in eradicating the siege of Sennacherib. Even if the author of First Isaiah did not compose this passage, he or a subsequent redactor likely employed it unchanged because it resonated with his desire to illustrate that YHWH alone was responsible for Judah's welfare. The redactor of Isaiah[147] thought that dependence on YHWH precluded dependence upon Cush/Egypt. Providing too much detail about Cush's role in the defeat of Sennacherib would mean diminishing YHWH's role. Hence, it is likely that the Isaianic redactor intended to remember the Cushite role in this incident matter-of-factly, seeking not to depart from the larger theme of exclusive trust in YHWH and Cush/Egypt's failure to deliver (cf. Isa 20). Yet there still remains in the narrative the implication that the angel of YHWH in v. 36 had Cushite hands.

2.2.3.5. *Summary of Cush in First Isaiah.* The eighth-century prophet Isaiah presents a mixed portrait of Cushites. During his prophetic period, the Cushites were at the pinnacle of their historical prominence, exercising sway over a region that stretched from the headwaters of the Nile all the way to the Levant. In the first two passages that mention Cush (chs. 11 and 18), Isaiah presents them in neutral to positive ways. Chapter 18 stands out as a key chapter in the Hebrew

---

146. See O. Kaiser, *Isaiah 13–39*, 375 and 380, who attributes both sections to Dtr because of the theological *Tendenz* of the author. Childs (*Isaiah*, 271–72) proposes a similar argument, determining that 2 Kings contains the oldest version of this narrative.

147. That Isa 36–37 is a conflation of two of Sennacherib's assaults on Judah makes it likely that a redactor would have had to compile this story since the second Assyrian invasion did not occur until ca. 687 B.C.E. See Section 3.2.7.3 below, on Dtr.

Bible for the ample details it gives about both the land and the people. But Isa 18 stands in marked contrast to Isa 20, which portrays a humiliated and debased Cush, a Cush with which he would have been completely unfamiliar, save after the less dramatic defeat they suffered at Eltekeh. Isaiah 37 rehearses a narrative known from 2 Kgs 19 that was probably redacted into Isaiah's prophecies because it explicitly mentions the prophet. Here we see footprints of a larger Cushite contribution to the history of Judah, as will become clear in Section 3.2.7.3 below.

When Isaiah employed Cush in his prophecies, the most commonly mentioned aspect was that of "mighty-Cush." He also knew of their phenotypes and presents the first references to the "return from Cush" and the bringing of "gifts from Cush" that we encounter elsewhere in our study. Of all the Judean authors, Isaiah of Jerusalem produced the most complete picture of the Cushites, perhaps because of the prominence of the Cushites on the geo-political stage during the prophet's time. It would have been difficult for the prophet to ignore this mighty empire whose sovereignty stretched to the borders of Judah and whose ambassadors he likely saw in Jerusalem.

### 2.3. *Summary: Cush in Tenth- to Eighth-Century Hebrew Literature*

#### 2.3.1. *General Statement of Findings*
In the earliest strata of Hebrew literature, Israelite/Judahite authors were familiar with the people of Cush. The earliest traditions found in the Pentateuch suggest that while Cush represented the extent of the known world, it was not seen as being beyond YHWH's provision, since even this distant land was sustained by water from YHWH's own garden (Gen 2). Further, though it is plausible that Cushites were not fully represented in the earliest strata of the traditions under-girding the Palestinian version of the Table of Nations (Gen 10), the final universal version extant in the MT presents the Cushites as important members of the family of humankind, responsible for the origins of prominent nations to the south and north of Israel/Judah. The final occurrence of Cushites in the Pentateuch (Num 12) illustrates that the term "Cushite" could be used as a trope for dark skin color in the ancient world, but the general tone of the text favors an anti-racialist interpretation.

The earliest prophetic texts also present information about Cushites. From them we can discern that there was a Levantine Cushite community whose migration to their Palestinian home Amos (9:7) likened to the Hebrews' own Exodus. Further, Isaiah of Jerusalem portrays Cush as a distant land where the Israelites had settled (Isa 11), and as a powerful riparian nation of people with distinct phenotypical traits (ch. 18). The people of Cush, like the Egyptians, contributed to Judah's welfare (ch. 37), but were destined for destruction because of their reliance on human strength (ch. 20). Isaiah's prophetic portrait ultimately redeemed Cush, predicting a day when Cushites would return to Jerusalem, bearing gifts to YHWH.

### 2.3.2. *The Reason Why Cush Is Employed in Hebrew Literature*

Tenth- to eighth-century B.C.E. Hebrew authors used Cushites most frequently as tropes for human might (Isa 18; 20; 37). They also refer to "Cush" as an individual in genealogies (Gen 10) and "Cush" as a nation as a geographical marker (Gen 2). Twice Judean authors writing in this period mention Cushite phenoltypical traits (Num 12 and Isa 18). Yet, as is evident in Num 12, there was also a strong anti-racialist tendency in these early texts. Once a biblical author mentions the existence of a Levantine Cush (Amos 9 refers to "offspring of the Cushites"). Isaiah represents the eschatological future of Cush, predicting a return of a community of Israelites from this region (Isa 11) and the offering of gifts brought by proselytes (Isa 18).

Chapter 3

A WORD STUDY OF THE HEBREW ROOT "CUSH"
IN SEVENTH CENTURY TO EXILIC LITERATURE

*3.1. Introduction to the Exegesis of Hebrew Literature
from the Seventh Century to the Exilic Period*

Following the methodology employed in Chapter 2, we will explore the way
Israelite/Judahite authors writing between the seventh century and the end of the
Exile wrote about the Cushite Other. The majority of references to Cush-related
terms occur in literature dating to this period. This coincides with the zenith of
Cushite influence in the ancient Near East. In this chapter we will review the
references to Cush-related terms in Nah 3, Zephaniah, Hab 3, Deutero-Isaiah (Isa
43 and 45), Jeremiah, Ezekiel, and from the Deuteronomistic Historian (Dtr–Judg
3; 2 Sam 18; 2 Kgs 19).

Of note among these texts is Zephaniah, because a Cush-related term occurs in
each of its three chapters. Also significant are the Cush-related terms in Deutero-
Isaiah, where references appear to reverse the sense of equality of Amos 9:7.
Two passages in the book of Jeremiah merit particular attention. The first deals
with the rhetorical questions about a Cushite's skin (13:23). The second is the
narrative describing the fidelity of Ebed-melech, the Cushite courtier who rescued
the prophet Jeremiah. Also important are the two genealogical references to
ancestors identified only as "Cushi" (Jer 36; Zeph 1), the image of the conquered
Cushites (Ezek 29 and 30), and the most significant passage regarding a Levantine Cush (Hab 3).

*3.2. Analysis of the Term "Cush"
in Seventh Century to Exilic Literature*

*3.2.1. Nahum 3: Cush, the Might of Egypt*
The term כוּשׁ occurs once in Nah 3, in v. 9, in another comparison and in connection with yet another rhetorical question.[1] Nahum asks the city of Nineveh
"are you better than Thebes?," thereby questioning whether Nineveh was better
than Thebes in some way that it should escape the total destruction that Thebes
could not avoid.

---

1. Cf. a similar comparison associated with a rhetorical question in Amos 9:7. There, the purpose
is to prepare Israel for its impending disaster. In this instance, Nineveh's doom is prophesied. Cush
also appears in the rhetorical questions in Jer 13:23.

This passage reflects knowledge of the disastrous demise of Thebes and the imminent or recent destruction of Nineveh. Soggin suggests that the text dates to either the siege of Nineveh in 625 by the Medes or to the one in 612 by the Medes and Babylonians, after which the city was defeated.[2] Similarly, Coggins recognizes that the fall of Thebes was apparently a significant recent memory for the author. Noting that it was likely rebuilt soon after its destruction, he dates the text to the period after the time when Thebes was destroyed and immediately prior to the destruction of Nineveh (ca. 625–612 B.C.E.).[3]

Thebes ("No-Amon" in Hebrew) was the principal city of the Egyptian Empire from ca. 2000 B.C.E. until its destruction in 663 B.C.E. by the Assyrian king Asshurbanipal.[4] During the period of the XXVth Dynasty (mid-eighth to mid-seventh centuries), Thebes was the capital of both Cush and Egypt; it retained its theological importance because it was the city of Amun, the principal deity of both Cush and Egypt, not unlike Jerusalem was to Judah. Because Cush ruled Egypt during this period, the use of either the term "Egypt" or "Cush" in this period would imply the other national entity;[5] also the mention of the Egyptian capital would imply its Cushite rulers. The Assyrian destruction of Thebes effectively ended Cushite hopes of regaining control over the Delta region to the north and marked the final decline of the XXVth Dynasty,[6] making the fall of Thebes the end of the Cushite administration of Egypt.

The destruction of Thebes was no mean feat and no easy loss; the human toll the Cushites paid for their opposition to Assyrian imperial ambitions was extremely high. Craigie recalls the evil that the Assyrians did to Thebans when they abused and dehumanized the people of that great city, treating them with infamous cruelty.[7] Nahum employs the memories of Assyrian atrocities at Thebes to set the stage for the Assyrians' own destruction.

Several of the savage acts the Assyrians committed are chronicled in Nah 3:10, including imprisoning the populace and practicing infanticide. We should, of course, recognize the artistic license that the author of the book of Nahum may be exercising in composing his account, for he was not an eyewitness to these events;[8] yet, as Ashurbanipal recorded in his annals, the Assyrians were particu-

---

2.   Soggin, *Introduction*, 325–26.

3.   Richard J. Coggins, *Israel among the Nations* (Grand Rapids: Eerdmans, 1985), 52. Also see Kevin J. Cathcart, "Nahum, Book of," in *ABD* 4:998–1000.

4.   The only periods when another city was more prominent was between 1750–1550 and between 1364–1347. For histories of Thebes, see Elizabeth Achtemeier, *Nahum–Malachi* (Atlanta: John Knox, 1986), 25; Peter C. Craigie, *The Twelve Prophets*, vol. 2, *Micah, Nahum, Habakkuk, Zephaniah, Haggai, Zechariah, and Malachi* (Philadelphia: Westminster, 1985), 74; Donald B. Redford, "Thebes," in *ABD* 6:442–43.

5.   So Samuel R. Driver, *The Minor Prophets: Nahum, Habakkuk, Zephaniah, Haggai, Zechariah, Malachi* (New York: Oxford University Press, 1919), 40. Also see 2 Kgs 19:9 where Tirhakah, a Cushite king of Egypt, is described only as the "king of Cush."

6.   Redford, *Egypt*, 360–64; Miller and Hayes, *History*, 369–70.

7.   Craigie, *The Twelve Prophets* 2:75.

8.   Coggins, *Israel*, 53–54. Haldar has noted that there are other inaccuracies in this pericope as well, including Nahum's description of the geography of Thebes as a coastal city. He suggests that the waters are actually the mythical rivers of the netherworld symbolizing chaos; see Alfred Haldar,

larly brutal.[9] The author strikes an ironic chord when he likens the fate of the Assyrian capital to that of a prominent national capital they had destroyed. YHWH would provide the balance upon which Assyrian malevolence would be weighed.[10]

Nahum's reference to Cush in this passage is not mere happenstance. A cursory reading of the text might erroneously lead us to conclude that Cush was just another member of a larger Egyptian army. Yet we must remember that Cush ruled Egypt during this period.[11]However, Nahum does not need to explicitly identify Cush because by contrasting the fate of its former capital, Thebes, with Nineveh he conjures the image of utter defeat that gives this passage its rhetorical potency. Nahum employs Thebes as a metonym for the Egyptian empire, focusing on the virtual impregnability of the empire's political-military center and the host of nations operating at its behest. Thebes, the decimated capital, is an appropriate parallel to the besieged or still smoldering ruins of Nineveh in this synecdoche, and Cush is relegated to an incidental reference in v. 9.

Because Nahum chose to contrast the capital cities of these two superpowers, Egypt and Assyria, he obscures the fact that the Cushites were rulers of Egypt. The intended audience probably would have understood that Cushites were not just the "strength" behind Thebes, but the rulers of that great city also. Although the text does not disclose such information, the author presumes that the audience would have been fully aware of the power relationship between Cush and Thebes; hence, the pericope does not denigrate or disparage the Cushites. On the contrary, the description כּוּשׁ עָצְמָה ("Cush [was] its [Thebes'] strength"), was a complimentary reference to the imposing strength represented by the Cushite warriors. Thus this is another reference to the "mighty" Cushite nation.

In this pericope the "might" is qualified; it was said to have been וְאֵין קֵצֶה ("and without end"), demonstrating the near limitless military resources available to the Cushite rulers of Egypt. References to this "might" often occur in contexts where an alliance of nations with Cush, including the Egyptians, the Libyans, and the Putim, is implied. For example, such alliances are implied in Gen 10 and frequently in 2 Chronicles, suggesting a political league that was prevalent from the time of the XXIInd Libyan Dynasty in Egypt throughout the reign of the XXVth Cushite Dynasty, and perhaps began earlier under pharaohs of the XXIst Dynasty.[12]

The tradition of the fall of Thebes would have been familiar to Nahum's late seventh-century B.C.E. audience. His use of the Cushites in this oracle is plausible

---

*Studies in the Book of Nahum* (Upsala: A. B. Lundequistska Bokhandeln, 1947), 138–39. Also see the discussion on Nahum's knowledge of Theban facts in Walter A. Maier, *The Book of Nahum: A Commentary* (St. Louis: Concordia Publishing House, 1959).

9. Cf. Maier, *Nahum*, 325.

10. Craigie, *The Twelve Prophets*, 75.

11. Maier (*Nahum*, 321) suggests that the reason for the separate references to Cush and Egypt when both were under Cushite administration was that Nahum wanted to emphasize that Thebes could rely on the might of Cush, but could also draft the northern populace of Egypt for its military efforts.

12. See below, Sections 4.2.1.2–5.

only if his audience could reasonably understand them to have been an imposing force, one unlikely to be defeated in battle. Nahum's pronouncement that Cush was Thebes' strength supports my earlier contention that other Judean authors understood Cush in a similar way (i.e. 2 Kgs 19; Isa 18; 20; 37), particularly in association with Egypt. In addition, this poetic reference indicates the role that Cush was often perceived to play in world politics. Here, and in the references already examined, the Cushites were depicted as Egypt's enforcers, likely making up significant portions of Egypt's armies even prior to their political hegemony over their northern neighbor (cf. 2 Chr 12; 14; 16; 21). The value of might frequently associated with the term Cush made it a trope for military power.

Yet Thebes fell. In spite of the best efforts of the Cushites and their armies, the Assyrians overcame the legendary coalition. Still, we can discern no evidence that Nahum intended the Cushites to be seen as having any defect, save the arrogance implied in vv. 8–9, which precipitated this outcome. In this instance, likening Nineveh to Thebes would suggest to the prophet's audience that no matter how strong you perceive yourself to be, you too are vulnerable. We can therefore understand this passage in the way Elizabeth Actemeier has:

> [as] an oracle directed against false security, against those nations and individuals who think they can preserve and save themselves in the onslaughts and sea-changes of human history…for there is no hiding place from God and no defense against his anger.[13]

Even mighty Thebes, who relied on Cush as its strength, and the aid of the Putim and Libyans, was vanquished.

Though this pericope contrasts Thebes with Nineveh, hence Cush with Assyria, another contrast could have been implicit in the text for Nahum's Judean audience. Cush epitomized human strength, which served to inspire pride in fallible human might; such strength was not enough. The fall of Thebes was a particularly great tragedy because it was wholly unexpected. Yet even Cushite might failed, as inevitably it must, when confronted with a more powerful adversary. Only YHWH could be relied on to such an extent. A careful reading suggests that Nahum exploited the commonplace understanding of Cushite strength to contrast this "arrogant" Other with the trustworthiness of YHWH. On this point, Coggins notes that here and in Ps 68:31, this powerful "enemy" of Israel/Judah was "rendered harmless by the power of God."[14] Further, because Nineveh had failed to trust YHWH, its fate was certain destruction. The lesson for the people of Judah implicit in Nahum's words was "Don't trust in nations or human might, only YHWH can save you."

In sum, Nahum used the Cushite Others as symbols of overconfidence in human power. The prophet employs their recent defeat and the destruction of their sacred capital as a means to taunt the Assyrians about their imminent or recent destruction and to reify Judean reliance on YHWH. For Nahum, Cushites serve as tropes for human strength, a pattern we will observe frequently in this study.

13. Achtemeier, *Nahum*, 26.
14. Coggins, *Israel*, 52–53.

### 3.2.2. Cush in Zephaniah

The book of Zephaniah is a brief book, consisting of only three chapters. One of its most remarkable aspects is that each of its chapters has a reference to Cush or a Cush-related term. Zephaniah was a mid-to late seventh-century Judean prophet thought by some scholars to trace his lineage back to King Hezekiah.[15] We will examine the validity of the relationship between Hezekiah and Zephaniah in greater detail below.

In the next three sections I will examine the variety of ways that Cush-related terms are employed in Zephaniah. In Zeph 1:1, one of these terms is used in a prophetic genealogy. The section devoted to that verse addresses various issues concerning the term "Cushi." The second section pertains to the enigmatically brief oracle against Cush in Zeph 2:12. The final section examines the reversal of YHWH's opinion about Cush for in Zeph 3:10, where proselytes or Judean émigrés come before YHWH bearing gifts. We will begin with the most contentious issue: Was one of Judah's own prophets actually a Cushite?

### 3.2.2.1. Zephaniah 1: Son of a "Cushi".

The term כוּשִׁי occurs once in Zeph 1, in v. 1, the genealogy of Zephaniah. The Hebrew Bible provides little information about the life of this prophet. Though the name Zephaniah is used to designate at least four different people in the Hebrew Bible (1 Chr 6:21, the ancestor of a Levitical singer; Jer 21:1, the "Second Priest" of Jerusalem; Zeph 1:1, the prophet; and Zech 6:10, the father of a man named Josiah),[16] it is only used here (Zeph 1:1) to refer to the prophet. What little information there is about this mysterious oracle bearer has been gleaned from this verse. However, the limited extant information has inspired an enormous amount of controversy and numerous theories regarding its interpretation.[17]

Zephaniah 1:1 contains a brief statement of Zephaniah's prophetic call, an extended linear patronymic, and a temporal marker. The verse reads as follows:

> The word of YHWH which came to Zephaniah, son of Cushi, son of Gedaliah, son of Amariah, son of Hezekiah, in the days of Josiah, son of Amon, king of Judah.

The controversy arises from the unusually long genealogical list given for this prophet. Zephaniah is the only prophet in the Hebrew Bible with such an extensive genealogy, naming as it does four of his paternal ancestors. This has evoked scholarly speculation regarding its length and its constituents, two of whom are viewed as problematic. The first of these is Hezekiah, a name borne by one of the greatest reforming kings of Judah. The second is Cushi, the only one of Zephaniah's ancestors not to have a Yahwistic name, and the possessor of a name which can also be used as a gentilic designating a person from Cush. To assess what can be known about Zephaniah, scholars have posed the following arguments.

---

15. John S. Kselman, "Zephaniah, Book of," in *ABD* 6:1077–80.
16. John M. Berridge, "Zephaniah," in *ABD* 6:1075.
17. Including the position that we can learn absolutely nothing about the prophet from this unusual prophetic prolegomena. Cf. Maria Eszenyei Szeles, *Wrath and Mercy: A Commentary on the Books of Habakkuk and Zephaniah* (Grand Rapids: Eerdmans, 1987), 62. See below for others who hold this position.

One group of scholars claims that there is nothing that moderns can learn about Zephaniah by reading this verse. They conclude that the Hezekiah that is mentioned is a random Judean who at most confirms the fact that the prophet stems from a good Yahwistic Judean family. These scholars identify Cushi as another random Judean, bearing a name which, though it could be taken as a gentilic, is actually a respectable Judean name. Hence there is nothing about the prophet's social position or ethnic identity that can be learned from this lengthy introduction.[18] We will return to the suggestion that Cushi was simply a personal name below.

Another closely related school of thought builds on the relationship between the two problematic members of the prophet's lineage, "Hezekiah" and "Cushi." Fohrer, perhaps the best spokesperson for this position, believes that the long genealogy does not point to King Hezekiah, but rather to a generic Judean who is only significant because he demonstrates the authentic Judean lineage of this prophet and "avoid[s] the *embarrassing* misconception that Zephaniah's father, Cushi, was an Ethiopian and not a Judean."[19] John Berridge holds a similar, yet more diplomatically phrased version of this argument. He concurs that the lengthy patronymic has been added "to demonstrate that the prophet was in fact of native descent."[20] This theory presupposes that the name "Cushi" could have been taken as either a gentilic or a personal name given to a person of Cushite ancestry. Only in either of those instances would it have been necessary for the author of Zephaniah or a subsequent redactor to reaffirm the prophet's Judean heritage. The theory also presupposes that Judean citizenship is incompatible with Cushite heritage, for only if it had been deemed problematic to be both a descendant of Cushites and a Judean would such a genealogical confirmation of the prophet's Judean identity be necessary. Hence, this theory postulates that in order to mediate the potential damage Zephaniah's father's name or ethnic origins might cause, the prophet is given an extended genealogy, which proves he is of good Judean stock.[21]

---

18. Cf. Craigie, *The Twelve Prophets*, 106. Ben Zvi believes that there is nothing of Zephaniah's origin or position that can be gleaned from this long introduction; see Ehud Ben Zvi, *A Historical-Critical Study of the Book of Zephaniah* (Berlin: de Gruyter, 1991), 42–51. Larue argues that Cushi is simply a proper name, not an ethnic designation; see Gerald A. Larue, *Old Testament Life and Literature* (Boston: Allyn & Bacon, 1968), 237. Kapelrud argues against royal descent saying that Hezekiah was a common name and that if the author wanted to say that Zephaniah was related to the king, it would have been made more explicit; Arvid S. Kapelrud, *The Message of the Prophet Zephaniah* (Oslo: Universitetsforlaget, 1975), 43–45.

19. Georg Fohrer, *Introduction to the Old Testament* (Nashville: Abingdon, 1978), 456 (emphasis added).

20. Berridge, "Zephaniah," 1075.

21. Szeles (*Wrath*, 62) also suggests that this verse is a redactor's gloss inserted to have the prophet's pedigree conform with the dictates of Deuteronomistic law (cf. Deut 23:7–8). However, if this is a valid reading of the text and we should understand that the rules applied to Egyptians also applied to Cushites, then Zephaniah could be authentically Yahwistic, fully able to participate in Judean society and have Cushite heritage. Deuteronomy 23:7–8 does not make Cushite heritage and Judean citizenship mutually exclusive; these verses provide a means of legitimating an Other, here Zephaniah, for service in "the assembly of Y.

Yet another theory suggests that the reason for the extended patronymic has less to do with Cushi, and more to do with the final name mentioned in Zephaniah's lineage, Hezekiah. Those holding this theory[22] believe that the four-stage genealogy indicates that Zephaniah was a direct descendant of Hezekiah the reforming Judean king. Thus, Zephaniah was not a "newcomer to the reform movement and was, perhaps, among those urging it even before Josiah instituted it."[23] Those holding this position argue that King Hezekiah was the best known of all the Hezekiahs mentioned in the Hebrew Bible, hence the simple mention of his name would bring the king to the minds of listeners during and after the seventh century. Also, they argue that it is plausible for Zephaniah and Josiah to have been contemporaries even though there were only three generations between Josiah and Hezekiah, while there were four generations between Zephaniah and Hezekiah. The difference in the number of generations between Zephaniah and Josiah and the common ancestor Hezekiah might be due to Manasseh's long life and the early age of marriage in the Iron II period.

Finally, those holding this position suggest that the use of Yahwistic names, a common feature in the Judean ruling family, means that Zephaniah may have been of royal lineage.[24] In addition, Wilson argues that there would be no other legitimate reason to have such an extended genealogy except to identify an important ancestor, and that only King Hezekiah was significant enough for this long list.[25] King Hezekiah's fame as a reformer provides an additional reason for the author to mention him in the introduction to a book that sought religious and administrative reform.

Other theories have arisen to deal with the second element of concern in Zeph 1:1, the name Cushi. For example, Watts suggests that the name of Zephaniah's father may indicate a partial Cushite heritage, for it means "the Cushite."[26] His theory does not preclude Zephaniah's extensive Judean heritage, for it was possible to be both Judean and Cushite.[27] Watts also calls attention to the narratives about Ebed-melech, a Cushite who served on the palace staff and saved Jeremiah's life, thereby securing YHWH's protection during the fall of Jerusalem. Watts argues that this event probably occurred during the life of Zephaniah; hence the presence of Cushites in prominent positions in Jerusalem, even in the royal court, is not too farfetched a notion (Jer 38:7–13; 39:15–18).[28]

22. For instance, Adele Berlin, *Zephaniah: A New Translation with Introduction and Commentary* (AB 25A; Garden City, N.Y.: Doubleday, 1994), 65.

23. Berlin, *Zephaniah*, 65.

24. J. N. Boo Heflin, *Nahum, Habakkuk, Zephaniah, and Haggai* (Grand Rapids: Zondervan, 1985), 113–14; Rice, "African," 21–22.

25. Robert R. Wilson, *Prophecy and Society in Ancient Israel* (Philadelphia: Fortress Press, 1980), 279–80.

26. John D. Watts, *The Books of Joel, Obadiah, Jonah, Nahum, Habakkuk and Zephaniah* (Cambridge: Cambridge University Press, 1975), 154.

27. McCarter, *II Samuel*, 408.

28. Watts, *The Books*, 154.

Rice takes a similar position. Considering the name Cushi, he notes that gentilic names typically refer to the ethnicity of the named party.[29] He firmly associates Cushi with Cush, the portion of the Nile Valley south of Syene.[30] Yet Rice does not believe that Cushites dwelt only in the land of Cush; he argues for their continued presence in the land of Canaan from the fourteenth through the seventh century B.C.E., the time of Zephaniah's prophecy.[31] He also suggests that some of these Cushites, though initially Egyptian and Assyrian mercenaries, remained in Levantine regions.[32]

Similarly, Rice traces the history of Yehudi ben Nethaniah ben Shelemiah ben Cushi,[33] an official of King Jehoiakim (Jer 36:14, 21, 23), to Cushites coming into the kingdom of Judah during the reign of Hezekiah and the historical moment of his alliance with the XXVth Cushite Dynasty of Egypt. He reasonably proposes that an exchange of people and ideology was likely due to what is known about such alliances in the ancient world. Rice then proceeds to mention the Cushite, Ebed-melech,[34] an official in the royal court of King Zedekiah. The presence of both of these men who were near contemporaries of Zephaniah in royal contexts, he argues, makes the likelihood that Zephaniah's father was Cushite and was associated with Judean royalty more plausible. Rice therefore suggests that Zephaniah's Cushite heritage could best be assumed to have come through Gedaliah's wife, who was perhaps the daughter of a Cushite diplomatic family in Judah.[35]

A further modification to this argument was made by Copher, who argues that there were

> black persons in the native Hebrew–Israelite–Judahite population from earliest times . . .
> [O]ne must conclude that Zephaniah was indeed a native Judahite, black in color, and related to none other than Hezekiah, king of Judah, of the house and lineage of David.[36]

Though his terms are anachronistic, introducing racialist concepts likely alien to the text of the Hebrew Bible, Copher's point is well taken. There is no need for

29. For instance, Rice notes that the name Gadi refers to a Gadite (2 Kgs 15:14), the name Hachmoni refers to a Hachmonite (1 Chr 11:11; 27:32), and the name Buzi refers to a Buzite (Ezek 1:3; Job 32:2). As in each of these instances, where the gentilic has become a personal name representing a man from that ethnic group, we should understand Cushi as a name for a man from Cush; so Rice, "African," 22–23.

30. Rice, "African," 22 n. 3.

31. Cf. the Sections above on Judg 3 (3.2.7.1); Amos 9:7 (2.2.2) and Hab 3:7 (3.2.3), where I discussed the biblical evidence for Cushites in the Levant. Though Cushi may be part of a later Cushite infusion into the region, an indigenous population of Cushite descendants could prove important to understanding this passage.

32. Rice notes, for example, that there were Cushites in many military campaigns from the fourteenth century downward. Tell el-Amarna Letter 287 puts Cushite troops near Jerusalem in fourteenth century B.C.E. There were also Cushites in David's army 2 Sam 18:21–32 (one man Cushi could not have been extent of Cushite presence.), in Shishak's raid against Judah in fifth year of Rehoboam 918 B.C.E. (2 Chr 12:3), and in Pharoah Neco's armies in 605 B.C.E. (Jer 46:9); so Rice, "African," 24.

33. Yehudi will be discussed more fully below (see Section 3.2.5.2).

34. Ebed-melech will be discussed more fully below (see Sections 3.2.5.3-4).

35. Rice, "African," 28. Also see Adamo, "Africa," 211.

36. Copher, "Black," 161.

Rice to look outside of Judah to find the source of Zephaniah's Cushite lineage; there are plausibly an adequate number of Cushites in the Judean population to suggest an indigenous locus for Zephaniah's Cushite heritage. Hence, the prophet could be a legitimate Judean, capable of delivering the "oracle of YHWH," participating in the Jerusalem cult, and even being a descendant of the royal family, while still acknowledging a connection to Cush.

In this regard, contrary to the positions held by Craigie and Ben Zvi mentioned above, the introduction may provide valuable information about the heritage and the social location of the prophet Zephaniah.[37] There are certain features of this prophetic book that seem obscure without the dual assumption that Zephaniah is both a man of royal blood and a man with a connection to Cush. For example, perhaps Zephaniah failed to critique the office of the king as he did priests, prophets, and judges in Zeph 3:3–4 because he was a member of the royal family. Further, the noticeably brief oracle against the people of Cush may reflect the fact that the prophet himself had Cushite ancestry. In fact, Rice suggests that the reason Zephaniah listed Cush at all in Zeph 2:11 was to include the land of his heritage among those doomed in his oracles, so as not to appear to be demonstrating favoritism by leaving it out. Logically, we would expect him to include Egypt and not Cush in his list of fallen nations in order to balance out Judah's traditional adversaries,[38] Philistia, Moab and Ammon, and Assyria.[39] Hence, the personal information about the prophet Zephaniah given in the superscription in Zeph 1:1 provides interpreters with a hermeneutical framework for understanding the subsequent text.

That Zephaniah had Cushite ancestry is a plausible understanding of this text. Yet the term "Cushi" could also be a personal name that implies nothing about ethnicity.[40] To this end, Lipiński has identified other people named "Cushi" in Assyrian epigraphic sources. In fact, he has determined that the name "Cushi" was "quite common among the Western Semites at the time of the 'Ethiopian' rule in Egypt and during the period that followed."[41] He locates a number of people with the names *kuši(y)* in Hebrew and Phoenician and *kušay* in Aramaic. Lipiński cites epigraphic sources from Nineveh that discuss men named *ku-ša-a-a* and *ku-ša-ia-a*.[42] Independently, Avigad translates a seventh- to sixth-century Hebrew seal belonging to a *"Cushi ben Yedayahu."*[43] In spite of the scarcity of

---

37. This is consistent with Wilson's hypotheses regarding biblical genealogies. Wilson posits that genealogies are given precisely to confer status upon a particular individual and to ensure their authority; R. R. Wilson, "Genealogy."

38. Rice, "African," 29.

39. More will be said about other solutions to this dilemma in the commentary on 2:12 below; see Section 3.2.2.2.

40. Cf. Haak, "'Cush,'" 250; Szeles, *Wrath*, 62.

41. Eduard Lipiński, Review of A. S. Kapelrud, *The Message of the Prophet Zephaniah: Morphology and Ideas*, *VT* 25 (1975): 688–91 (689).

42. Lipiński, Review of Kapelrud, 689.

43. Nahman Avigad, "Six Ancient Hebrew Seals," in *A Book for Shemuel Levin* (ed. Shmuel Abramski and Yohanan Aharoni; Jerusalem: Kiryat-Sepher, 1970), 305–6 (Hebrew), *apud* Haak, "'Cush,'" 250.

epigraphic evidence from the pre-exilic period, the ample data containing the name Cushi indicates that people bearing the name were not uncommon in the Levant.

Though Lipiński's argument adequately demonstrates the popularity of the name in the eighth–seventh-century Levant, he fails to provide adequate support for his contention that the name Cushi says nothing about Cushite ethnicity. For example, in support of this position, he considers the case of one man from Hurran named *ku-ša-a-a* who was mentioned in conjunction with his father *si-i'-a-qa-ba* and his brother *se-er-ma-na-ni*. Based upon this statement, Lipiński argues that "both his father and his brother bore genuine Aramaic names. This decidedly proves that we cannot regard him as an Egyptian or an Ethiopian captive."[44]

Lipiński's argument is vulnerable at this point. The occurrence of a man with a gentilic name meaning "Cushite" alongside two authentically Assyrian names tells us no more than the mention of Cushi in Zeph 1:1 in conjunction with three authentically Yahwistic Judean names. This by no means precludes any association of the name "Cushi" with Cushite ethnicity, since, as Rice observed, the existence of Cushites throughout the Levant would make it likely that they assimilated into other nations.[45] Similarly, Heidorn argues for an increased population of Cushite mercenaries, equestrians, and other royal officials in Assyria in the late eighth century.[46] Men named Cushi could have Cushite heritage and have vertical and horizontal kin with names related to the ethnic group among whom the Cushites lived due to their adoption of the local customs and names. Do we not see a similar scenario at work in the Hebrew Bible where the Hittite soldier in King David's army had an authentic Yahwistic Israelite name, אוּרִיָּה ("Uriah")? We also see this phenomenon with another character definitively identified as belonging to the Cushite Other. In 2 Chr 14:8 we find זֶרַח הַכּוּשִׁי ("Zerah the Cushite"), a Cushite leader with a name that appears to relate to the Hebrew word for "arise," "shine," or "dawn." Hence it is imprudent to discount the effects of assimilation on naming, for foreigners did acquire names alien to their own ethnic affiliations.

In another instance, Lipiński argues that a man named *kšy*, whose script was found on a Phoenician graffiti from Abu Simbel, could not be Cushite because he would have had to be a Phoenician "capable of writing in his native language."[47] Again, his conclusion does not logically follow. Nothing in the evidence he presents precludes the author of the graffiti from being a Phoenician Cushite or even a Cushite diplomat who was familiar with Phoenician script. In fact, the narrative discussed below in Jer 36 describes a Yehudi, who is arguably a descendant of Cushites, working as a Judean courtier, reading a Hebrew scroll of Jeremiah's prophecy to King Jehoiakim. Reading, even reading in a non-Cushite language, is not incompatible with Cushite ethnicity!

44. Lipiński, Review of Kapelrud, 689.
45. Rice, "Africa," 23–25.
46. Lisa A. Heidorn, "The Horses of Kush," *JNES* 56 (1997): 105–14 (106–10).
47. Lipiński, Review of Kapelrud, 689.

Hence, the hypothesis that "Cushi" was a personal name is by no means mutually exclusive of the proposition that "Cushi" was also a gentilic designation. It is entirely likely that the name was given to some Cushites living in the Levant. We must also consider that to have the name "Cushi" may say nothing about the bearer's ethnicity. Nonetheless, the increased popularity of the name in the Levant correlates with the rise to prominence of the Cushites in the eighth century B.C.E. In light of such historical factors we should thus consider that the use of the name may illustrate the extent to which Judeans esteemed the people of Cush.[48]

However we interpret the name "Cushi," there are several implications for our argument. Should we choose to interpret "Cushi" as a gentilic, we can see by its use here in this context that it was not deemed a matter of shame that would damage the credibility of the prophetic voice or contradict the identity of the prophet as a Judean Yahwist—otherwise a conscientious scribe would have quietly omitted the name. Rather, its presence here would illustrate that the author of the text could see Zephaniah as both a descendant of Cushites and a member of the Judean royal court (cf. Jer 36:14; 38:7–12; 39:16). Hence, Cushite ancestry was not mutually exclusive with Judean citizenry or noble status.

Alternatively, if we interpret the term as a personal name unrelated to the bearer's ethnicity, we could not avoid the fact that the name was also a gentilic and that the prophet's audience probably would have recognized it as such because the term "Cushi" could have referred to a citizen from a renowned world power. To give a child the name "Cushi" would automatically call to mind the powerful southern Other that until recently was one of the principal power brokers in the ancient Near East. Assuming "Cushi" is a personal name would lead to the conclusion that the Cushites were deemed honorable enough to merit such rehearsal.

In Zeph 1:1, either the prophet who bore the name had Cushite ancestry or the name Cushi was an acceptable designation for a good Yahwistic Hebrew.[49] In either instance, the author does not demean or devalue the Cushites. Both hypotheses have positive implications for the Judean representation of the Cushites. In the first instance, a faithful Yahwistic Judean prophet could be identified as a Cushite without it demeaning his person or his message. In fact, it was included

---

48. Perhaps it would be possible to see the name Cushi used for someone with Cushite phenotype. Both Lipiński and Kapelrud posit that this was a plausible reason why some were given the name Cushi. See Lipiński, Review of Kapelrud, 689, and Kapelrud, *Zephaniah*, 44. At present I am unaware that names were employed in such a manner in Judah, but it is not impossible, particularly since the term Cushite had commonplace value meaning "dark" (cf. Num 12:1; Jer 13:23). However, if this name were in any way disparaging, it is unlikely that it would have been so common a name in the eighth to the seventh centuries. Hence, this alternative hypothesis would not alter the conclusion that it demonstrated Judean esteem for the people of Cush.

49. Here Szeles is again relevant. Though committed to the proposition that the prophetic prolegomena says nothing about the prophet's identity, Szeles determined that is was possible under YHWH's sovereign election for Zephaniah to have been either a prophetic prince or a Cushite slave and to have served authentically as God's instrument; see Szeles, *Wrath*, 62. Though the notion of "Cushite slave" seems to be the exegete's eisegetical insertion, the concession is duly noted.

in his patronymic in order to validate his authority to speak the word of YHWH.[50] It would also illustrate that Cushites had integrated into Judean society and participated in its political and religious spheres in prominent positions.[51] Most significantly, a Cushite could also have been a descendant of King Hezekiah.

In the second instance, the name Cushi would represent the Judean esteem for this foreign people who symbolized might in the Near Eastern world.[52] This superscription from Zephaniah, therefore, suggests that the name Cushi could occur in a larger recitation of Yahwistic names without proving troublesome to its author or its audience, not to mention the host of redactors and scribes who had the opportunity to delete it had they deemed it inappropriate. However we choose to read this pericope, Zeph 1:1 demonstrates the extent to which Cushite identity was acceptable, even favorable, in late seventh-century B.C.E. Judah.

3.2.2.2. *Zephaniah 2: A Thimble of Woe.* The term כּוּשִׁים occurs once in Zeph 2, in v. 12. This is an obscure verse that seems to have little in common with the overall context. Verses 4–7 of this chapter address YHWH's punishment of the Philistines. Immediately preceding v. 12 is a four-verse description of YHWH's wrath against the Ammonites and Moabites (vv. 8–11). The verses immediately following v. 12 address YHWH's assault against the Northern Kingdom of Assyria (vv. 13–15). Amid these three multiple-verse oracular pronouncements against specific nations, each with a history of animosity with the Israelite/Judahites, there is no more than a single verse dedicated to Cushites: גַּם־אַתֶּם כּוּשִׁים חַלְלֵי חַרְבִּי הֵמָּה. We should also note that there was no extensive history of conflict between the Cushites and the people of Judah.[53] How we interpret this verse will have implications for how it fits into its context.

In the NRSV, this verse reads "You also, O Ethiopians, shall be killed by my sword." A more literal translation of the MT would be "Moreover you, O Cushites, shall be wounded ones of my sword they." Despite the brevity of the Cush reference, there is a disagreement between the pronouns in first and second stichoi of v. 12, the first stichos refers to אַתֶּם ("you" [2 m.pl.]), while the second refers to and emphasizes הֵמָּה ("them" [3 m.pl.]). Such confusion is unsettling in such a succinct account and should make us suspect that there may be some corruption in the text.[54]

---

50. R. R. Wilson, "Genealogy," 931.

51. Again, see 2 Sam 18; Jer 36; 38–39. A similar genealogy is found in Jer 36:14 for an official in the court of King Jehoiakim of Judah.

52. Consider the discussion of Nah 3:9 (see Section 3.2.1) where Cush is identified as the "strength" of Thebes. Also consider the numerous other instances where Cush is a trope for might, as identified in this study.

53. See the Sections on 2 Chr 14:8 (4.2.1.3); 16:8 (4.2.1.4); 21:16 (4.2.1.5). Each of these texts portrays Cush acting at the behest of the XXIInd Egyptian Dynasty, not as independent agents. When sovereign, Cush allied itself with Judah (cf. 2 Kgs 19:9; Isa 18; 20; 37:9).

54. Kapelrud (*Message*, 34) suggests that v. 12 could be a gloss on the larger text, or that a section of the verses has been lost. See also Szeles, *Wrath*, 97. However, Eric Meyers suggested in personal conversation that this manner of pronominal usage would have the effect of emphasizing the fate of the Cushites.

In this instance there is no mention of the Egyptians, or even the Sabeans, Arabs, or Libyans, who are all often considered national powers on Israel's southern front and who were allied with Cush.[55] Scholars have been particularly intrigued that there is no oracle against the Egyptians in this list. Of all the nations at the time that were not included, the Egyptians are most noticeably absent. Some have speculated that it was due to the conflation of Cush and Egypt during the period of the XXVth Dynasty. Cush was considered to have been the principal southern superpower during its domination of Egypt, which would have ended approximately a half-century before this oracle was uttered.[56] Hence, to say Cush would have sufficed, since it would clearly have included all the peoples under Cushite purview, including Egypt.[57] Against this, Ben Zvi has argued that biblical authors in no other place have conflated these two nations (e.g. Gen 10:6; Isa 20:3, 4; 43:3; Ezek 29:10; 30:5; and most significantly, these nations are distinguished in 2 Kgs 19:9 and Isa 37:9).[58] However, 2 Kgs 19:9 and Isa 37:9 do not support Ben Zvi's conclusion.[59] Driver and others have concluded that Cush was simply a distant nation; hence, the reference to Cush was intended to show how YHWH's authority reached to the nations at the ends of the world.[60] Because Egypt was closer, with a more extensive history of interrelationships with Israel/ Judah, would it not merit mention?

For a theory about why there is no anti-Egyptian oracle, we should ask when the text was composed. Achtemeier claims that it originates prior to the predicted events (mid- to late seventh century), foretelling future events on the eschatological horizon.[61]

Conversely, others, including Watts, conclude that this prophecy dates to the latter part of the seventh century, after the Cushite dynasty had been driven out of Egypt and into Cush proper. In such a scenario, Cush would have already suffered a tragic defeat at Thebes in 663. Noting the verbal ambiguity in v. 12, Watts concludes that the verse should be read as past action;[62] hence, the Assyrian defeat of the Cushites would still be part of recent lore in the late seventh century. Ben Zvi, who shares Watts' conclusion, suggests that the "prophecy" was written, as were all the others in this set of oracles against the nations, because each of these nations had previously been defeated; hence, Egypt, Babylon, and

---

55. For examples of these alliances, see Gen 10; 1 Chr 1; 2 Chr 12:3; 16:8; 21:16; Isa 20; 43:3; 45:14.

56. Berlin, *Zephaniah*, 120.

57. So Achtemeier, *Nahum*, 77.

58. Ben Zvi, *Zephaniah*, 176–77.

59. We should note that Cush and Egypt are conflated in 2 Kgs 19:9 and in Isa 37:9, for the reference to Tirhakah designates him the king of Cush. We know that he was also king of Egypt and that the absence of a reference to Egypt here in no way limited his sovereign sphere to Cush alone, but included his northern territories as well. It is also likely that Cush and Egypt are conflated in Nah 3:8–10.

60. Cf. S. R. Driver, *The Minor Prophets*, 128; Daniel Hojoon Ryou, *Zephaniah's Oracles against the Nations: A Synchronic and Diachronic Study of Zephaniah 2:1–3:8* (Leiden: Brill, 1995), 238.

61. Achtemeier, *Nahum*, 78.

62. Watts, *Joel*, 172.

Edom would have been omitted. Yet, these three nations had not had a significant recent defeat, and the prophecies would have been unfulfilled. This also led Ben Zvi to date all these prophecies to the post-monarchic period.[63] In this instance, the defeat at Thebes may be what is recalled in this obscure and corrupted verse.

Szeles takes a similar position to those of Watts and Ben Zvi. Based upon her conclusion that text was composed after 605 B.C.E., she posits that the defeat described in the text refers not to the people of Cush, but to an Egyptian expeditionary unit composed largely of Cushites dispatched by Pharaoh Neco II to reinforce the Assyrians in their wars against the Babylonians. According to Szeles, the slain Cushites in this chapter represent Egyptian mercenaries sent to Carchemish to aid the Assyrians in their war against Babylon, but who never made it home alive. What is most interesting about her proposition is that she deems Zeph 2:12 and its reference to slain Cushites to be part of Zephaniah's anti-Assyrian propaganda.[64] Szeles suggests that there is an implicit taunt of the Assyrians who have relied on "human efforts" to save them, similar to the taunting of the Assyrians we saw above in the section on Nah 3:9. Following this hypothesis, we could read Zeph 2:12 as a reference to Cushites employed as a trope for human might; here, the tenuous nature of relying on human might is apparent.[65]

Following either of these latter two hypotheses, Zephaniah's remarkably brief oracle against the Cushites can hardly be deemed an attempt to denigrate them. The defeats suffered by the Cushites at Thebes or by Cushite mercenaries at Carchemish would have been matters of historical memory. In Zephaniah's account, the historical memory has been recast in theological terms. As Ryou observes, the prophet evokes YHWH in divine warrior imagery, especially in the reference to those slain by the "my sword."[66] It was YHWH who defeated the Cushites. YHWH was not only in charge of Judah's history, but was active in the unfolding history of nations to the end of the earth. That Zephaniah recalled Cush's defeat at this juncture would provide a much-needed balance for the structure of this chapter that focuses on the nations round about the people of Judah. With the inclusion of the Cushites, Zephaniah has presented a portrait of YHWH's sovereign power over the nations to the west, east, south, and even north of Judah.[67]

But one significant issue remains unresolved: Why did Zephaniah devote so little time to the demise of the Cushites? Watts' conclusion that the oracle's brevity relates to the historical nature of the reference is unsatisfactory in light of Ben Zvi's proposition that all of the "prophesied" events had previously come to

---

63. Ben Zvi, *Zephaniah*, 306.

64. Note the proximity of this oracle and the anti-Assyrian oracle that begins in the next verse. This textual positioning may suggest that the demise of the Cushite mercenaries was viewed by the author as a contributing factor in the subsequent demise of Assyria.

65. Szeles, *Wrath*, 97–98.

66. See Ryou, *Zephaniah's Oracles*, 239, particularly n. 208.

67. For a distinctively different view of this passage, see Berlin, *Zephaniah*, 117–24. There, Berlin suggests that the reference to Cush here is to the northern Cassites and alludes to the Table of Nations in Gen 10.

fruition.[68] Unfortunately, through conjecture alone may we propose any solutions to this dilemma. We have to consider: If Zephaniah had Cushite ancestry, could he have had reservations about casting them as YHWH's enemies? Even if his father's name were merely a personal name unrelated to ethnicity, we can specu- ·late that it may have caused him some cognitive dissonance to pronounce doom on the people whom his father's name honored. Perhaps his desire to redeem the people of Cush[69] moved him to add an eschatological reference to 3:10 declaring that Yahwists will come specifically from that nation bringing offerings to YHWH. The hint that Zephaniah had Cushite ancestry further complicates this obscure verse.

In the end, this text remains enigmatic. We are left uncertain about whether it was all of Cush, only soldiers at Thebes, or mercenaries at Carchemish who were actually put to YHWH's sword. We cannot definitively say whether the text refers to a future event or to an historic occurrence, though the latter option seems most plausible because of late seventh-century Levantine politics. We cannot even be certain why Cush is mentioned amid a host of Judah's most visceral rivals, since instances of Cushite/Judahite conflict do not suggest an extensive history of ani- mosity. What we can say with the most certainty, based upon what we have already seen about references to Cushites, is that the reference here in Zeph 2:12 most likely employs Cush as a trope for the southernmost extreme of the known world to which YHWH's sword could reach. It also alludes to Cushites as tropes of human might, might that failed inasmuch as their countrymen would be slaughtered by YHWH's own hand.

### 3.2.2.3. *Zephaniah 3: From Beyond the Rivers of Cush.* The phrase נַהֲרֵי־כוּשׁ

("the rivers of Cush") occurs in v. 10 of Zeph 3. Isaiah 18:1, 2, and 7 are the closest parallels.[70] In an oracular pronouncement of the day of YHWH (Zeph 3:11, "on that day") Isaiah speaks of the land "beyond the rivers of Cush," with "swift messengers" (18:2), "tall and smooth" people (18:2, 7), and "a nation mighty and conquering" (18:2, 7) bringing gifts to "YHWH of Hosts" at Jerusalem. Isaiah there describes the Cushites favorably. Several of the themes in Zephaniah's prophecy appear to be echoes from Isa 18.

Zephaniah 3:10 seems at first irrelevant because in v. 9 *all the people* have been gathered, purged, and united in the worship of YHWH. Why are the Cushites once again mentioned following that inclusive reference? If Zephaniah were closely patterning this proclamation after Isaiah's, one would expect him to mention Assyria, Egypt, Aram, Moab, and Philistia. Or, if the prophet wanted to provide a redemptive footnote to the oracles of doom in ch. 2, he should have

---

68. However, Ben Zvi's further conclusion that the oracle against the Cushites is an appropriate introduction for the oracle against the Assyrians, who conquered the Cushites at Thebes, merits our attention in light of Nah 3:8–10; see Ben Zvi, *Zephaniah*, 306.

69. Rice ("Africans," 30) suggests that Zephaniah sought to shield his own people from harsh chastisement and that, hence, he redeemed them in Zeph 3:10.

70. Kapelrud (*Message*, 35–36) also suggests Isa 19:21 as a parallel noting the similarity of the Egyptians coming to serve God.

mentioned the Philistines, Moab, Ammon, and Assyria. Yet in 3:10 Zephaniah seems to leave out all but Cush. Rice postulates that Zephaniah rescues his own people from the obscurity of the "peoples," whose lips need to be purified, thus indicating that there may already be Cushite people who worshipped and served YHWH. Rice notes that this verse is awkward unless we can assume the prophet had some historical affiliation with Cush.[71]

Exegetes havereached no consensus about the subjects of this prophecy, עֲתָרַי בַּת־פּוּצַי. Note b to v. 10 in the MT (*BHS*) presents the LXX and the Syriac versions of Zeph 3:10, where the phrase עֲתָרַי בַּת־פּוּצַי is absent. The note in *BHS* suggests that we read עַד יַרְכְּתֵי צָפוֹן, meaning "and to the northernmost parts." This reconstruction, though in seeming violation of the spirit behind the principle of *lectio difficilior*, is not without merit. Perhaps the author of Zephaniah employed Cush as a trope for the furthest southern extremes of the known world.[72] Hence, the reference becomes a vision of universal submission to YHWH. However, though the phrase עֲתָרַי בַּת־פּוּצַי is cumbersome, we do not have to reconstruct the text to comprehend it. Further, in order to accept the proposed reconstruction we would have to presume that a scribe copied this verse from a very poor text, or that considerable homoioteleuton or homoioarchton occurred, thus producing עֲתָרַי בַּת־פּוּצַי from עַד יַרְכְּתֵי צָפוֹן, or visa versa. Hence, we should consider the plausibility of the phrase in the MT, עֲתָרַי בַּת־פּוּצַי.

Rice suggests that there are two distinct groups referenced in this phrase. He views the בַּת־פּוּצַי ("dispersed") as Judean refugees and the עֲתָרַי ("worshippers") as native Cushites.[73] Copher believes that they are all simply native Cushite worshippers of YHWH.[74] Ben Zvi proposes that YHWH created all peoples from one man and one woman, therefore YHWH's dispersed are the "peoples" scattered throughout the world. The people of the world will all come to worship YHWH on YHWH's day.[75] This reading reflects Gen 11:1–9, where all of humanity was initially united and then, following a collective attempt to reach the heavens, scattered across the earth. Hence, Ben Zvi understands vv. 9–10 as Zephaniah's vision of the gathering of scattered humanity.[76]

---

71. Rice, "African," 30.

72. See Esth 1:1 and 8:9 (cf. Section 4.2.4) for examples of this variety of Cush usage. We could come to similar conclusions based on Gen 2:13.

73. Rice, "African," 30.

74. Native African worshippers of YHWH will come from beyond the rivers of Ethiopia and bring offerings. Copher, "Black," 161.

75. Ben Zvi, *Zephaniah*, 227–30.

76. See Szeles, *Wrath*, 108, for a similar perspective. She understands בַּת־פּוּצַי to refer to "the masses of pagan peoples" in contrast to the phrase בַּת־צִיּוֹן, which she associates with the "chosen people." Similarly, rejecting the notion that there could have been Israelite/Judahites in Cush in the pre-exilic period, Berlin (*Zephaniah*, 134–35) suggests that the text refers to a future when Yahwism will be universal. See also Heflin (*Nahum*, 151–52) who suggests three possible interpretations for this verse: (1) the subjects are repentant gentiles coming to bring offerings to God in their own lands (see 2:11 where people of all the coasts and islands bow to YHWH in their own place); (2) the subjects are scattered Judeans who will return and bring themselves as an offering or re-institute the sacrificial system; (3) the subjects are gentile worshippers who bring exiled Judeans back to the land as tribute to the grace of YHWH.

However, we note that reading all the "peoples" of the earth as the subject of this particular verse does not take seriously the phrase מֵעֵבֶר לְנַהֲרֵי־כוּשׁ ("from beyond the rivers of Cush").[77] Though v. 9 does suggest universal worship of YHWH, v. 10 narrows its focus to one particular region, Cush. But does it actually limit the focus to Cush? Could the phrase "from beyond the rivers of Cush" have been used as a cliché for "from the ends of the earth"? This is certainly a reasonable conclusion based upon what we know about Cush, which was considered the farthest extent of the known world. There are even instances where it appears to have been employed by Hebrew authors in a similar manner.[78] Two significant Isaianic references discussed in Chapter 2 (11:11 and 18:7) describe processions brought from Cush to Jerusalem during the eschaton.[79] Because this pattern occurs in prophetic and liturgical literature, it is unlikely that this text specifically mentioning Cush would depart from it.

In light of v. 10 and its similarity to Isa 11:11 and 18:7, Zephaniah's intended subject may have been one of the two that Rice suggested. Surely, v. 10 could refer either to native Cushite Yahwists, as in Isa 18:7, or native Israelite/Judahite refugees in Cush, as in Isa 11:11. Isaiah 18:7 suggests that native Cushites will come to worship YHWH: the pilgrims are identified by their phenotypical traits— "tall and smooth (without facial hair)." So, here we could also identify native Cushites with עֲתָרַי ("my worshippers"). Stonehouse also holds that this refers to Cushites bringing offerings to either Elephantine or Jerusalem, likely at a post-exilic period.[80] Jeremiah 39:15–18 indicates that YHWH's blessing can come to foreigners, particularly Cushites, because of their trust in Judah's God.[81] Thus we could have a depiction of the mighty southern Other coming to worship Judah's God.[82]

Isaiah 11:11 predicts that the Lord would recover a remnant from an assortment of nations, including Cush. If this is an eighth-century B.C.E. authentic Isaianic text, the remnant must either be a group of northern Israelites who fled to

---

77. The editors of *BHS* have deemed this section, in fact all of v. 10, to be an addition according to note 10a. However, it is not clear how the editors came to this conclusion since it is attested in the LXX and in the Dead Sea Scrolls, Mur XII.

78. For example, Esth 1:1 and 8:9. Genesis 2:13 may have been used in this manner, emphasizing that the Garden of Eden sustained the people in the rich land located at the farthest extent of the known world. Indeed this concept may be behind the reference in Zeph 2:12, though this is not the most likely conclusion.

79. Note also the related theme of proselytes from Cush in Ps 68:32 and possibly even in Ps 87:4. These texts suggest that proselytes or gifts coming from Cush had ideological significance in Hebrew literature.

80. George G. V. Stonehouse, *The Books of the Prophets Zephaniah and Nahum* (London: Methuen, 1929), 62.

81. See the Sections on Jer 38–39 below (3.2.5.3 and 3.2.5.4).

82. Carol Meyers and Eric Meyers, *Zechariah 9–14: A New Translation with Introduction and Commentary* (AB 25C; Garden City, N.Y.: Doubleday, 1993), 474, also note the parallel in Zech 14:16–21 where the "family of Egypt" will come to Jerusalem as pilgrims for the Feast of Booths. It is likely that Cush is implicitly included in the metaphorical "family" and that they, too, were expected to make this pilgrimage at the eschaton.

this distant region[83] or members of a Judean settlement in Cush at this pre-exilic moment.[84] These are the most likely referents for בַּת־פוּצַי ("daughter of my dispersed ones", v. 10).[85]

By evaluating these two phrases, בַּת־פוּצַי and עֲתָרַי, as references to two distinct groups, Rice postulates that they refer respectively to native Cushites and dispersed Jews. Yet it is likely that in the absence of a *waw* intervening between the two terms—עֲתָרַי ("my worshippers") and בַּת־פוּצַי ("daughter of my dispersed")—we should probably consider the entire phrase together. The only plausible group to be subsumed under both descriptions would be dispersed Israelites/Judahites. Hence, we again find possible literary support for a group of Israelites living in Cush in the pre-exilic period.

Zephaniah, therefore, in his final chapter casts a more favorable light upon Cush than he did in 2:12. He presents Cush as a land where it is likely that Israelites (בַּת־פוּצַי) sought refuge, sojourning among the indigenous population following the destruction of their land by the Assyrians in 722. The very people the Assyrians removed the Cushites welcomed. Thus, we could interpret this passage as a prophecy of the return of the dislocated Israelites.

However, we cannot rule out that the dispersed worshippers may have been Judahites, who for reasons of commerce or politics emigrated to Cush, or indigenous Cushites.[86] In either instance, Zephaniah's negative attitude toward this region or its people in his stunted reference to the defeat of Cush in Zeph 2:12 has changed in this passage.

Zephaniah may have felt a kinship to these people, whether Israelite/Judahite or Cushite, because however their identity might have been constructed, they were Yahwists bringing gifts to the God he served. The ambiguity of the text does not alter the conclusion that the Cushite affiliation or ethnicity did not preclude Yahwistic fidelity. However we understand the enigmatic phrase עֲתָרַי בַּת־פוּצַי in this pericope, it is obvious that Zephaniah bore them no ill will because of their association with this southern region. To the contrary, he envisioned a future where people would come from Cush bearing gifts to YHWH.

---

83. See Section 2.2.3.1 on Isa 11:11. Note also that Isaiah uses this phrase שְׁאָר עַמּוֹ ("remnant of his people") to describe the group coming from Cush. The term שְׁאָר is often used in reference to a portion of YHWH's people who remain faithful. When this is read in conjunction with Isa 10:20–21, where Jacob and Israel are also discussed, it becomes clear that the "remnant" likely refers to those who were displaced by the destruction of the Northern Kingdom of Israel ca. 722 B.C.E. The literary evidence from this pericope suggests that there was a group of refugees from Israel that fled south, settling in Cush.

84. This also would not be unlikely noting the diplomatic ties between Cush and Judah between the mid-eighth and mid-seventh centuries B.C.E., particularly evident during the reign of Hezekiah (cf. 2 Kgs 18–19; Isa 36–37). Still, the former suggestion seems most likely based on Isa 10:20–21.

85. The phrase בַּת־פוּצַי seems to parallel more familiar phrases, including בַּת־יְהוּדָה בַּת־עַמִּי בַּת־צִיּוֹן and בַּת יְרוּשָׁלָם. It appears to have been the likely trope for Judeans living in the Diaspora, particularly since it is used in proximity to בַּת־צִיּוֹן and בַּת יְרוּשָׁלָם in 3:14. This supports the hypothesis that 3:10 describes a return of Yahwists settled in Cush in the pre-exilic period.

86. Thus Szeles' proposition (*Wrath*, 108) that בַּת־פוּצַי was deliberately juxtaposed with בַּת־צִיּוֹן to denote foreign pagan Others whom YHWH also claimed is plausible. Here the first-person possessive suffix would demonstrate YHWH's concern for this Other.

**3.2.2.4.** *Summary of Cush in Zephaniah.* The three references to Cush-related terms in Zephaniah provide us with a host of interesting data about Cush. Zephaniah 1:1 presents us with a prophet with possible Cushite links. Whether he himself was ethnically Cushite, as evidenced through his father's gentilic name, or was a Judean whose patriarchal lineage illustrates his grandfather's esteem for the Cushites, Zephaniah provides us ample material for our discussion and analysis. In spite of the ambiguous nature of the references in this prophetic book, there are a few conclusions that we can state with reasonable certainty.

However we interpret the patronymic "Cushi" in 1:1, we understand that the author and subsequent redactors did not perceive it as a mark of shame. If such had been the case, it would have been omitted from the text to prevent the reference from diminishing the authority of Zephaniah to bear YHWH's word. But the reference remains in the MT as testimony that an association with Cushites, either by bearing a name that honored the mighty southern Other in a Yahwistic pedigree, or by intermarrying with them did not impede prophetic service to YHWH.

The greatest puzzle in Zephaniah is the brief oracle in 2:12, which presents a portrait of Cushites devastated by YHWH's sword. Because we cannot clearly comprehend this text based upon its larger literary context, we have to rely on other clues to ascertain its meaning. Based upon what we know from other passages in which the name Cush appears, we know that Cush could serve as both a trope for a distant land and also for human might. Both of these interpretations may lend meaning to this verse, suggesting that YHWH's sovereignty and ability to judge reached not only to Judah's foes round about, but also to the end of the earth, where YHWH could vanquish even the overwhelming might of the Cushites. The negative tenor of Zeph 2:12 does not single out the Cushites for harsh treatment, but includes them in an array of Others who have tasted YHWH's wrath. Because Cush is included in this array and other nations we might expect to see (i.e. Egypt) are omitted, this prophecy was likely born of historical exigencies and not a desire to demean.

The final Zephanian use of a Cush-related term recalls the Isaianic references in 11:11 and 18:7, which state that Yahwists will come forth from Cush bearing gifts. Zephaniah 3:10 falls within the larger pattern of texts that depict gifts and worshippers from Cush (e.g. Ps 68:32 and perhaps even Ps 87:4). Again, we should note Zephaniah's redemption of a group of God-fearers from Cush, though we cannot unequivocally identify them. The phrase עֲתָרַי בַּת־פוּצַי ("my worshippers, daughter of my dispersed"), most likely describes Israelite exiles in Cush, although the worshippers could be Judean settlers or native Cushites who will make a pilgrimage from Cush to Jerusalem at the eschaton. In any event, Zeph 3:10 counters the oracle of doom in 2:12 with a prophecy of a blissful faithful future for the people from "beyond the rivers of Cush."

Zephaniah has no hint of constituent elements of racialist thought. If anything, the Cushites are othered in a manner similar to the various nations mentioned above in Chapter 2, except that the Cushite's doom is mentioned only cursorily among the more extensive descriptions of YHWH's wrath against the Judah's traditional enemies. The two other passages are instances where the lines between

Cushite and Judean identity are somewhat blurred. In the first case (Zeph 1:1), the adoption of a gentilic as a personal name implies Cushite presence in Judean community or the ideological acceptance of the name "Cushi," a gentilic designation employed for a known Other, in conjunction with Yahwistic theophoric names. That this occurs in the context of an extended prophetic patronymic, where the integrity of the delivered word rests upon the audience's perception of the prophet's pedigree, denotes the level of comfort Judeans had with the idea of Cush. Further, the association of Cushi with Hezekiah and the royal house of Judah may suggest the extent of Cushite participation in the Judean hegemony.

The final reference to a Cush-related term, found in Zeph 3:10, contains no constituent elements of racialist thought. The prophet has portrayed a scenario where either dislocated Yahwists dwelt in pre-exilic Cush or where Cushites could be welcomed into the most intimately Israelite/Judahite practice, Yahwism.

### 3.2.3. *Habakkuk 3: The Tents of Cushan*

The term כּוּשָׁן ("Cushan") occurs once, in v. 7, in the psalm-like prayer, which constitutes all of Hab 3 (vv. 1–19). In this chapter the prophet depicts a Yahwistic theophany proceeding from the desert regions far to the south toward Judah. The late seventh-century prophet Habakkuk (610–605), a contemporary of Zephaniah, Jeremiah, and Nahum, is thought to have worked at the Temple, where he would have delivered his oracles to the people of Judah.[87] Chapter 3 is a particular type of Hebrew poetry, resembling a hymn that, some postulate, could have been performed in the Temple. As Craigie suggests, Habakkuk's Temple context likely influenced the liturgical form of this particular oracle.[88]

The term כּוּשָׁן is used in parallel with the term מִדְיָן ("Midian") in 3:7. As often in Hebrew poetry, when terms such as these occur in this structural arrangement, they should be viewed as similar or identical.[89] This has led some to posit a relationship between these two nations. For instance, Driver claims that Cushan was a neighboring tribe to Midian.[90] Baker suggests that Cushan may be a subgroup of Midianites or a location in the vicinity of their main settlements.[91] Albright notes that Cushan was "a probable archaic designation for southern Transjordan."[92] Hidal concludes on the basis of this verse that there was an Arabic Cush. This group, Cushan, was distinguished from Cush in Hab 3:7 by the Arabicized *–an* ending, and was definitively related to the southern Other.[93]

---

87. Craigie, *The Twelve Prophets*, 77.
88. Craigie, *The Twelve Prophets*, 102.
89. Achtemeier calls the terms "synonymous" in this pericope; see Achtemeier, *Nahum*, 57. For a discussion of parallelism in Near Eastern and Hebrew poetry, see Adele Berlin, "Parallelism," in *ABD* 5:155–62; Robert Alter, *The Art of Biblical Poetry* (New York: Basic Books, 1985), 3–26.
90. S. R. Driver, *The Minor Prophets*, 90.
91. David W. Baker, "Cushan," in *ABD* 1:1219–20.
92. William F. Albright, "The Psalm of Habakkuk," in *Studies in Old Testament Prophecy* (ed. H. H. Rowley; Edinburgh: T. & T. Clark, 1950), 15 n. v.
93. The reader should see Hidal's argument ("Cush," 1011–3) in this regard. He suggests that the *–an* ending is an element found in Arabic *nomina propria*. Hidal cites the biblical references to other peoples found in the Arabian peninsula (i.e. Jokshan, Medan, and Midian of Gen 25:2) to support this

Based on Hidal's theory, we may hypothesize that there was a people identified as "Cushan" known to the people of Judah in the seventh century and located somewhere near Judah's southern border, likely in a region that overlapped with that of Midian.[94]

The precise relationship between this Cushan and the focal Other located in the region south of Egypt remains unclear. Whether this was a group of people that possessed similar phenotypical traits, a similar genealogy, or was distinct in some other regard is uncertain. As I noted in my discussion of Judg 3, the term "Cush" is an Egyptian loan-word unrelated to any Semitic root. Because of this it is improbable that "Cushan" was a designation originating in Israel or Judah for a people unrelated to Cush.[95] Cushan may have been the offspring of a group that migrated from Cush, or even the descendants of Cushite soldiers in the Egyptian army who were assigned to the Levant.[96]

The basis of the prayer in Hab 3 is an account of YHWH's journey from the southern regions of Teman and Mt Paran to the land of Israel. The term "Teman" comes from the Hebrew תֵּימָן and means, literally, "south." Teman is thought to have been a region in southern Edom in the mountain range on the eastern side of the Jordan Rift Valley. It was also used as metonym for Edom (see Jer 49:20; Obad 1:9). The biblical association between YHWH and Teman was strengthened by the discovery of an ostracon at Kuntillet 'Ajrud with the epithet "YHWH of Teman."[97] Edom is also associated with YHWH in the Song of Deborah (Judg 5:4) and in the Song of Moses (Deut 32:2), two of the oldest traditions found in the Hebrew Bible.[98] Paran is by no means synonymous with Teman. Though also

contention. He further notes that the Assyrian term for Cush, *Meluhha*, was used for South Arabia and for Cush. Hence, he contends that there was an Arabian Cush identified as "Cushan." In light of my discussion of the Table of Nations (Gen 10), I should note that Gen 25:3 describes Jokshan as the father of Sheba and Dedan. Sheba and Dedan are also identified as the descendants of Raamah son of Cush in Gen 10:7. Though we should not draw firm conclusions about historical matters based solely upon biblical evidence, the narratives suggest that Cushites were somehow affiliated with people on both sides of the Red Sea.

94. Some have chosen to see this as a direct reference to Cush; for example, Watts, *Joel*, 148. However, this conclusion has several problems: (1) Why is the term Cushan employed instead of Cush? (2) Why would Cush be so closely linked with Midian, a people separated from them by Egypt? (3) Why would Cush occur in a discussion about YHWH's migration to the Promised Land? Traversing through Cush would have required a considerable detour from the various proposed Exodus roots.

95. See the discussion above about Judg 3 (Section 3.2.7.1) for a more thorough analysis.

96. See the discussion above about Amos 9 (Section 2.2.2). The people of Cushan may well be the intended meaning of the unusual construction "offspring of the Cushites." In fact, reading this verse in conjunction with Amos 9:7 helps us to see that the intended audience likely knew of a group or even groups Cushite immigrants on the southern borders of Judah. Also see the discussion on Num 12. Moses' Cushite wife may have been a member of one such community, if she was not herself a participant in Israel's own exodus.

97. Ernst Axel Knauf, "Teman," in *ABD* 6:347–48; Zeev Meshel, "Did Yahweh Have a Consort?," *BARev* 5 (1979): 24–34; Meyers and Meyers, *Zechariah 9–14*, 152; Mark S. Smith, *The Early History of God: Yahweh and the Other Deities in Ancient Israel* (San Francisco: HarperSanFrancisco, 1990), 85–88.

98. Szeles, *Wrath*, 47.

south of Judah, this region occupies the easternmost portion of Sinai, principally the western side of the Jordan Rift Valley.[99] It is also mentioned in Deut 33:2 in a similar context as a location visited by the Hebrews during their wandering in the wilderness.

The chaos in this passage as YHWH passes through the southern deserts is not uncommon in theophanies, which often mention plagues and pestilence, earthquakes and cosmic disruption, and imagery of the deity as a divine warrior.[100] It is in such a context that the reference to the אָהֳלֵי כוּשָׁן ("tents of Cushan") occurs. In this theophany, when YHWH passes through the region south of Judah on his northern trek, there is great turmoil in his wake. This turmoil is manifest in the "affliction" of the tents of Cushan and the "trembling" of the tent-curtains of Midian.

Habakkuk does not indicate what Cushan and Midian did to deserve this fate. Perhaps this is simply a reference to the Midianite wars with the people of Israel during their experience in the wilderness and during their initial attempt at settlement in Canaan (Num 31; Judg 6–8; Ps 83:9–12). Though Cushan is here associated with one of Israel's early enemies, it is not apparent that Israel's enmity toward Midian was transferred to Cushan in this passage, for Cushan's fear may have resulted from the potency of the theophany. After all, Habakkuk seeks to recreate the dread that a deity traversing the land would evoke. However, some scholars have noted the contrast between YHWH the warrior and the fearful camps trembling in YHWH's wake,[101] or have associated this divine warrior passage with judgment against Midian.[102] In light of the affiliation between Cushan and Midian in this text, I find it difficult completely to disassociate these two groups.

Other exegetes perceive the reason for Cushan's mention in the text of Habakkuk in different ways. Marbury thinks the following factors came into play:

> Cushan, or Ethiopia, took its name from Cush the eldest son of Ham, the youngest son of Noah, Gen. X. 6, to show, that though Canaan, the son of Ham, be only named in Noah's curse, yet the smart thereof should also light upon Cush also, and he should taste also of affliction.[103]

Marbury also uses the reference to the curse of Ham to declare the divine authorization for the affliction of the people of Cushan. However, there is little in the text of Habakkuk that would support his contention. He does consider the notion of tents, suggesting that they were images of military preparation. Yet he never takes into account that there were Midianite migratory pastoralists who, though they did dwell in cities, also spent significant portions of their lives in tents as

---

99.    Cf. Jeffries M. Hamilton, "Paran," in *ABD* 5:162; M. S. Smith, *History*, 3 and 50.

100.    Cf. Theodore Hiebert, "Theophany in the Old Testament," in *ABD* 5:505–11. On the notion of the Divine Warrior in this passage, see Szeles, *Wrath*, 48–49.

101.    For example, William P. Brown, *Obadiah through Malachi* (Louisville, Ky.: Westminster John Knox, 1996), 95.

102.    Achtemeier, *Nahum*, 57.

103.    Edward Marbury, *Obadiah and Habakkuk* (Ann Arbor: Sovereign Grace Publishers, 1960), 626.

they tended their flocks.[104] In fact, the curse of Ham is not employed in this manner in the Hebrew Bible.

The value of this text for our study is at least twofold. This is the best evidence for the existence of an Arabian Cush in the Hebrew Bible. But how frequently did biblical authors refer to this region when discussing Cushites in the Hebrew Bible? Only in Judg 3, Amos 9, and in this text is an Arabian Cushan plausible.[105] On the occasions when Judean authors intended to refer to Cushan, they clearly distinguished between this southern Levantine people and the nation south of Egypt, Cush proper. In these instances, Cushan is clearly indicated by the suffix *–an* to the term for Cush (Judg 3; Hab 3) or by identifying them with Amos' unique moniker, בְּנֵי כֻשִׁיִּים (9:7). In both instances, the philological relationship between Cushan and Cush is evident and the relationship between the peoples of those nations is implied, particularly in the Amos reference.

### 3.2.4. *Cush in the Work of Deutero-Isaiah*

The material in Isa 40–55 has traditionally been assigned to an anonymous prophet called Deutero-Isaiah. For a variety of reasons, all but the most conservative scholars agree that these chapters represent a separate corpus from those associated with the eighth-century prophet, Isaiah ben Amoz.[106] Though included in the book bearing the prophet's name, the corpus of Isa 40–55 never mentions Isaiah by name or otherwise attempts to place its prophecies in the eighth-century prophet's mouth.[107] Soggin dates Deutero-Isaiah's material to the period between 550–539 B.C.E.[108]

Inasmuch as the emphases of Deutero-Isaiah tend to be on comfort for an abused people, rather than judgment, doom, or dread,[109] this book seeks to elevate the esteem of the people of Judah, who had been brutalized, subjugated, and exiled by Babylon. Deutero-Isaiah's message of restoration was intended to boost the collective morale of a broken nation and to reassure them that YHWH their God was still in control of their destiny and, in spite of their tragic circumstances, their God still cared deeply for them. In fact, Deutero-Isaiah also reveals to his

---

104.   George E. Mendenhall, "Midian," in *ABD* 4:815–18.

105.   We could reasonably conclude that Num 12:1 and 2 Chr 21:16 imply an Arabian Cushan. However, both of those texts, particularly the latter, can also be explained on the basis of the region south of Aswan.

106.   Soggin, *Introduction*, 365–67, provides a thorough summary of the elements of Deutero-Isaiah that distinguish it from the work of Isaiah of Jerusalem: (1) the exile had already occurred; (2) Babylon was now the clear enemy and Isaiah's foe, Assyria, is not mentioned; (3) Babylon is depicted on the brink of destruction; (4) Cyrus, the sixth-century Persian king, is mentioned twice by name; (5) prophecies are intended to console not deride Judah; (6) there are stylistic differences between this book and the material of Isaiah of Jerusalem; (7) hope for the future has replaced visions of doom.

107.   Bernhard W. Anderson, *Understanding the Old Testament* (4th ed.; Englewood Cliffs, N.J.: Prentice–Hall, 1986), 474.

108.   Soggin, *Introduction*, 365–67.

109.   So B. W. Anderson, *Understanding*, 474; Bright, *History*, 355; Frank S. Frick, *A Journey through the Hebrew Scriptures* (Forth Worth, Tex.: Harcourt Brace, 1995), 410.

people that their God, YHWH, will soon exercise authority over the very nations who sought to control Israel/Judah's destiny. YHWH's dominion will be universally recognized, as all the nations of the world will do obeisance before Israel/Judah's God in their capital, Jerusalem.[110]

Each of these factors comprises the context in which Deutero-Isaiah uttered his oracles. Without taking into consideration the context for their utterance, it is difficult to comprehend the purpose of the particularly harsh portrayals of Cush found in this unknown prophet's typically jubilant predictions. For it seems that Deutero-Isaiah has singled out the Egyptians, Sabeans, and the Cushites for ignominy, and predicated the liberation and restoration of Israel/Judah upon their demise.

3.2.4.1. *Isaiah 43: The Cost of Redemption.* The term כּוּשׁ appears once in the prophecy of Isa 43, in v. 3, where it is partnered with סְבָא ("Seba") and מִצְרַיִם ("Egypt"), recalling a set of political alliances also reflected in Gen 10, Isa 45:14, and in numerous instances in 1 and 2 Chronicles.

Some scholars have rearranged the MT's order of verses in ch. 43. For example, Whybray prefers viewing the passages as two distinct salvation oracles: vv. 1–3a and vv. 3b–7.[111] However, we can discern a pattern in vv. 3 and 4 where v. 3a and 4a are parallel constructions, as are v. 3b and v. 4b. Verses 3a and 4a are parallel explanatory clauses: v. 3a identifies whom YHWH is to redeem Israel and 4a identifies who Israel is to YHWH. In vv. 3b and 4b, YHWH offers parallel promises to nations תַּחַת ("instead of") Israel. Hence, there is no need to reconstruct this passage, particularly vv. 3–4; the author intended them to be read as a unit.[112]

Deutero-Isaiah's here prophesies redemption for the dispersed people of Israel. But one nation's redemption comes at a high cost; in order to ransom Israel, YHWH would give מִצְרַיִם כּוּשׁ וּסְבָא in its stead. It is YHWH's offering of Egypt, Cush, and Seba to redeem Israel that is most significant, and our understanding of the implications of this act depends upon what we infer about it.

There are several quite contradictory ways to interpret the author's valuation of Cush and its partners. The first is to observe that these nations were of great value to YHWH, for they were regions rich in natural resources which had at various times been significant military and political forces in the Levant. Deutero-Isaiah may have chosen these nations to emphasize what a great sacrifice YHWH made to redeem Israel: to offer in exchange for a beloved but weaker and poorer nation such mighty powers. Were these nations of no repute, this exchange would be meaningless. Hence, we may conclude that Cush is of great value.[113]

---

110.  Bright, *History*, 357.

111.  Roger N. Whybray, *Isaiah 40–66* (Grand Rapids: Eerdmans, 1981), 81–82.

112.  For others who have taken vv. 1–7 as a unit, see Wade, *Isaiah*, 276. Verses 3–4 are so deemed by Andrew Wilson, *The Nations in Deutero-Isaiah: A Study on Composition and Structure* (Lewiston, N.Y.: Edwin Mellen, 1986), 243. Westermann divides the pericope into vv. 1–4 and vv. 5–7; see Claus Westermann, *Isaiah 40–66* (Philadelphia: Westminster, 1969), 114–19.

113.  See Adamo, "Africa", 233, and Wade, *Isaiah*, 277 n. 3, for a similar position.

Another interpretive strategy leads to a different conclusion. The author's deliberate elevation of Israel above these three southern nations—Egypt, Cush, and Seba—in an undeniably hierarchical manner confers value upon Israel at the expense of the dignity of its southern neighbors. The restoration of Israel is predicated on the subjugation of not just one, but three prominent nations.

A third possibility could be that the author mentioned these nations, all of which are in Africa,[114] to represent the farthest extent of the world. Hence, the message is that YHWH would give the whole world to ransom favored Israel from its Babylonian captivity.[115]

Finally, this prophecy may have a real world historical referent. Depending upon when Deutero-Isaiah composed this prophecy, he could have perceived a period when Cyrus' political ambitions would have led him to seek the unconquered territories in Egypt and further south.[116] Although he never acquired Egyptian territory, like his successor Cambyses,[117] the prophet seems to suggest that a contract existed between YHWH and Cyrus. Because Cyrus was YHWH's anointed (Isa 45:1), the prophet may have envisioned an arrangement between YHWH and this Persian king whereby YHWH would ensure the fruition of the king's plan for world domination if Cyrus repatriated the exiled people of Judah. The most significant lands left for Cyrus to subjugate would have been those in northeastern Africa; hence, the metaphor of nations given "instead of" Israel.[118] However we choose to interpret this passage, several points are clear: Israel is deemed more important to YHWH than these other three nations;[119] the freedom and autonomy of these other nations can be compromised for the sake of Judah's redemption; Judah is given hierarchical priority over other nations, including Cush.

Isaiah 43 provides the clearest instance of a reference to Cush within the framework of an ethnic hierarchy. What makes this passage particularly troubling is that the inferior position ascribed to Cush is sanctioned by YHWH's action. The deity is the agent willing to forfeit Cush and the other nations for the sake of Israel. Though this is not unexpected in that the Hebrew Bible is a collection of Israel's sacred texts, we cannot ignore the implication of YHWH's patently pro-

114.   So Arthur S. Herbert, *The Book of the Prophet Isaiah Chapters 40–66* (Cambridge: Cambridge University Press, 1975), 49; Whybray, *Isaiah*, 83; John L. McKenzie, *Second Isaiah: Introduction, Translation, and Notes* (AB 20; Garden City, N.Y.: Doubleday, 1968), 50.

115.   Herbert, *Isaiah 40–66*, 49.

116.   The relationship between this prophecy and Cyrus is implied by Isa 45:14. Here we see the image of YHWH delivering Egyptians, Cushites, and Sabeans into Cyrus' hands as implied in 43:3. However, there are problems with the identification of Cyrus as the recipient of the people of these three nations in 45:14. (See the discussion below.) Still, following Soggin's dating (*Introduction*, 367) of this material (550–539 B.C.E.), Deutero-Isaiah, having written during Cyrus' tenure, would not have known that he would never conquered this southern triumvirate.

117.   Adamo, "Africa," 232; Wade, *Isaiah*, 277 n. 3.

118.   So Adamo, "Africa," 232, and Whybray, *Isaiah*, 83. Also consider A. Wilson's caution that "no geopolitical import should be read into [this] prophecy" (*Nations*, 243).

119.   This pericope seems antithetical to that found in Amos 9:7. There, the implication is that YHWH has cared for a number of nations, not just Israel alone, hence Israel is equally responsible for its iniquity. Here YHWH favors the Judean exiles above the people of Cush, Egypt, and Seba.

Israel position in Isa 43. This Israel-centered, divinely sanctioned hierarchy could have led the audience to view Cush and its two partners as less worthy of ontological merit than Israel.

But does this hierarchy represent what we would call Deutero-Isaiah's racialist thinking with regard to Cush? Though a hierarchical prioritizing of human beings is a constituent element of racialist thought,[120] several other factors are important to consider. First, Cush is not singled out for special mention. Although it seemingly diminishes Cush's worth to have it as one of three nations given in exchange for one smaller nation, Cush was not denigrated in a manner unlike other nations, for its lot was shared by Egypt and Seba.[121]

Second, Deutero-Isaiah makes no appeal to any essentializations about Cush or the other nations to justify YHWH's prioritization of Israel. He does not employ phenotypical or behavioral traits to justify this hierarchy. There is no "legitimating ideology"[122] in place, save, perhaps, the elect status of the Judeans for whom the book was composed.

However, should we overlook the ideological import of this pericope? Just as Cush, Egypt, and Seba are ransomed for Israel figuratively in this literary construct, does not this metaphorical ransoming compromise the humanity of the nations who are delivered up? Does not this passage reduce the value of the people given for ransom and elevate those ransomed? In this instance, the latter is the precise intent of the prophecy and the former is an unfortunate, though no less real byproduct. We are left with what could be perceived as a theologically charged statement about the value of Cushite lives in comparison to those of Israelites.[123]

Yet, the overall goal of Deutero-Isaiah was to build the fragile self-esteem of a nation recovering from a tragic series of events that threatened its future. To this end the purpose is primarily Judeo-centric, seeking to reassure the people that YHWH still had their welfare at heart despite the trauma they had recently endured. Further, the author perceives Judah as a covenant community,[124] bound to YHWH by a unique and enduring relationship. Thus parity between nations in YHWH's sight was not the author's principal aim, for his initial goal was to produce a theology that redeemed Judah, to reinforce their covenantal relationship with their God. Deutero-Isaiah's liberation strategy in this text requires that the powerful must be sacrificed for the sake of a disenfranchised and despairing people in exile.

120. See Banks, *Ethnicity*, 54; Rigby, *African Images*, 1–5.

121. Depending on how v. 4b is interpreted, it could indicate that other nations and peoples would also be given as ransom. However, it would be equally plausible to suggest that v. 4b reflects the nations mentioned in v. 3b.

122. Again, by "legitimating ideology," Banks (*Ethnicity*, 54) means the political or ideological valuation of perceived phenotypical or behavioral differences between racial types.

123. Note the distinctly different message of Amos 9:7 where Israel and the offspring of the Cushites are valued equally in YHWH's eyes.

124. Though rehearsals of YHWH's covenantal relationship with the people of Israel/Judah occurs less frequently in Deutero-Isaiah's works than in other texts, it also functions in this corpus; see Isa 42:6; 49:8, and 54:10.

If we take this into account, the author's social location precludes any notion of authentic subjugation of the Cushites or their colleagues,[125] for Deutero-Isaiah's people are in the most tentative position, holding power over no one or nothing, including their own lives. The only real power they possessed was ideological and their power to affect the outcomes of other nations was limited to the spoken and written word. Hence, any hint of self-elevation must be understood in this context, as an ahistorical ideological projection meant to buoy Israelite/Judahite floundering self-esteem.

3.2.4.2. *Isaiah 45: The Price of Esteem*. The term כוּשׁ occurs once in Isa 45, in v. 14. Here Cush is again united with its allies מִצְרַיִם וּסְבָא ("Egypt and Seba"). There are several similarities between this text and 43:3. The concept of redeeming those exiled from Israel (v. 13), in close proximity to v. 14 where the subjugation of these three nations is described, resembles ch. 43, where Egypt, Cush, and Seba are ransomed for the sake of Israel. However, something has changed in the interim. The Hebrew phrase לֹא בִמְחִיר וְלֹא בְשֹׁחַד ("not by price nor ransom") in 45:13 implies that the situation recounted here is distinct from the former one. Yet the situation described in ch. 45 can be perceived as equally grave.

Certain exegetical issues must first be resolved. The initial issue is: Who was the recipient of the gifts described in v. 14? The extant text contains an ambiguous referent, עָלַיִךְ ("to you"), לָךְ ("to you"), אַחֲרַיִךְ ("after you"), etc. But who is the "you?" We might plausibly suppose that the "you" refers to Cyrus, the assumed subject of v. 13, the one who will rebuild Jerusalem and free the exiles of Israel/Judah. In Isa 44:28 and 45:1, Cyrus is deemed respectively YHWH's "shepherd" and "anointed." However, the gender of each of the "yous" mentioned in this passage is feminine; hence, they can not refer to Cyrus.

Rather than emend the text, many scholars have chosen to view the referent as Zion employed as a metonym for Israel/Judah.[126] However, this does not significantly alter our understanding of Isa 43:3, since YHWH may have offered these nations to Cyrus as ransom and he may be the one delivering them to Israel/Judah where they can submit to and worship YHWH.[127]

A similar issue is the structural division of this passage. Whybray claims, following Westermann, that v. 14 begins a unit distinct from the preceding one (vv. 11–13).[128] If we accept this division, the problem discussed above concerning the recipient of YHWH's "gifts" can be resolved with greater certainty. If v. 13 belongs to another discrete literary unit, the "you" in v. 14 may not refer to Cyrus, the assumed subject of the prior verse.

A further exegetical issue concerns the subject of the prophecy in v. 14. The first two members of this chain appear to be exported goods, יְגִיעַ מִצְרַיִם וּסְחַר־ כּוּשׁ, and are translated in the NRSV as "the wealth of Egypt and the merchandise

---

125.  Cf. Rigby, *African Images*, 1–5.
126.  For example, Adamo, "Africa," 234–35; Herbert, *Isaiah 40–66*, 70; Whybray, *Isaiah*, 109; A. Wilson, *Nations*, 243.
127.  Whybray, *Isaiah*, 109.
128.  Whybray, *Isaiah*, 109; Westermann, *Isaiah 40–66*.

of (Cush)." However, the last member in the chain poses a problem, that is, וּסְבָאִים אַנְשֵׁי מִדָּה ("and the Sabeans, tall of stature [lit. 'men of measure']"),[129] a translation that suggests that the subjects of this prophecy are not an assortment of commodities, but human beings! The phrase at the end of v. 14 supports this hypothesis, אַחֲרַיִךְ יֵלֵכוּ בַזִּקִים יַעֲבֹרוּ וְאֵלַיִךְ יִשְׁתַּחֲווּ אֵלַיִךְ יִתְפַּלָּלוּ עַלַיִךְ יַעֲבֹרוּ וְלָךְ יִהְיוּ ("to you they will pass over and they will be yours, they will follow you in chains [reading with the note in *BHS*], they will pass over and to you they will bow, to you they will entreat/pray..."). The latter portion of v. 14 cited above requires human subjects who will "pass over," "follow in chains," "bow," and "pray." Thus, סחר and יגע should not be read as nouns, but as participles.[130] Understanding סֹחֲרֵי and יֹגְעֵי as participles makes this a reference to Egyptian "laborers" and Cushite "merchants,"[131] thus solving our exegetical problem.

However, we have exchanged a textual problem for a social dilemma, for the text now justifies the subjugation of the Egyptians, the Sabeans, and the Cushites. This prophecy is contrary to the beatific vision of universal Yahwism that we see in Zech 8:20–23. In that oracle, the prophet describes the assembled nations as willing worshippers of Judah's God, who intend לְבַקֵּשׁ אֶת־יְהוָה צְבָאוֹת בִּירוּשָׁלַ͏ִם ("to seek YHWH of the hosts in Jerusalem"), and further he notes a time when they will וְהֶחֱזִיקוּ בִּכְנַף אִישׁ יְהוּדִי לֵאמֹר נֵלְכָה עִמָּכֶם ("seize the hem of a Yehud-ite saying, 'let us go with you'").[132] But in Isa 45, Deutero-Isaiah metaphorically subjugates the Cushites and their allies, who are being led away in chains and forced to bow before Israel/Judah. Thus these Others are not willingly reverent, but are compelled to submit. Further, Cush and its allies are not forced to bow to YHWH but to the people of Judah, and herein is the crux of the problem.

Indeed, Isa 45:14 justifies Judah's enslavement of these three peoples and YHWH's sanction for it. Further, if we accept Adamo's conclusion that these three peoples represented "all African territories" known to the Israelite/Judah-ites,[133] then v. 14 seems to authorize the enslavement of African peoples.

However, before reaching such a conclusion, several details must be consid-ered. First, Isa 49:22–23 also describes nations similarly subjugated, submitting

129. Sabeans being tall are similar to the Cushites mentioned in Isa 18. Perhaps this is a general description of people from this region of Northeastern Africa. Cushites and Sabeans tend, on the main, to be of greater stature than the Israelites. If the Sabeans and the Cushites could be conflated, this is an interesting phenotypical description. However, since we are addressing explicit references to Cush, we will simply note this as a possible Cush-related notation of somatic type. Cf. Müller, "Seba," 1064.

130. As suggested by notes 14 a and b in *BHS*.

131. Cf. Wade, *Isaiah*, 295; Whybray, *Isaiah*, 109; A. Wilson, *Nations*, 243.

132. See Carol Meyers and Eric Meyers, *Haggai, Zechariah 1–8: A New Translation with Introduction and Commentary* (AB 25B; Garden City, N.Y.: Doubleday, 1987), 442–45, who note the "eschatological inclusiveness" (p. 445) of Zech 8:20–23. There, the prophet describes a time when people from across the world will make their way to Jerusalem, the seat of YHWH's rule, and acknowl-edge YHWH's dominion because of "those who already stand in relationship to God" (p. 445).

133. Adamo, "Africa," 232. Also see Mckenzie (*Second Isaiah*, 81) who describes these "north-east Africa[n]" nations as the first non-Israelite/Judahite people groups to profess Yahwism in the Hebrew Bible.

themselves to denigration by the people of Israel/Judah. So it is not just these "African" nations singled out for submission; in Deutero-Isaiah's vision, all nations will eventually bow before YHWH. These specific nations are "used as representatives of the entire world serving Israel,"[134] and not as those singled out for distinct abuse.

Also, though the scene appears to pertain to the enslavement of these three peoples, contemporary biases should not dictate the interpretation of this prophecy. Wilson concludes that this text does not represent the enslavement of these peoples but merely changes their status to vassals of YHWH. According to Wilson, the notion of subjugated people in "chains" in v. 14 represents the fate of the formerly idolatrous nations who will be released and promised a prosperous future should they willingly choose to bow before YHWH.[135] The text depicts the Cushites and their allies doing obeisance before Israel/Judah, but the nation here represents its deity. The image of Cushites, Egyptians, and Sabeans in chains genuflecting before Judah is a metaphor for their eventual submission to YHWH at the eschaton. In the end, we are left with a portrait of inclusive Yahwism at the eschaton. However, this inclusive portrayal is not based on consanguinity or choice as in Zech 8:20–23, but is predicated on force.

Finally, the subjugation of these nations generally reflects the historical context of King Cyrus' empire building but not historic events. No evidence suggests that Cyrus ever conquered Cush. Isaiah 45:14 is simply part of Deutero-Isaiah's effort to boost the self-esteem of his people by predicting a time of future glory. At that time, the wealthy, powerful, and influential nations of the world will come to a once debased but soon glorious Judah in order to bow before YHWH. However subversive to Cush and its allies this prophecy may seem to contemporary interpreters, such a perspective does not reflect the original context of the prophecy. In his ancient milieu, Deutero-Isaiah could not have imagined that his words of hope for his people could someday be employed to serve the purposes of those who perceived the world through racialist lenses.

3.2.4.3. *Summary of Cush in Deutero-Isaiah.* The Cushites in Deutero-Isaiah do not fair well; they are described as a subjugated people in both instances where they are mentioned in this corpus (43:3; 45:14). They are used by the author to suggest a future when great and powerful nations will make forced pilgrimages to Jerusalem to bow as vassals before the universal sovereign, YHWH, the God of Israel/Judah. In order for the Cushites and their colleagues to be depicted in this manner, their history as mighty and wealthy nations would have had commonplace value for the Judean author. Thus the author's knowledge of the sovereign status of Cush, Egypt, and Seba would strengthen the implied contrast between their actual independence and prosperity and his depiction of them as Judah's vassals. It is precisely because this trio maintained their sovereignty during the period when the larger world was subjected to the Babylonians and Persians that

---

134. Adamo, "Africa," 236.
135. A. Wilson, *Nations*, 244.

this prophecy would have been potent; YHWH would cause the very nations the northern powers could not conquer to bow to a restored Judah.

Deutero-Isaiah's use of the Cushites in his prophecies, though establishing a hierarchy of human beings and representing the Cushites negatively, neither represents the racialization of Cushites or "Africans." The Cushites and their allies are included in these texts because they were nations not under the dominion of Babylon and Persia during the author's lifetime. They represented the final, unconquered frontier of the known world; because they are autonomous, their subjugation represents a marked change in world affairs. Their subjugation could only come at the hand of YHWH; only with the intervention of Judah's God could Cyrus hope to gain sovereignty over them. But their ultimate fate is as vassals not to Cyrus but to YHWH (45:14), represented in this text by Judah.

Further, the images of Cushite submission to Israel/Judah are best perceived as part of the Deutero-Isaian agenda to comfort and restore his people. It is a boost to the self-perception of a subjugated people to view the free, wealthy, and mighty as subject to them and their God. Because they exercised no real power over their southern neighbors, we cannot conclude that this was an ideological ploy intended to restore a disenfranchised people's self-esteem. Though in the future this prophecy would prove to have negative ramifications for the Cushites, Egyptians, and Sabeans, there was no racialist intent in Deutero-Isaiah's original ideological hierarchy.

A final note on the composition of these texts is in order. Because both Isa 43 and 45 address a scenario whereby the people of Judah would exercise authority over Cush, and because Isa 43 suggests that this will happen as a result of Cyrus' efforts, this prophecy was probably composed during his reign and not subsequent to it. Had the prophecies been uttered after that period, an audience aware that Cyrus never conquered Cush would have readily dismissed them.

### 3.2.5. *Cush in Jeremiah*

Jeremiah offers one of the most consistently positive and fascinating views of Cush in the Hebrew Bible. There are references to Cushites in five chapters; three among them are narratives that describe men with Cushite affiliations in the Judean royal court. This prophetic book indicates that there were Cushite elements in Judah over a number of generations, that those elements occupied positions of prominence in Judean society, and that some were even Hebrew literati, functioning as scribes in the Judean court. Because literacy was a valuable and rare skill in ancient Israel/Judah, the possibility that Cushites may have served as Judean scribes takes on added importance.

### 3.2.5.1. *Jeremiah 13: Can a Cushite Change His Skin?* The term כּוּשִׁי occurs once in Jer 13, in v. 23, where it is used in a riddle comprised of a rhetorical question intended to solicit a negative response from its audience.[136] The question posed is

---

136.  Holladay notes that this rhetorical style was borrowed from the wisdom literature genre; see William L. Holladay, *Jeremiah: A Commentary on the Book of the Prophet Jeremiah Chapters 1–25* (Philadelphia: Fortress, 1986), 414.

הֲיַהֲפֹךְ כּוּשִׁי עוֹרוֹ וְנָמֵר חֲבַרְבֻּרֹתָיו ("Is a Cushite able to change his skin or a leopard his spots?"). Of course they cannot. The answer to the question then forms the basis of YHWH's response to the people of Judah's query in v. 22. Why had an unpleasant fate befallen Judah? The answer: they were incapable of change! Jeremiah's response is more eloquent: גַּם־אַתֶּם תּוּכְלוּ לְהֵיטִיב לִמֻּדֵי הָרֵעַ ("then you too will be able to do good, you who are taught evil"). In a circuitous manner, Jeremiah declares that the people of Judah were unable to change their ways and were consequently destined to suffer a horrendous fate.[137]

Let us first examine the phrase הֲיַהֲפֹךְ כּוּשִׁי עוֹרוֹ ("Can a Cushite change his skin?").[138] What is it about the skin of the Cushite that is under consideration in this rhetorical question? Isaiah 18:2 and 7 is the text that provides the best ethnography for Cushites in the Hebrew Bible. It refers to a Cushite phenotype that likely relates to skin. The land of Cush is described as the home of "a nation tall and smooth" (NRSV). Because this is an accurate presentation of the Cushite phenotype, we could restate Jeremiah's question: "Can a Cushite change [the smoothness of] his skin?"

However, the purpose of these rhetorical questions is to present a scenario where change would be impossible. Though it would not be easy for a man with a hairless face to grow a beard, Cushites with facial hair were known in antiquity.[139] Judean people probably knew of such Cushites. So we should look for another aspect of Cushite skin as the focus of this question.

The other significant aspect of a Cushite's skin that might have had commonplace value in the ancient world was its color. In fact, Brenner has classified the term Cushite as one of a series of Hebrew terms like those for "snow" and "wine" that had idiomatic value and could replace specific color terms, particularly in poetry.[140] The verb יַהֲפֹךְ ("to turn or overturn") is used frequently in reference to the color, particularly in relation to skin disease in Lev 13:3, 4, 13, 20, 55. In each of these instances the root הפך is associated with turning "white"; hence, it is not beyond the realm of possibility that the transformation of the Cushite's skin to a "white" complexion is the paradox raised by Jeremiah. If this were the image Jeremiah intended to evoke in his audience, the startling contrast between "whiteness" and a Cushite's dark complexion would impress upon his audience the implausibility of Judah's repentance. However, though this contrast would strengthen the riddle, turning the Cushite's skin "white" is by no means the certain implication.[141]

137. Note the image of sexual assault associated with their punishment in v. 26: "I myself will lift up your skirts over your face, and your shame will be seen" (NRSV).

138. Holladay (*Jeremiah*, 411, 415) translates the phrase with a conditional or interrogative sense: "Does the [Cushite] ever change his skin, or the leopard his spots?"

139. See, for example, Plates 43, 54, 55, 71, 73, 93 and 95 in Frank M. Snowden, *Blacks in Antiquity: Ethiopians in the Greco-Roman Experience* (Cambridge, Mass.: Harvard University Press, 1970).

140. Brenner, *Colour Terms*, 47.

141. For references to Cushite skin color, see Andrew W. Blackwood, Jr., *Commentary on Jeremiah* (Waco, Tex.: Word Books, 1977), 129; Robert P. Carroll, *Jeremiah: A Commentary*

Besides Isa 18, Jer 13:23 is the most obvious reference to a Cushite phenotypical trait in the Hebrew Bible, making it one of the only opportunities we have to examine how Judean authors view the skin coloration of Cushites.[142] Because of the nature of the riddle, the only thing that was emphasized about the color of the Cushite skin was its inability to change.[143] We find a similar proverb in Egyptian wisdom literature in the "Instructions of 'Onchsheshonqy."[144] These instructions, thought to have been composed in the fifth century B.C.E., contain a series of lessons an imprisoned member of a failed assassination plot against an unknown pharaoh composed for his son. The proverb provides a fitting answer to the rhetorical question asked in Jer 13:23. As 'Onchsheshonqy declares, "There is no Negro who lays off his skin."[145] From this, we may conclude that the color of Cushite skin had commonplace value to the Judeans, the Egyptians, and other peoples in the ancient Near East.[146] Still, we have to be careful how far we take this conclusion since there is little emphasis on phenotypical difference in most references to Cush in the Hebrew Bible.

At the same time, there also does not appear to be any clear value ascribed to skin color.[147] It would have been simple to equate darkness to evil in this passage, as has been done in subsequent Christian and Jewish post-biblical literature. Hood, for example, notes that in his

> study of the images of blackness in the West, for example, the following characteristics are associated with the color black: gloom, woe, darkness, dread, death, terror, horror, wickedness, mourning, defilement, annihilation. By contrast, the color white evokes the following traits: triumph, light, innocence, joy, purity, regeneration, happiness, gaiety, peace, femininity, delicacy.[148]

He goes on to demonstrate that such associations of "blackness" and negative themes were common in the cultures of the Chinese, Arab, Indian, and later Greek and Romans to various degrees from the second millennium B.C.E. to the contemporary period.[149] However, though other ancient societies appear to have correlated negative themes with concepts of "blackness" and dark skin color, such a contrast does not appear in the present instance, nor in general in the Hebrew Bible.

(Philadelphia: Westminster, 1986), 305; Robert Davidson, *Jeremiah*, vol. 1 (Philadelphia: Westminster, 1983), 115.

142.   I would argue that Num 12:1 implies the same recognition of color, but Jer 13:23 is far more explicit.

143.   Cf. Drake, *Black*, 5.

144.   Berend Gemser, "The Instructions of 'Onchsheshonqy and Biblical Wisdom Literature," in *Congress Volume: Oxford, 1959* (VTSup 7; Leiden: Brill, 1960), 102–28 (105–6).

145.   Gemser, "Instructions," 126.

146.   Numbers 12 would lend further support to this hypothesis in regard to the Israelite/Judahite community.

147.   Blackwood (*Jeremiah*, 129) notes that the "[Cushite's] skin pigment is under discussion, not his character," further noting the Cushite official Ebed-melech's role in rescuing Jeremiah.

148.   Robert E. Hood, *Begrimed and Black: Christian Traditions on Blacks and Blackness* (Minneapolis: Fortress, 1994), 1–2.

149.   See Hood, *Begrimed*, 1–21.

There are a number of references to black in relation to skin color, but this is not associated with Cushite skin coloration. For example, Job 30:30 has עוֹרִי שָׁחַר ("my skin is black"), while Song 1:5 has the phrase שְׁחוֹרָה אֲנִי ("I am black") and 1:6 has שֶׁאֲנִי סְרְשֶׁחַרְחֹרֶת ("because I am black"). Similarly, Lam 5:10 contains the phrase עוֹרֵנוּ כְּתַנּוּר נִכְמָרוּ ("our skin as an oven has been blackened"). Each of these statements represent the effect of the sun that has darkened the subject's skin. This darkening would likely not be deemed pleasing less for aesthetic than for health reasons, for essentially the authors are saying that they have been sun-burnt. In Jer 8:21, the prophet proclaims that קָדַרְתִּי ("I am black"). This appears to be more a poetic assessment of his affective state, where "blackness" denotes mourning, than a description of his phenotypical traits. These are but a few of the instances where terms for blackness are used in description for people of Israel/Judah. A more thorough study of these terms is in order. However, our initial cursory review has revealed no racialist assessment when these terms are employed or any type of bias against Cushites where these or other color terms are used disparagingly. In fact, the term Cush never occurs in relation to an explicit Hebrew term for "blackness."

In fact, YHWH in Num 12:1 seems to counter such prejudices against the color of the Cushites' skin by punishing Miriam for her disdain at Moses' marriage to a Cushite woman.[150] This brief reference to Cush is incorporated to say something about Israel. Jeremiah's rhetorical question emphasizes Israel's stubborn refusal to repent of their deviant disposition (cf. Hos 5:3d–4).[151]

Another question arises: Why does skin coloration, such an obvious means for Othering and a constituent element of racialist thought, play such a limited role in the Hebrew Bible? Further: Why, once skin color was finally acknowledged, was it given so little attention? Could it be that such differences were neither remarkable nor off-putting in the ancient Judean context? Was the ancient Levant a region replete with people of various hues where a Cushite's complexion was a common feature? We will return to these questions below. Suffice it to say here that even when Cushite coloration was acknowledged, the distinctiveness of Cushite skin was not negatively evaluated or granted ideological significance as it would be under a racialist paradigm.

### 3.2.5.2. *Jeremiah 36: A "Cushi" in the Family*.

The phrase בֶּן־כּוּשִׁי ("son of Cushi" or "son of a Cushite") occurs once in Jer 36, in v. 14. This passage pertains to events during the fifth year of the reign of Jehoiakim (ca. December 604 B.C.E.)[152] and addresses matters in the royal court of Judah. It is occasioned by the fact that the prophet Jeremiah, who had been barred from the Temple (cf. v. 5)

---

150. For a more thorough discussion of Num 12:1, see Section 2.2.1.5 above.

151. Clements, *Jeremiah*, 87; Holladay, *Jeremiah*, 415; Douglas Rawlinson Jones, *Jeremiah* (Grand Rapids: Eerdmans, 1992), 203; Elmer Leslie, *Jeremiah: Chronologically Arranged, Translated, and Interpreted* (New York: Abingdon, 1954), 75.

152. Robert Davidson, *Jeremiah, Vol. 2, and Lamentations* (Philadelphia: Westminster, 1985), 114.

for unspecified reasons,[153] wanted to deliver his prophetic message to the people who were assembled there for a fast. In his stead he sent his colleague Baruch to read his prophecy. Later, when word of Jeremiah's words reached King Jehoiakim's officials, they sent a messenger to procure Jeremiah's scroll from Baruch.

The messenger they chose, one Yehudi, was the raison d'être for the Cush reference. In what has been deemed an unusually long genealogical list,[154] Yehudi is declared to be the son of Nethaniah, son of Shelemiah, son of Cushi. The list traces Yehudi to his great grandfather Cushi, about whom nothing else is mentioned.

The author may have employed this uncharacteristically long patronymic for a specific purpose. Carroll suggests that lists of this length are usually reserved for significant characters.[155] However, because Yehudi's importance is limited to this narrative,[156] Cushi may have been the significant one. Perhaps this Cushi would have been recognizable to the prophet's audience as the name of a character in biblical tradition. Two possible candidates would be the characters from Ps 7:1 (כּוּשׁ בֶּן־יְמִינִי) or 2 Sam 18 (הַכּוּשִׁי). Hutton, in his exegetical study of Ps 7, claims that these were one and the same person.[157] However, if this were the case, there would have had to have been a number of unmentioned generations to tie this late seventh-century court official to a tenth-century courtier active during David's reign. Further, it is based upon the implausible hypothesis that there was only one Cushi[158] or Cushite[159] active in previous Judean history.

Another possibility is that Cushi was not a personal name, but was a gentilic designation.[160] Hence, the extended patronymic would represent the author's

---

153. Perhaps this was a result of his earlier prophetic activity at the Temple in chs. 7 and 26.

154. Cf. Zeph 1:1 for a similar genealogy.

155. Carroll, *Jeremiah*, 659.

156. Noting this, Carroll suggests that there may have been a conflation of two names here and that the text should be emended following the note in *BHS* to read, "Yehudi ben Nethaniah and Shelemiah ben Cushi"; see Carroll, *Jeremiah*, 659, and Blackwood, *Jeremiah*, 253. Though it is not implausible to have transposed בֶּן for וְאֵת, this confusion seems unlikely since Yehudi appears to have been the only person sent to collect Baruch and Shelemiah ben Cushi does not recur anywhere else in this narrative, though a שֶׁלֶמְיָהוּ בֶּן־עַבְדְּאֵל ("Shelemiah ben Abdeel") does participate in v. 26 of this chapter. To equate the two Shelemiahs, we would have to equate Cushi and Abdeel or presume that one of these designations was a title and not a personal name (i.e. "the Cushite" or "the servant of God"). Though this is unlikely, the figure of Ebed-melech the Cushite from chs. 38–39 would be a plausible parallel character to Abdeel the Cushite, if we argue that by "servant of the king" we actually mean servant of "El" or God, the true king of Israel/Judah. This solution requires too much speculation to be plausible. It is reasonable to assume the pedigree is authentic to Yehudi.

157. Rodney R. Hutton, "Cush the Benjaminite and Psalm Midrash," *HAR* 10 (1986): 123–37.

158. Recall Lipiński's conclusion that the name Cushi was popular in eighth- to seventh-century Semitic nations, as discussed in the Section on Zeph 1:1 (3.2.2.1); see Lipiński, Review of Kapelrud, 689.

159. Recall Adamo's and Rice's positions that there were Cushites active in Judah throughout the history of the United and Divided Monarchies; see Adamo, "Africa," 211, and Rice, "African," 28.

160. Though the inclusion of an ethnic marker in a genealogy like this one would not be typical, it would certainly not be impossible. In Amos 9:7 we see a similar, though plural construction בְּנֵי כֻשִׁיִּים. This is clearly intended to denote people from Cush. Also note the בְּנֵי כוּשׁ in the genealogical lists found in Gen 10:7 and 1 Chr 1:9. The present construction, בֶּן־כּוּשִׁי, could indicate ethnicity.

attempt to delineate Yehudi's ethnic background, perhaps apparent to those who knew of him. Though for two generations his ancestry could be traced to indigenous Judeans with characteristic Yahwistic names, his lineage could ultimately be traced to an unnamed Cushite. Rice posits that if we trace the genealogy, it is likely that Cushi lived during the time of Hezekiah. Due to his close political ties with the Cushite dynasty in Egypt, a Cushite may well have served in Hezekiah's administration to help conduct diplomacy with Judah's southern allies.[161]

Why would we expect to find a Cushite in the Judean royal court at the moment referenced in Jer 36? The period under investigation is less than half a century after the demise of the XXVth Egyptian Dynasty. We also know that there were Cushite emissaries in Judah during the time of Isaiah of Jerusalem (Isa 18) and an alliance between Judah and Cush during the reign of King Hezekiah (2 Kgs 19; Isa 37). Below we will even examine literary evidence suggesting a significant Cushite presence among the Egyptian forces in the Levant as early as the late ninth century (2 Chronicles). Prudence and politics may have inspired prior kings (i.e. Hezekiah) to incorporate Cushite elements into the royal court as messengers, ambassadors, and scribes. Though this hypothesis is at best speculative, the biblical data support such a theory.[162] In Jer 38–39, Ebed-melech, another courtier contemporaneous with Yehudi, is described as a Cushite. The author of the narrative may have intended to demonstrate that there were a number of Cushites present in the royal court and that this Yehudi was one of these figures.

If Yehudi was of Cushite descent, that would indicate that Cushites could both be Hebrew literati and serve as scribes in the Judean court. A prominent Cushite is thus depicted in Jer 36 as the possessor of a rare and valuable skill in the ancient world, the ability to read and write.[163] He was not ignorant but educated, and not alienated but granted access to the central administration of Judah, and hence able to stand in the presence of the king.

*3.2.5.3. Jeremiah 38: Ebed-melech the Cushite*. The term הַכּוּשִׁי occurs three times in Jer 38, in vv. 7, 10, and 12. In these verses is the most positively portrayed Cushite in the Hebrew Bible, one עֶבֶד־מֶלֶךְ הַכּוּשִׁי ("Ebed-melech the Cushite"). It is unclear from the context whether to understand this as a name, meaning "Ebed-melech the man from Cush" or "Ebed-melech the man with Cushite ancestry" or as a title, "the Cushite servant of the king." Each of these possibilities has important implications.

---

161. Rice, "African," 27–28.

162. So Rice, "African," 21–31. Copher takes this argument further and hypothesizes that there were Cushite elements in Israel/Judah since its inception; see Copher, "Black."

163. Scholars are still uncertain as to the level of literacy in monarchic Israel/Judah. Crenshaw suggests that though there was an increase in literacy in the last century and a half of the Judean monarchy, the extent to which common people were literate is uncertain. In fact, Crenshaw concludes that there was little incentive for common people to seek literacy or formal education and, due to the presence of scribal guilds, literacy was a carefully regulated skill. See James L. Crenshaw, *Education in Ancient Israel: Across the Deadening Silence* (New York: Doubleday, 1998), 29–40. For more on literacy in Israel, see Alan R. Millard, "Literacy (Israel)," in *ABD* 4:337–40.

The first option takes Ebed-melech to be a personal name and not a title.[164] "Ebed-melech the man from Cush" is understood to be a foreign national in the employ of the Judean king Zedekiah. On the other hand, the second option takes Ebed-melech to be a personal name but re-envisions the intended meaning of the term "Cush". Thus, "Ebed-melech the man with Cushite ancestry" supposes that he could be a citizen of Judah who traced his lineage to a Cushite ancestor. In this way he would be in the company of such a character as "Uriah the Hittite," who had foreign ancestry but was born in and swore allegiance to Judah. Such a conclusion would lend further support to the hypothesis that there could have been Cushites dwelling in Jerusalem over a period of time who were integrated into the socio-political world of the Judean capital.[165]

The third option is the more problematic, for it supposes Ebed-melech to be a titular description in lieu of a name and thereby eliminates the possibility of a personal identity for this character. Just as הַכּוּשִׁי in 2 Sam 18 was denied personal identity and referred to solely by the ethnic group to which he belonged, this "Cushite servant of the king" would be denied the dignity of having a name. Though he played an active role in two chapters of this book and a critical role in rescuing Jeremiah, he would remain a character whose identity is circumscribed by his occupation.[166]

The first hypothesis seems more likely because the author explicitly describes Ebed-melech's occupation: סָרִס, meaning either "eunuch" or "court official."[167] Such a hypothesis strengthens the thematic subtext, contrasting a faithful foreigner with the obdurate indigenous courtiers of the Judean king. This in no way contradicts Copher's hypothesis that Ebed-melech was indigenous to Judah, for there is evidence for Judean born people of Cushite ancestry. Indeed, Cushite

---

164. So Ernest W. Nicholson, *The Book of the Prophet Jeremiah Chapters 26–52* (New York: Cambridge University Press, 1975), 121. That Ebed-melech was a personal name is also likely because his title was also given: אִישׁ סָרִים ("a man [who was an] official/eunuch").

165. Copher, "Black," 160–61.

166. The reader will find a similarly constructed name in 1 Kgs 18, where a character is identified as Obadiah, "servant of YHWH." Hence, we should not think the name Ebed-melech, "servant of the king," unusual. It may even be theophoric, referring to a heavenly king (i.e. Melchiah in Jer 21:1). Cf. Nahman Avigad, *Hebrew Bullae from the Time of Jeremiah: Remnants of a Burnt Archive* (Jerusalem: Israel Exploration Society, 1986), 23–25, who describes several bullae dating from the time of Jeremiah. Two of these bullae bear a title similar to Ebed-melech's name. The first is לאלשמע [ע]בד המלך ("belonging to Elishama servant of the king"). The second is לגדליהו עבד המלך ("belonging to Gedalyahu servant of the king"). Both of these titles differ slightly from the name עֶבֶד־מֶלֶךְ by the addition of the article to the term for king. They are most similar to the title for the named character Asaiah servant of the king (2 Kgs 22:12; 2 Chr 34:20). If Ebed-melech is taken to be a title, then Avigad's work is significant inasmuch as he determines the title was only used for high ranking officials in the king's inner circle, in the case of Elishama, for a scribe (p. 24).

167. The reader should consider Tov's recent article in regard to Ebed-melech's status as a eunuch ("The Book of Jeremiah: A Work in Progress," *BRev* 15 [2000]: 32–38, 45). Tov examines the text of Jeremiah and determines that two distinct editions of the text are extant, one contained in the MT and one in the LXX. He determines that the shorter LXX version was actually closer to the oldest version of the text and that the MT provides additional information and glosses on the older story. Most significant for our study is his conclusion that the oldest version of the narrative in ch. 38 does not call Ebed-melech a eunuch. This only appears in the later version reflected in MT.

identity is precisely what is emphasized in this instance. The author intentionally juxtaposed the faithful foreigner, "the only person whose concern for Jeremiah drove him to act,"[168] with the native-born sycophants surrounding the king, who refused to help the prophet, "lest (they) be tainted with suspicion of treason."[169]

Ebed-melech's role in this story is important for this study. Because Jeremiah dared to prophesy against Jerusalem, predicting its imminent demise, several officials in Zedekiah's court sought to take his life. The king, refusing to stand up for Jeremiah, consented to their plan; and his officials eventually lowered the prophet into muddy cistern to starve him to death.

When Ebed-melech learned what happened to Jeremiah, he entreated the king to allow him to rescue the prophet. With the king's permission, he led a team that raised the prophet from the cistern. Had it not been for the compassion of Ebed-melech, Jeremiah would have died alone, abandoned by those to whom he prophesied.

The recollection of this Cushite's act of kindness contrasts him with the nefarious officials who chose to abuse the prophet of YHWH instead of heeding his message.[170] The man denoted as a foreigner demonstrates loyalty to YHWH and thereby implicitly illustrates the deafness of the people of Judah to the word of YHWH. The audience is left to ponder how far the leaders of Jerusalem had fallen in their infidelity to YHWH when the most faithful man to be found is the one of alien extraction.

Further, Ebed-melech is identified as a *saris*. The phrase אִישׁ סָרִיס ("a man [who was a] *saris*") has also been a matter of contention. Some have suggested that this phrase denotes "a man who was an official" because the term *saris* has the meaning of a royal officer in Egyptian, Assyrian, Babylonian, Persian, and even Judean contexts.[171] Others have noticed the extraordinary ability of Ebed-melech to persuade the king to follow his counsel instead of that of the four princes who placed the prophet into the well. Such ability to influence and access the king led Blackwood to conclude that Ebed-melech was an important court official.[172] Further, the unnecessary additional element, אִישׁ ("a man"), in this phrase implies that he was not emasculated.

Still others have determined that Ebed-melech was likely a eunuch, for his status as a eunuch would further alienate this foreigner in the king's court. As an emasculated and hence unclean man, he would be the least likely instrument of YHWH's will.[173] The ancient audience would have recognized the irony of an unclean, emasculated foreigner as the only person in Judah's royal court willing

168. Leslie, *Jeremiah*, 247.

169. D. R. Jones, *Jeremiah*, 460.

170. Carroll, *Jeremiah*, 683.

171. John A. Thompson, *The Book of Jeremiah* (Grand Rapids: Eerdmans, 1980), 639 n. 7; Rice, "African," 28.

172. Blackwood, *Jeremiah*, 258–59.

173. D. R. Jones, *Jeremiah*, 461. See also Cottrel R. Carson, " 'Do You Understand What you are Reading?' A Reading of the Ethiopian Eunuch Story (Acts 8:26–40) from a Site of Cultural Marronage" (Ph.D. diss., Union Theological Seminary, 1999), 94–106, for a thorough discussion of ancient perceptions of eunuchs.

to heed YHWH's voice. Though this interpretation seems particularly powerful, it does not preclude the possibility that he was a high ranking court official and counselor to King Zedekiah.

Some scholars however, have called the historicity of this account into question. Carroll labels it "historical fantasy."[174] Jones counters that it was "founded in history, however it was subjected to the storyteller's art."[175] Evidence of such artistry may be seen in the similarity of this account to 1 Kgs 18, where Obadiah, "servant of YHWH," rescues 150 prophets and intercedes for Elijah with another obdurate king, Ahab of Israel. However, Carroll offers no legitimate reasons for concluding that this text is authorial "fantasy."[176]

Whether historical or not, this narrative is significant in presenting a picture of the Judean royal court that included an influential Cushite who had the ear of the king and a heart for YHWH. It depicts a Cushite who is more faithful to YHWH than all the other high officials in the court[177] in spite of the impending disaster that Jeremiah prophesied for Jerusalem. Further, as a character, he has depth, demonstrates insight, and is granted the dignity of a name. In this regard, the author of Jeremiah has created a more fully developed character than Dtr's "the Cushite" seen above in the section discussing 2 Sam 18. Because the author portrays him sympathetically, Ebed-melech could also experience YHWH's blessing, as we will see in the next section.

*3.2.5.4. Jeremiah 39: The Reward for Fidelity.* The term הַכּוּשִׁי occurs once in Jer 39, in v. 16. Jeremiah 39 continues the narrative of ch. 38 and provides the reward for Ebed-melech's fidelity to Jeremiah and hence to YHWH. His fidelity is described as given not to Jeremiah, but to YHWH, and the reward is a promise of protection, not by Jeremiah, but by YHWH. In this manner, the promise of Jer 17:7–18 is fulfilled: the one trusting in YHWH will be blessed.[178]

The term used for the type of "rescue" Ebed-melech is to receive has been the source of debate. In v. 18, the phrase נַפְשְׁךָ לְשָׁלָל means "your life for war booty," suggesting the interpretation "your life will be a prize of war." This expression recalls the promise made in Jer 21:9. Some scholars suggest that this was a minimalist redemption, that no great blessing was promised to Ebed-melech, just his life as if a souvenir from a military campaign.[179] However, Carroll claims that this was YHWH's activity on Ebed-melech's behalf to rescue and reward his fidelity.[180]

The author makes good use of Ebed-melech. This official with a foreign lineage is promised a pleasant fate, the protection of YHWH, and deliverance from

---

174. Carroll, *Jeremiah*, 683.

175. D. R. Jones, *Jeremiah*, 461.

176. As pointed out by D. R. Jones, *Jeremiah*, 461.

177. Consider also "the Cushite" in 2 Sam 18. He also was the most favorably portrayed character, however problematic it was for him to be the only unnamed character in the narrative.

178. Carroll, *Jeremiah*, 697.

179. Davidson, *Jeremiah*, 131; D. R. Jones, *Jeremiah*, 466; Leslie, *Jeremiah*, 250.

180. Carroll, *Jeremiah*, 695–96.

the Babylonian menace[181] (vv. 15–18). This contrasts with the treatment of the other officials of the Judean court: the king was blinded and led away in chains; Zedekiah's son's and Judah's nobles were slaughtered before the king's face; and many of the inhabitants of Jerusalem were exiled to Babylon. Here fidelity to YHWH is shown to trump Judean identity as that which ensures YHWH's blessing!

Ebed-melech's "foreignness" is clearly identified in this chapter because this aspect of his identity is most useful for the author's purpose: to demonstrate the lack of fidelity to YHWH among the urban elite in Jerusalem. The Cushite Other illustrates how far the elect had fallen from grace. The only one of the king's inner circle to respect the life of YHWH's prophet and to continue to place credence in YHWH's word as Jerusalem literally crumbled around him is a foreigner. Thus, the author contrasts a Cushite with the people of YHWH (cf. Amos 9:7). Such contrasts are frequently used to demonstrate lapses in the fidelity of YHWH's people.[182] In two instances where Cush has been so employed (here and Amos 9:7), the comparisons precede the immanent judgment of YHWH against Israel/ Judah, the destruction of their respective capitals, and the exile of their elite.

As in ch. 38, the Cushite Ebed-melech is described positively. The author has no bias against Cush or Cushites, but exalts a Cushite; YHWH's favor could come to a son of this southern land even as indigenous Judeans face their deity's wrath.

3.2.5.5. *Jeremiah 46: Cushites in Neco's Army.* The term כוש occurs once in Jer 46, in v. 9. The larger prophetic context addresses YHWH's judgment on Egypt. Egypt, described with overtones of arrogance in vv. 7–8, charges into a battle that YHWH has predestined them to loose. The Cushites too are destined to suffer defeat together with the Putim[183] and Ludim,[184] who have again allied

---

181. Carroll, *Jeremiah*, 696. Others have concluded that it was the princes of Judah that Ebed-melech would have feared since he rescued the prophet that they sought to destroy for his treasonous words. See J. A. Thompson, *Jeremiah*, 649. However, Carroll rightly points out that they had ready access to Ebed-melech. Had they intended to do him harm, they would not have waited for the destruction of Jerusalem to do so.

182. Not only are Cushites used this way by Judean authors, but other Others are as well. Consider as examples the contrasts established in the narratives of the proactive Jael the Kenite and the hesitant Barak (Judg 4), the faithful Uriah the Hittite and the flawed King David (2 Sam 11–12), the generous Namaan the Aramean and the greedy Gehazi (2 Kgs 5), the disobedient people of Judah and the obedient Rechabites (Jer 35), and the people of Israel/Judah who were unrepentant in most prophetic books and the people of Nineveh who repented after hearing Jonah's one-sentence oracle (Jonah). Each of these Others were employed in narratives to contrast the negative qualities portrayed by indigenous Yahwist children of Israel with the fidelity of aliens. In addition, there are narratives that focus on other faithful Others as well. For examples, see the story of Rahab the prostitute from Canaanite Jericho (Josh 2), Ruth the Moabite (Ruth), the woman of Zarephath who sustained Elijah (1 Kgs 17), and Jonadab the Rechabite (2 Kgs 10).

183. Carroll and Jones do not read the Putim as Libyans, but as the people from Punt, near the modern Somali coast; see Carroll, *Jeremiah*, 762; D. R. Jones, *Jeremiah*, 493.

184. Nicholson suggests that Ludim does not mean the Lydians from Asia Minor, but should be emended to read the Lubim, or Libyans; see Nicholson, *Jeremiah*, 169. Carroll does not think that the Ludim are Libyans, but an unknown ethnic group active in North Africa; see Carroll, *Jeremiah*, 762. Others have argued that based upon the Rassam Cylinder II:95–96 that they were the Lydians. The alliance between Lydia and Egypt may date to the time when Gyges and Psmmetichus, respectively,

themselves[185] with Egypt in an attempt to regain their prominence in the Levant. Ezekiel 30 contains a similar description of the destruction of the composite Egyptian armies.

The events in this prophecy relate to the defeat of the motley hosts of Pharaoh Neco in 605 B.C.E. by the Babylonians under Nebuchadnezzar at Carchemish. Prior to this time, actually since 609 B.C.E., Judah had been Egypt's vassal. But this defeat shifted the balance of power significantly so that Judah came under the aegis of Babylon.[186] The destruction of the Egyptian expeditionary force was a crushing defeat for Neco II's imperial ambitions, though his Babylonian foes never represented a serious threat, for he defeated Nebuchadrezzar's forces soundly at Migdol.[187]

This prophecy belongs to a type that we will encounter frequently in this study. This type portrays Cushites as members of a larger Egyptian army.[188] As discussed above, several biblical narratives suggest a Cushite presence in the Levant from the time of the tenth century until the late seventh century.

What is unique about this passage is that it represents a Cushite contingent in Pharaoh Neco II's army in the late seventh century, after the fall of the XXVth Dynasty. This would imply that Cushites continued to participate in the Egyptian military after they were no longer the ruling force in Egypt; whether this was with the official sanction of Cush or due to the activity of mercenaries is unclear.

As in similar accounts, Cushites are here portrayed as warriors. Their might is legendary,[189] and their presence, usually in connection with Put or Libya, ensures a formidable military force. Also as elsewhere, the othering of Cush in this pericope is comparable to that of Egypt, Put, and Lud. Hence, we can infer Cush was again a confederate in a regional army but subjected here to Neco II and destined to suffer tragic defeat with their allies.[190] Jeremiah's othering of Cush has no racial component, nor does it portray Cushites in a negative light apart from their relationship with Egypt.

In fact, based upon what we know of the history of the battle this prophecy foretells, Jeremiah misconstrued its outcome. His desire to see the hand of YHWH manifest in Nebuchadrezzar, who would deliver a serious blow to the Egyptians, never came to fruition. This desire was likely motivated by Jeremiah's disdain for Egyptian hegemony over Judah from 609–605 B.C.E., and not due to any traits of the Egyptians or their allies. The reference to the Cushites is yet another instance where they were known for their might, bolstering the armies of Egypt.

---

ruled these nations in the seventh century. Cf. Daniel I. Block, *The Book of Ezekiel: Chapters 25–48* (Grand Rapids: Eerdmans, 1997), 159; Walther Zimmerli, *Ezekiel 2* (trans. James D. Martin; Philadelphia, Fortress, 1983), 129.

185.  Or served as mercenaries as suggested by v. 21. See D. R. Jones, *Jeremiah*, 493.

186.  Clements, *Jeremiah*, 248–49; Leslie, *Jeremiah*, 161.

187.  Redford, *Egypt*, 452–59.

188.  This phenomenon appears particularly in the sections on Deutero-Isaiah, Ezekiel, and 2 Chronicles as well as a number of other books.

189.  As confirmed by Nah 3.9.

190.  Cf. Bright, *History*, 327.

3.2.5.6. *Summary of Cush in Jeremiah.* The author of Jeremiah employs the Cushites for a variety of reasons, exploiting aspects of their identity known to his audience. The immutability of a Cushite's skin-color is used as a metaphor for Judah's indelible sin (13:23); and the "mighty" Cushites are found in a narrative prophesying Egypt's doom (46:9). Apparently the term Cush had become a commonplace that could be evoked by Judean authors to particular ends. In neither of these instances is there a hint of racialist thought, in spite of the recognition of Cushite phenotypes. Even in the latter instance, the prophecy of doom was likely directed at Pharaoh Neco II's Egypt. Cush was only incidentally involved, based upon the presence of Cushite mercenaries who served in Neco II's armies. Hence, the destruction Jeremiah prophesied was limited to those Cushite mercenaries, not reaching into the borders of Cush.

Two of these references are significant because they indicate that Cushites were present in the Judean royal court. The reference to Yehudi, a descendant of "Cushi," supports the hypothesis that Cushites had intermarried with indigenous Judeans and had likely become Yahwists. Further, if we understand that Yehudi was of Cushite lineage, a descendant of Cush was literate in Hebrew and served as a court scribe. Should we come to the alternative conclusion, that Cushi was simply a personal name, we would see emphasis on the esteem that Judeans had for this powerful and wealthy Other to the south, such that they would allow the name to disrupt a chain of Yahwistic theophoric names.[191]

The references to Ebed-melech, however, are more explicitly representative of a Cushite presence in the Judean royal court. The author uses the faithful foreign Other to contrast the infidelity of the indigenous Judean courtiers who attempt to kill the prophet Jeremiah to silence YHWH's word. As a result of Ebed-melech's actions on behalf of Jeremiah, this Other escapes the horrendous fate that befell many prominent members of the urban elite in Jerusalem.

Cushites fare well in Jeremiah, a prophetic book that includes one of the most comprehensive assortments of Cush references. There is one clear reference to phenotypes (13:23), one instance of a Cush-related term in a genealogy (36:14), two chapters where a Cushite is used in an implicit narratological comparison with Judeans (38–39), and one instance where the mighty-Cushite trope is employed. As is true in the other books discussed in this chapter, it is clear that Jeremiah and his audience were familiar with the Cushites, who still participated in the history of Judah in the late seventh century though they were no longer the sovereigns of Egypt.

### 3.2.6. *Cush in Ezekiel*
The events recorded in the book of Ezekiel seem to come from the same period as those in Jeremiah. For example, Ezekiel refers to Pharaoh Neco and his exploits. The defeat of the Egyptians, the Cushites, and their allies herein described likely

---

191. See also Section 3.2.2.1 on Zeph 1:1, where I discussed the fact that the name "Cushi" came into vogue in the Levant during the eighth and seventh centuries—that is, precisely during the period when Cushites were in control of Egypt and certainly present in regions as far north as Assyria.

stem from this period, following Neco's assault on Syria and Judah. After conquering all of the Levant as far as the Euphrates, Neco was defeated by Nebuchadnezzar and his forces were driven back to traditional Egyptian borders in 605 B.C.E.[192] It appears that the Egyptians later offered their support to subsequent Judean rebellions against the Babylonians in 602 and 589; yet they were only partially successful in their efforts, evoking the metaphor of Egypt as a "staff of reed."[193] However, the notion that there was a chance of freedom from their Babylonian overlords made the people of Jerusalem willing to trust in the might of the Egyptians and their allies and to shun Ezekiel's call to submission to Babylonian dominance.[194] It is against such sentiments or because of them that Ezekiel prophesies.

3.2.6.1. *Ezekiel 29: "And unto the Border of Cush."* The term כּוּשׁ occurs once in Ezek 29, in v. 10. The occasion for this reference was an oracle against Egypt, reminiscent of Jer 46 and its prophecy of the destruction of Egypt at the hands of Nebuchadnezzar. Cush plays a seemingly nominal role in this pericope because the prediction of Egypt's demise does not explicitly implicate Cush. Yet the interpretive strategy we employ may indicate a greater role for Cush. There are two ways to understand this chapter.

The first interpretive strategy, the one favored by the majority of biblical commentators,[195] emphasizes Egypt's destruction. Egypt was to receive the brunt of Babylon's venom, as is evidenced by the phrase וְעַד־גְּבוּל כּוּשׁ ("and unto the border of Cush"), which depicts a destruction of Lower and Upper Egypt that ceases at Cush's northern border.[196]

Another interpretive strategy envisions a more comprehensive destruction that would include both Egypt and its partner Cush. In this regard, וְעַד־גְּבוּל כּוּשׁ may mean "unto the [southern] border of Cush." Ezekiel's reference to מִגְדֹּל[197] and סְוֵנֵה[198] could thus describe the traditional boundaries of Lower and Upper Egypt, for Syene is roughly the southern border of Egypt. In this paradigm the border of Cush would refer to Cush's southern border, for the northern border of Cush

192.    So Walther Eichrodt, *Ezekiel: A Commentary* (trans. Cosslett Quin; Philadelphia: Westminster, 1970), 400.

193.    See Eichrodt, *Ezekiel*, 400; Isaac G. Matthews, *Ezekiel* (Philadelphia: Judson, 1939), 111.

194.    See Eichrodt, *Ezekiel*, 400; Zimmerli, *Ezekiel 2*, 103–4.

195.    For example, Joseph Blenkinsopp, *Ezekiel* (Louisville, Ky.: John Knox, 1990), 130; Eichrodt, *Ezekiel*, 405; Zimmerli, *Ezekiel 2*, 103–4.

196.    See Eichrodt, *Ezekiel*, 405, though Eichrodt was uncertain about the exact location of the northern border of Cush during this period.

197.    Eichrodt considers מִגְדֹּל ("Migdol") to be in the northern section of Egypt, reading with Jer 44:1; see Eichrodt, *Ezekiel*, 405. Blenkinsopp suggests that Migdol was one of the regions where Diaspora Jews would have settled in the Delta region, following Jer 44:1 and 46:14; see Blenkinsopp, *Ezekiel*, 130. Zimmerli further identifies Migdol as Tell es-Samut or Tell el-Her; see Zimmerli, *Ezekiel*, 113.

198.    Typically understood to have been located in the site of modern Aswan. Blenkinsopp also notes that Syene is also close to a known Jewish settlement—that of Jeb, known from the Elephantine papyri; see Blenkinsopp, *Ezekiel*, 130.

would only be a few miles to the south of Syene. If the phrase מִמִּגְדֹּל סְוֵנֵה ("from Migdol [to] Syene") is similar to the traditional united Israel border formula "Dan to Beersheba," as some have postulated,[199] it would be unnecessary to mention the "border of Cush" at all, particularly since the phrase in 30:6 suffices for all of Egypt without any reference to the border of Cush. The addition of the phrase "and unto the border of Cush" is plausible only if the reference was intended to include, not exclude, Cush. Further, the subsequent narrative in Ezek 30 pertaining to the same historical events (see the discussion below) portrays the destruction extending from Egypt into Cush (as in Jer 46). Hence, the author likely intended the tragic demise depicted in ch. 29 to extend from Egypt into Cush because Cushite soldiers figured prominently in Neco's armies as they had in the armies of his predecessors.

This second option may have further implications if we note that, when used in geographic references, Cush often represents the extent of the known world (cf. Esth 1:1 and 8:9). Hence, in this general reference to the destruction of Egypt, the use of Cush as a geographic point may mean the destruction would extend from Egypt to the southern extent of the world, possibly encompassing Put and Lud if we understand them to be other nations south of Egypt. The resulting destruction would thus extend from Egypt to the lands of its allies, resembling that found in Ezek 30.

Further implications arise from both interpretive options. Should we accept either the hypothesis that interprets the phrase "and unto the borders of Cush" as a reference to Cush's northern border or as a reference to all of Egypt and Cush, then this chapter delineates the location of Cush. Following the southward progression of the sites listed, Cush is definitively located to the south of Syene, which is south of Migdol. This seemingly insignificant mention of Cush provides substantive evidence as to where Cush was located.

Should we accept the latter option that the geographical reference was intended to include both Egypt and Cush, we must also accept that the Judean author of this book prophesied the destruction of the Cushites along with the Egyptians (and likely all their constituent troops outlined in ch. 30). The destruction of the Cushites in this instance would, again, not be due to any perceived Cushite defect or Judean malice toward this southern people. Rather, their destruction was due to one thing: their failure to defend Judah. Because the southern alliance forces failed to support and deliver the people of Judah from their northern aggressors, Babylon would come forth and decimate their land. (We will return to this issue below.) Perhaps the most significant reason to accept the second interpretation, that Cush was included in the prophesied crisis in ch. 29, is the content of ch. 30. If the prophet foresaw the comprehensive destruction of Egypt and the regions to its south, we have, as we will see in the next section, continuity between the prophecies found in chs. 29 and 30.

---

199. So Block, *Ezekiel*, 142; Millard C. Lind, *Ezekiel* (Scottdale, Pa.: Herald Press, 1996), 245; John W. Wevers, *Ezekiel* (London: Thomas Nelson, 1969), 224; Zimmerli, *Ezekiel*, 113.

3.2.6.2. *Ezekiel 30: Anguish Comes to Cush.* The term כוש occurs three times in Ezek 30, in vv. 4, 5, and 9. Like the previous chapter, ch. 30 posits Egyptian political alliances similar to those in Jer 46 and also refers to the last decade of the seventh century B.C.E.[200] However, some scholars have viewed the prophesied destruction of these nations not as historical but as eschatological,[201] noting that it does not correspond to known events.[202] Cush is mentioned along with other nations, including Put, Lud, Arabia, and Libya. If the destruction is part of a larger historical event, then it likely reflects the impact of the destruction of Judah by Nebuchadnezzar. The effect will be felt to the ends of the known world.[203]

It is necessary to determine the composition of the military alliance described in v. 5. Clearly Libya was part of this alliance; however, scholars have derived Libyan involvement from two different terms. Some read פוט as a reference to Libya,[204] while others have interpreted the hapax legomenon כוב a scribal error for the intended לוב as in the לובים of 2 Chr 12:3, and hence identified Libya. The latter argument is most plausible, requiring an emendation of the text to read כוב as לוב. פוט is not Libya, but ancient Punt, roughly corresponding to modern Somalia.[205]

The term לוד ("Lud") deserves attention. It may denote a minor nation in North Africa because of its association with this set of nations from that region. However, the Rassam Cylinder (II:95–96) suggests that there was an alliance between Lydia in Asia Minor and Egypt when Gyges and Psammetichus, respectively, ruled these nations in the seventh century.[206] So, we cannot rule out Lydia of Asia Minor as the לוד of v. 5.

The structure of v. 4 merits mention. Cush is used in parallel to Egypt in a discussion of the prophesied destruction. Ezekiel describes a metaphorical sword that is poised to destroy Egypt, while Cush will suffer anguish. This parallel construction likely reflects the perception that the Cushites were powerful in a manner distinct from that of the other confederate nations mentioned in this Egyptian alliance; their prowess rivaled that of Egypt.

Though Cush is singled out for special mention among the various nations, it is likely not the principal focus of the predicted destruction. Zimmerli suggests that the political entity of Cush was not the intended recipient of the destruction, but rather the soldiers or mercenaries from Cush alluded to in this chapter.[207] Egypt is the apparent impetus for the prophecy and, hence, will be destroyed. The Cushites' mercenaries will suffer loss because of their association with their northern benefactor, Neco's Egypt.

---

200.  See Section 3.2.6 above.
201.  Cf. Matthews, *Ezekiel*, 114.
202.  See Blenkinsopp, *Ezekiel*, 133.
203.  Eichrodt, *Ezekiel*, 415–16.
204.  As many have argued. Consider Blenkinsopp, who identifies Phut with Cyrenaica, though he does not fully account for another term, לוב, that should be identified with the Libyan people; see Blenkinsopp, *Ezekiel*, 134.
205.  Westermann, *Genesis*, 511.
206.  So Block, *Ezekiel*, 159, and Zimmerli, *Ezekiel*, 129.
207.  Zimmerli, *Ezekiel*, 129.

Verse 5 at first seems distinct in the literary context of this chapter for it is a prose statement that interrupts the poetry that precedes and follows it. Some scholars have deemed it a marginal gloss on v. 4, employed to clarify the constituent forces of the Egyptian military alliance that found its way into the text.[208] Against this, Block notes that v. 5 may well be a gloss, but he found no reason why it could not have been the work of Ezekiel's own hand, clarifying his intended meaning.[209]

To understand v. 5 better, we need to examine several of its components. The first is the phrase וְכָל־הָעֶרֶב. Authors have favored two principal interpretations of this phrase, stemming from the multiple interpretive options for the root ערב. Some translate the phrase "all the mixed assembly,"[210] following Exod 12:38 and understanding the root to represent the noun עֶרֶב, meaning "mixture" or "mixed company."[211] Another interpretation of the root ערב yields the phrase "all the Arabs,"[212] noting that the word, עֶרֶב can refer to the people to the southwest of Arabia.[213] The Arabs were also found in a similar alliance in 2 Chr 21:16.

In addition to these two possible interpretations, there is a third, potentially disturbing one: "all the black (ones)." This would be a plausible translation considering that the root ערב can also have the denotative sense of "blackness."[214] Further, all the nations in this passage stem from regions of northern Africa that were then dominated by the Egyptians and Cushites. This understanding would provide the strongest evidence yet for Judean authors essentializing various ethnic groups based upon phenotypical traits.

However, the reading "all the black (ones)" is unlikely because there is no single obvious instance in the Hebrew Bible where the Hebrew root ערב is used to describe "blackness." Moreover, there is no other instance in the Hebrew Bible where Cushites are associated with the notion "blackness."[215] Further, since the

---

208. Eichrodt, *Ezekiel*, 414, and Zimmerli, *Ezekiel*, 123.

209. Block, *Ezekiel*, 158.

210. Note that the LXX favors this interpretation inasmuch as it employs the phrase πάντες οἱ ἐπίμικτοι, which means "all the mixed ones." Cf. NRSV Jer 25:20; 50:37 (though both are not wholly convincing). Also see Wevers, *Ezekiel*, 228; Zimmerli, *Ezekiel*, 129–30; Moshe Greenberg, *Ezekiel 21–37: A New Translation with Introduction and Commentary* (AB 22A; Garden City, N.Y.: Doubleday, 1997), 621–22.

211. Cf. BDB, 786, definition I.

212. Cf. NRSV of 1 Kgs 10:15 and Jer 25:24. Also see Matthews, *Ezekiel*, 116. Matthews prefers Arabs to "Mongrel races."

213. Cf. BDB, 787, definition IV.

214. Reading with the sixth definition for the root ערב in BDB, 788. Acknowledging an Arabic parallel word, which means to "be black," we come up with the Hebrew word עֶרֶב for "raven," a bird known for its "blackness." Hence it is possible, that the phrase וְכָל־הָעֶרֶב could be translated "and all the black [horde]," further distinguishing the ethnic groups that precede this statement from those that follow it based upon phenotypical traits. In this regard, we would have to assume that the people of Judah considered the people of Cush, Put, and Lud to be "black," and somehow distinct from the people of Libya and the "sons of the land of the covenant," discussed below. This hypothesis could have implications for our reading of 2 Chr 21:16, וְהָעַרְבִים אֲשֶׁר עַל־יַד כּוּשִׁים, which might then be translated "and the black ones who are under the authority of the Cushites."

215. As I have noted above, there are instances where I believe Cushites are used to denote "darkness," for example, Num 12:1 (see Section 2.2.1.5 above) and Jer 13:23 (see Section 3.2.5.1).

form of the noun used here is singular, the term הָעֶרֶב should have a collective sense. Because of these factors, as well as the ethnically diverse composition of Egyptian armies, I would suggest that the best understanding of the phrase וְכָל־הָעֶרֶב is "and all the mixed assembly."

Another issue in v. 5 is the identity of those called בְּנֵי אֶרֶץ הַבְּרִית ("the sons of the land of the covenant"). This could be read as the author's recognition of the military alliance between these various nations. However, this definite construction, הַבְּרִית, is typically used in reference to YHWH's covenant with Israel/Judah. Further, the phrase "all the mixed assembly" takes into account any alliances that may have existed between diverse ethnic groups. Thus, וּבְנֵי אֶרֶץ הַבְּרִית likely refers to people from Israel/Judah who served as mercenaries in the larger Egyptian force.[216] Hence, Israelites or Judahites were complicit with the military aggression of the Egyptians and would fall alongside their ill-fated allies.[217]

Note too that v. 9 contains a familiar allusion. This verse describes messengers going forth from what must be Jerusalem, though it is not explicitly stated,[218] to the Cushites with news that will terrify them. As Eichrodt notes, this text bears a remarkable resemblance to the account in Isa 18:1, demonstrating the prophetic tendency to recycle previous oracles when they pertain to current events.[219] The author has rehearsed the theme of Jer 46 and incorporated elements familiar from Isa 18 into this passage. Some of the comments mentioned above about the representation of Cush in Isa 18 (cf. Section 2.2.3.2) pertain to this pericope.

What is being said about the Cushites here in Ezekiel? The Cushites and their allies will endure what appears to be a devastating military conquest. Perhaps what is most troubling in this instance is that these horrors were predicted and consented to by YHWH. Does this mean that Israel's God condoned the oppression of Cush?

Oppression is not the issue here at all, but rather a military defeat that Cush and its allies would suffer at the hands of Nebuchadrezzar. Ezekiel perceived such a defeat theologically as the just result of the Egyptians' and their allies' own offenses. As in Amos 9, YHWH would not withhold the sword even from Israel when it is guilty of an offense. And what would Cush's offense be? Though

---

Yet, there are no instances in the Hebrew Bible where a Cush-related term is used in association with a Hebrew term for "blackness."

216.   Cf. Eichrodt, *Ezekiel*, 414; Patrick Fairbairn, *Ezekiel, and the Book of his Prophecy: An Exposition* (Edinburgh: T. & T. Clark, 1863), 336; David Muir Gibson Stalker, *Ezekiel: Introduction and Commentary* (London: SCM Press, 1968), 226; Wevers, *Ezekiel*, 228; Greenberg, *Ezekiel 21–37*, 622.

217.   Block, *Ezekiel*, 160.

218.   The Hebrew simply says that the messengers went out מִלְּפָנַי ("from before me"). Because YHWH was thought to dwell in the Temple, it is probable that the messengers were returning from Jerusalem to Cush with news of an imminent disaster already on the horizon. Zimmerli suggests that this indicates YHWH's direct involvement in the disasters that will befall Cush; see Zimmerli, *Ezekiel*, 124.

219.   Eichrodt, *Ezekiel*, 414. See also Blenkinsopp, *Ezekiel*, 134; Block, *Ezekiel*, 161; Zimmerli, *Ezekiel*, 130.

Ezekiel does not explicitly state it, it appears that the Cushites and the larger Egyptian alliance were guilty of having גְּאוֹן עֻזֹּה, or pride due to their strength (v. 6), as well as being idolatrous (v. 13). They have foolishly depended on their false gods, wealth, and the fear of their military machine for their security.[220] This negates hypotheses that presuppose an aspect of Cush's identity merited the prophesied doom. The prophesied devastation of Cushites and Egyptians (and even members of the covenant community) was the result of their hubris and godlessness. An ironic reversal of fortunes comes at the end of this prophecy. Because they trusted in their seemingly limitless might, this "mixed assemblage" would eventually be impotent before a superior foe; as Block notes, "The feared become the terrorized."[221]

3.2.6.3. *Ezekiel 38: The Armies of Gog.* The term כּוּשׁ occurs once in Ezek 38, in v. 5. This reference is part of a description of a mythic battle being waged by one Gog from the land of Magog against the restored people of Israel.[222] There is no clear consensus about the identity of this Gog, but Eichrodt offers the plausible explanation that Gog represents the legendary mid-seventh-century figure, Gyges of Lydia, projected as a future figure presenting terror from the north during a peaceful period subsequent to the return of the exiles.[223]

In order to accept that Gog referred to Gyges, we also have to conclude that this is a secondary addition to Ezekiel's prophecies, added by a later member of his prophetic school perhaps uncertain of Gyges' chronology. Block offers a modified version of this proposition, contending that it was to Gyges' great grandson Alyattes that Ezekiel refers, for this Lydian monarch ruled during the period when Ezekiel prophesied and returned the kingdom to a position of international prominence. Because the dynasty Gyges established would have borne his name, Alyattes might be identified as Gyges, as Block proposes.[224] But I suggest that the absence of any evidence that Alyattes was known by Ezekiel and of any reference to Lydia by name in the list in chs. 38–39 of numerous nations makes the identification of Gog with any Lydian king unlikely. As Zimmerli cautions, we should not rule out the possibility that this eschatological prophecy

220. Block, *Ezekiel*, 162.
221. Block, *Ezekiel*, 162.
222. Stalker recounts four strategies for identifying Gog: (1) as an historic individual, that is, Gagi of Assyria, King Gyges of Lydia, Alexander the Great, Antiochus Eupator; (2) as a collective for the Scythians, the Cimmerians, or the Babylonians who are not elsewhere mentioned in Ezekiel; (3) as the Babylonian god Gaga; (4) as darkness from the Sumerian word "gug"; see Stalker, *Ezekiel*, 261. For a more complete review of this history of interpretation, see Blenkinsopp, *Ezekiel*, 183–84; Zimmerli, *Ezekiel*, 299–302.
223. Gyges, founder of the Mermnad dynasty, was a potent early to mid-seventh century king of Lydia thought to have been an early advocate for the use of coins, who is also known in the Annals of Ashurbanipal as *gugu*. Cf. Eichrodt, *Ezekiel*, 519–22; Blenkinsopp, *Ezekiel*, 184; Block, *Ezekiel*, 432; David G. Mitten, "The Synagogue and the 'Byzantine Shops,'" *BASOR* 177 (1965): 17–37 (34); Zimmerli, *Ezekiel*, 301–2.
224. Block, *Ezekiel*, 433.

actually belongs to the later activity of the prophet Ezekiel himself.[225] Further, following Lind, we can plausibly conclude that the character Gog may be a mythic figure with no historical referent.[226]

In Ezekiel, Gog is mentioned as leading an assembly of troops from the north against Palestine. Cush and פּוּט (Put), two southern nations, find themselves embroiled in the armies of this northern coalition that includes troops from as far away as Persia.[227] The inclusion of Cush and "Put" in an account of a battle with a northern adversary supports the theory that v. 5 is a secondary addition to the text.[228] Gog's allies should have been those northern nations found in v. 6. Cush and the other nations from north Africa would be unlikely allies for this northern king if this were an historical account.

Another possibility is that Ezekiel intentionally produced this peculiar arrangement of northern and southern nations for literary balance. He may well have intended to construct the motley assemblage found in v. 5 from the lands most distant from Judah, by gathering together people from what Lind calls the "rim nations" of the then known world.[229] The literary portrait thus has a logical balance, including elements from the northern and southern limits of the earth.[230] The prophet has provided precisely seven of these fringe nations. The number seven, representing completeness, is also reflected in the number of nations against whom Ezekiel prophesies in chs. 25–32 and the number of allies found with Egypt in Sheol in 37:17–32. Thus, Ezekiel may have chosen to emphasize these seven nations because he wanted this prophecy to have universal import.[231]

Exactly how this coalition would have come into existence is not clear. Cushite troops did participate in northern armies as mercenaries; Snowden recounts the presence of Cushites in the armies of Xerxes of Persia.[232] Cushites were also part of the equestrian forces in the Assyrian army early in the first millennium (eighth to seventh centuries).[233] Evidence of Cushite troops in armies so distant from their native land could indicate that significant numbers of Cushite mercenaries were active in other regions north of Israel/Judah throughout various periods. However, the apocalyptic nature of the prophecy in Ezek 38 and the probability that the author employed the Cushites and the people of Put to provide geographical balance for the nations from the extreme north should dissuade us from seeking completely accurate historical information in chs. 38–39.

Cush and other nations are found in Ezekiel 38 to demonstrate YHWH's power to vanquish a mighty coalition in order to rescue the people of Israel/Judah. The

225. Zimmerli, *Ezekiel*, 304.

226. Lind, *Ezekiel*, 315.

227. Eichrodt suggests that פָּרַס is not Persia as most argue, but a nation in North Africa; see Eichrodt, *Ezekiel*, 518.

228. Wevers, *Ezekiel*, 287. Also see Eichrodt, *Ezekiel*, 518; Stalker, *Ezekiel*, 261; Zimmerli, *Ezekiel*, 306.

229. Lind, *Ezekiel*, 315.

230. Fairbairn, *Ezekiel*, 422.

231. Block, *Ezekiel*, 441.

232. Snowden, *Blacks in Antiquity*, 123.

233. R. W. Anderson, "Zephaniah," 64–65, and Heidorn, "Kush," 105–14.

commonplace association of might and ferocity with Cush is the likely reason the Cushites are mentioned. An assembly of nations represents a malevolent army that threatens YHWH's people and will subsequently be vanquished.

What is also clear is that Cush could be readily employed in Hebrew literature as a commonplace referent for an aggressive and fear-provoking people. Therefore, Ezekiel mentions Cushites because they are well known as a symbol of ferocious might that would lend credibility to the threat in this apocalyptic account of an unknown northern king.

3.2.6.4. *Summary of Cush in Ezekiel.* In Ezekiel 30 and 38, the prophet has employed the familiar image of the mighty Cush because Cush was known to be a source of mercenary strength in other nations' armies, not only as a military power acting independently. In ch. 30, Cushites are participants in the armies of the Egyptians and are arrayed alongside their traditional allies known from Gen 10, and 1 and 2 Chronicles—Put, Libya, and Lud.

The fate of the Cushites in the book of Ezekiel is always the same: destruction. They tend not to fare well, likely because of the nature of the author's understanding of the Cushites in history: they were a people that had depended on their might and not faith in YHWH. Because of the terrors that were about to befall the world at the hands of the Babylonians and in the immanent eschaton, their reliance on their might would make the Cushites arrogant, which would cause them to serve as mercenaries in Egyptian armies. Eventually, this would lead to the destruction ordained by YHWH.

Though the depiction of Cush is negative in Ezekiel, the author does not allude to any constituent elements of racialist thought, including phenotypic, social, or behavioral traits of Cushite identity.[234] Nor does the prophet utilize any of these aspects to justify the unfavorable outcomes of the Cushites. The Cushites are a people that may suffer sudden terrors and even devastation within their borders. Yet such terrors are not linked with any aspect distinct to Cushite identity, but are rather rooted in the ideology and theology of Judean prophetic thought.

### 3.2.7. *Cush in Works of the Deuteronomistic Historian*
In three instances, Cush-related terms occur in the work of the Deuteronomistic Historian. The first instance is in Judg 3, in reference to an enemy leader who launched an assault against the southern tribes during the pre-state period. The second is during the time of Israel's celebrated king, David, providing insight into the diverse composition of Israel's military and royal court in the early Iron Age II. The final reference is to Tirhakah, the renowned Cushite king of Egypt. His brief appearance in a narrative about Sennacherib's siege of Jerusalem provides an essential key for understanding the larger enigmatic text. Though the three references in this historical composition are minimal, they demonstrate

---

234. I wish to re-emphasize this point, particularly as regards the root עֲרָב. In Section 3.2.6.2 I examined the possible interpretive alternative of "blackness" for the root עֲרָב as a matter of thoroughness, and definitively rejected it as a viable translational option for the phrase הָעֶרֶב in 30:5. Thus, there is no racialist dimension present in Ezekiel.

that in every pre-exilic period of Israel/Judah's history, the pre-state period, the United Monarchy, and the Divided Monarchy, there was interaction with Cushites.

3.2.7.1. *Judges 3: Cushan-rishathaim*. Upon initial examination, Judg 3 seems to be of little value to our examination of Cushites in the Hebrew Bible. The author mentions כּוּשַׁן רִשְׁעָתַיִם מֶלֶךְ אֲרַם נַהֲרַיִם ("Cushan-rishathaim king of Aram-naharaim"), one who bears a name related to Cush, but who is apparently a non-Cushite, four times in this chapter, twice in v. 8 and twice in v. 10. In fact, the story is arguably an ahistoric[235] literary device meant to establish the five-element pattern for the subsequent narratives in Judges:[236] sin, punishment, crying out, salvation, and quiet.[237] Each of these boilerplate elements is found in this brief introductory passage, making it rich with formal elements but short on detail and content. Hence, it would appear that this passage is irrelevant to the present project about a southern Other inasmuch as it chronicles YHWH's victory through the judge Othniel over an otherwise unknown king who threatened the Israelite tribal confederation from the north. However, a simple textual emendation radically transforms the meaning of the text, making it a significant component in our analysis of the Hebrew image of Cushites.

Instead of reading מֶלֶךְ אֲרַם נַהֲרַיִם, a phrase that is employed elsewhere in regard to Mesopotamia, the land between the two rivers, several scholars have proposed reading מֶלֶךְ אֱדֹם ("king of Edom"). Proponents of this perspective base their conclusions on several factors: (1) "Aram" could readily have been mistaken for an original "Edom" when an early scribe transposed a *resh* for a *dalet*, as occurs elsewhere in the Hebrew Bible (2 Sam 8:12, 13; 1 Kgs 11:25; 2 Kgs 16:6; 2 Chr 20:2; Ezek 27:16);[238] (2) the element נַהֲרַיִם was a subsequent gloss meant to identify the supposed אֲרַם with the known northern Mesopotamian power; (3) נַהֲרַיִם is only connected with the initial mention of the אֲרַם in v. 8—it is noticeably absent in v. 10; (4) it is more reasonable that the southern hero Othniel, who hails from the tribe of Judah, would fight against a Edomite foe, than that he would have battled a northern aggressor.[239] For these reasons,

---

235.    J. Alberto Soggin, *Judges: A Commentary* (Philadelphia: Westminster, 1981), 47. Soggin refuses to regard the validity of textual emendations since he thinks the text has no historical basis. I would agree with Soggin that the story probably lacks historical merit, yet I would accept the emendation of Edom for Aram since it would resolve other implausible elements, such as the reason why a local southern hero battles a northern foe and how the gentilic Cushan could be employed as a pseudonym for the antagonist.

236.    Yairah Amit, *The Book of Judges: The Art of Editing* (trans. Jonathan Chipman; Leiden: Brill, 1999), 160.

237.    Amit, *Judges*, 45.

238.    Charles F. Burney, *The Book of Judges* (New York: Ktav, 1970), 65; James D. Martin, *The Book of Judges* (Cambridge: Cambridge University Press, 1975), 43.

239.    Cf. Burney, *Judges*, 64–66. Burney suggests, following August Klostermann, that this is a perspective that merits mention, though he favors a northern Cassite interloper. See also Barnabas Lindars, *Judges 1–5: A New Translation and Commentary* (Edinburgh: T. & T. Clark, 1995), 131–33, and J. D. Martin, *Judges*, 41–44.

we should emend the MT to read מֶלֶךְ אֱדֹם ("king of Edom"), both restoring a *dalet* for the *resh* we find in the MT and omitting the term נְהָרִים.[240]

Once we establish that Cushan is an Edomite, then his connection with the Cushites is more plausible. According to Hidal, Cushan was a term employed to describe the Cushite inhabitants of the Arabian Peninsula following Hab 3:7.[241] In this regard, an Edomite king called Cushan would not be as implausible as would a Mesopotamian king by the same name. In fact, this reference is one of those most likely to relate to the Arabian Cushan ethnic group posited by Hidal.[242]

The exact relationship between the people of Cushan and the people of Cush has not been clarified. We could postulate several different reasons for the similarity in names. First, the people of Cushan were a derivative ethnic group connected historically to the people of Cush.[243] In this instance it would have been significant to emphasize the *–an* ending of Cushan to distinguish this group from the wealthier and more powerful dynasty ruling Egypt. Second, the people of Cushan were historically unrelated to the Cushites, yet had similar phenotypical features to the Cushites. This conclusion would be particularly significant for our purposes since it would suggest the term כּוּשׁ had lost its ethnic specificity and could be used to describe a particular somatic type.[244] Third, the people of Cush were unrelated to the people of Cushan. This we could conclude is unlikely since כּוּשׁ is not a Hebrew root, but an Egyptian loan-word.[245] Further, the Assyrian term for Cush, *Meluhha*, was used to identify the people on both sides of the Red Sea.[246] Hence, it is probable that the term "Cushan" represents an Arabicized (*–an*) version of the foreign term, "Cush," denoting a derivative group of the southern Other, Cush.

Of these three options, the first seems to be the most plausible, particularly in light of Amos 9:7 and Hab 3:7. Habakkuk 3:7 clearly uses the name Cushan as an ethnic group, likely associated with the Midianites, dwelling in the regions south of Judah, through which some of the Hebrews traveled on their migration from Egypt. Further, our reading of Amos 9:7 supports the conclusion that there were "offspring of Cushites" living in the Levant. The phrase that Amos employs, בְּנֵי כֻשִׁיִּים, suggests that they are a derivative people, stemming initially from Cush. So, there are hints of a Cushite community in the regions near Edom that could form the basis of this reference. Still, to posit any position firmly would be largely speculative.

---

240.  Similarly, see Soggin, *Judges*, 43.

241.  Hidal, "Land," 97–106.

242.  See also the section above on Amos 9:7 (Section 2.2.2), which references the "offspring of the Cushites." The Arabian Cushan may represent this particular ethnic stock.

243.  Note the similar occurrence of two Shebas and two Havilahs, both set in African and Arabian geographical contexts. Cushan could represent an Arabian branch of the Cushite community, as Hidal concludes; see Hidal, "Land," 97–106.

244.  J. D. Martin (*Judges*, 43) determined that the author used the term Cushan because this people share phenotypical traits with the Cushites.

245.  Cf. James E. Hoch, *Middle Egyptian Grammar* (Mississauga, Ont.: Benben Publications, 1997), 291.

246.  See Hidal, "Cush," 103.

The name "Cushan-rishathaim" represents a further problem. It is not likely that a parent would have hung the appellation Cushan-rishathaim, which means "Doubly-wicked Cush(an)ite," on their child.[247] Thus this may not be a personal name, but rather a taunt that expresses the enmity between the author's community and the antagonist. Linking extreme wickedness with the name "Cushan" certainly denigrates an Edomite foe.[248]

Perhaps the Deuteronomistic historian (Dtr) or a later scribe engaged in word-play in this passage, intentionally crafting a name that sounded similar to the name received from an earlier tradition. The name of the foe known in the tradition may have sounded similar to Cushan-rishathaim,[249] and, by paronomasia, the association of words that are not identical in root or sound but share two root consonants and a phonetic similarity, this particular appellation was created.[250] But why would Dtr or a later scribe create this problematic name? The purpose could have been to indicate something about the bearer's character, noting that in the Bible names often are intended to represent essential traits.[251] For example, in 1 Sam 25:25 Dtr used the name נָבָל ("Nabal", meaning "fool") in the narrative describing David's affiliation with Abigail to illustrate the flawed nature of Nabal's character. We could also consider the name עֶגְלוֹן ("Eglon") for the Moabite king who was killed by Ehud in Judg 3:12–30. The name "Eglon" can be derived from עֵגֶל ("bull calf") or עָגֹל ("round") and is here used for a man who was depicted as very fat. Again, the name has been used to mock a trait of the bearer.

In the configuration extant in the MT, "Cushan-rishathaim," the troubling element is not the latter element, meaning "doubly-wicked." It would not be unusual for someone to describe a foreign foe as being particularly vile. However, the former element, "Cushan," is problematic. Why would this name for an ethnic group in the region south of Judah be employed in this jibe against a foe that was clearly not from Cushan?

Whether the association of this particular individual with a degrading name represents the denigration of Cush(an)ites[252] in general is questionable. It is likely that though it was a particularly negative reference, the negative association was limited to this particular individual. However, we cannot deny that it is troubling

247. J. D. Martin, *Judges*, 43. Martin goes further to suggest that "the name Cushan-rishathaim may the be thought of as referring to a villainous Edomite chieftain, whose negroid features may be reflected in his being named Cushan, 'the Nubian.'"

248. This opinion is not unique. That the name "Cushan-rishathaim" was employed to demean this foreign foe has been discussed by a number of exegetes. For example, Soggin (*Judges*, 46) calls this name "obviously a parody, a caricature ('the doubly wicked Ethiopian')." B. G. Webb (*The Book of Judges: An Integrated Reading* [JSOTSup 46; Sheffield: Sheffield Academic Press, 1987], 128) notes that the name represents an "intentional corruption." See also J. D. Martin, *Judges*, 43.

249. This is likely because the name in the LXX is a composite, Χουσαρσαθαιμ. If this represents an older version of the narrative than the MT, then it is possible that the earliest versions had no reference to Cushan at all. In this instance, we must ask: Why does the MT employ Cushan in this derision?

250. Edward L. Greenstein, "Wordplay, Hebrew," in *ABD* 6:968–71 (969).

251. Greenstein, "Wordplay," 968–71.

252. Note that I have intentionally used the term Cush(an)ite and not Cushite to distinguish this group from the southern people of Cush.

that a gentilic for Cush(an)ites is linked to an appellation correlating Cush(an) and extraordinary wickedness.

We should be suspicious that a term for a known ethnic group, Cushan, was used for a person of another group, an Edomite, in such a construction. We must consider the possibility that such an appellation is a pejorative that may utilize Cushan for the express purpose of deriding someone. Hence, Dtr or a subsequent scribe used this moniker either to belittle a particular Edomite ruler who had subjugated the Israelite tribes or else to demean an othered group, the Edomites, by calling their leader a "doubly-wicked Cush(an)ite." In the latter instance Cushan may have been used as such out-group ethnic terms are used in contemporary contexts. Allport notes that ethnic terms could acquire an association with negative qualities based upon prior uses of the terms in negative contexts. For example, such ethnic terms as Polish, Jew, and Black are used in taunts where the ethnic term becomes negatively charged and connotes an irrationally negative quality, despite its neutral denotation.[253]

If the term Cushan had a strong negative connotation, what are the implications for our study? Initially, Cush-related terms were not all met with universally positive regard by Judean authors. To evoke the term "Cushan" upon someone could have degraded him or her before the eyes of a Judean audience. The Other could be used to denigrate a foe. If we were prematurely to compare the union of the term Cushan with the notion of extreme wickedness with the correlation of "blackness" and antisocial behavior in contemporary racialist paradigms, we would have in this passage one of the strongest indications of racialist thought in the Hebrew Bible.

However, the terms Cush and Cushan were not identical. If Cushan was related to Midian, an ethnic group with whom the Hebrews had had periods of intense animosity, then this enmity may have been the source of the slight. The notion of extreme wickedness may arise from an historical memory of a political-military conflict between the Hebrews and Cushan not contained in the extant biblical narratives.[254] Also, this seldom-mentioned southern neighbor of Judah clearly did not share the power, wealth, and stature that the nation of Cush possessed. This is further evidenced by the presence of the term "Cushi" as either a name or gentilic used for ancestors of biblical characters.[255] If the term Cush had a negative connotation it could scarcely have been used in these patronymics. Otherwise later redactors would have emended them, particularly the patronymic of the prophet Zephaniah.[256] In fact, it is likely that as either a personal name or gentilic, Cushi was a badge of honor. Hence, it is improbable that any shame associated with the

---

253. Allport, *Nature of Prejudice*, 305–6.

254. Note that the reference in Hab 3:7 has negative overtones, since the people of Cushan are "in affliction" with Midian who "trembled" before YHWH's advance. This implies that there may have been enmity between the Hebrews and Cushan, as there was with Midian.

255. This name was used for an ancestor of Jehudi in Jer 36:14 (see Section 3.2.5.2) and Zephaniah in Zeph 1:1 (see Section 3.2.2.1).

256. See Section 3.2.2.1, below, on Zeph 1:1, where Zephaniah's genealogy was used to authenticate his prophetic authority.

term Cushan would have transferred to their ancestors, the people of Cush proper. Thus, a disparagement of Cushan cannot be associated with Judean perceptions of Cush or the Cushites!

We should consider two basic factors when determining the type of Cush reference we find in this passage. First, it is an indirect reference to a "Levantine Cushan." Second, it appears to be the only instance where a Cush-related ethnic term is used to mock or deride a foe in the Hebrew Bible.

### 3.2.7.2. *2 Samuel 18: A Cushite in King David's Court.* The term כּוּשִׁי appears seven times in 2 Sam 18, which recounts events at a pivotal moment in the rule of King David. Absalom's rebellion against his father had divided the nation in two; the larger part of the country supporting Absalom and a smaller but potent faction remained faithful to David. While David remained sequestered in Jerusalem, his troops were divided in thirds and met the rebels of Israel in the forests of Ephraim. The third led by David's renowned general, Joab, had the good fortune of locating the rebel leader, Absalom, then pursuing him until his head became lodged in the limbs of an oak. Joab then killed David's wayward son, actively violating the explicit request of his king and thereby ending the civil strife between David's house and the rest of Israel. Joab was subsequently faced with a choice that has implications for our study: whom should he send to give David news of his son's demise?

The choice is complicated by the overzealous ambitions of one Ahimaaz, son of Zadok the priest. Ahimaaz wanted to bring the report of the army's victory to David's ear, naively unaware of the effect the news would have on the king. But Joab recognized the potential political damage bearing this message might entail.[257] Without hesitation, Joab restrained Ahimaaz and compelled a Cushite confederate to take the message.

The details in this brief story reveal interesting aspects of the relationship between Cushites and Israelites. Initially, it is significant that Joab assigns the task to הַכּוּשִׁי. Joab thought that the task was inappropriate for Zadok's son, in spite of his ample pleas to perform it. Joab persistently attempts to dissuade Ahimaaz from running with the message,[258] implicitly acknowledging the aforementioned negative repercussions of delivering such patently bad news about Absalom's death to David. Yet Joab says nothing to the Cushite about this! Nor does he inform the Cushite that by killing Absalom, Joab has violated the will of the king, something that may provoke the king to wrath. Joab clearly places less value on the life of the Cushite than he did on the life of Ahimaaz.[259]

---

257.   David has a history of responding violently to bad news. In two prior instances the bearers of a report of which the king disapproved were promptly executed (see 2 Sam 1:1–16 and 4:9–12). But in all fairness to David, in both instances the bearers of the news were responsible for the death of prominent figures, hence the bad news that they reported.

258.   Robert P. Gordon, *1 & 2 Samuel: A Commentary* (Grand Rapids: Regency, 1986), 286. Gordon notes that this is a task Ahimaaz is familiar with (cf. 2 Sam 15:27; 36; 17:17–21).

259.   Cf. Charles Conroy, *Absalom, Absalom: Narrative and Language in 2 Sam 13–20* (Rome: Biblical Institute, 1978), 69. Conroy argues against such an obviously racial reason as that posited by Dhorme, de Vaux, and Blenkinsopp. These scholars posit that Joab would have chosen a "black" runner to

Similarly, Ahimaaz's actions betray no greater sense of compassion. Though he has reached David before the Cushite, his zeal has been replaced by a sense of self-preservation before David. Instead of revealing to David the fate of his son, he holds his tongue and waits for the unsuspecting Cushite to break the news. The Cushite is left alone and in peril before an unstable king, having been abandoned by both Joab and Ahimaaz; his life was deemed less valuable than theirs.

The manner in which the Cushite is portrayed is also significant. His few actions are those of a faithful and dedicated servant.[260] Before the king, his words express fidelity to David and stand in stark contrast to the deceit of Ahimaaz. Indeed, the Cushite shows respect. Whereas Ahimaaz challenges the prominent general and willfully violates his wishes, the Cushite bows before him. Though this could be described as the type of behavior typical of such flat characters as the Cushite, it is not unimportant. The occurrence of the verb וַיִּשְׁתַּחוּ ("and he bowed") represents the only time that a character bows before a military official in the Hebrew Bible. Though many bow to God,[261] to kings,[262] to prophets,[263] and even to kinsmen of higher social standing,[264] bowing to a general is mentioned only for the Cushite in this narrative. This Cushite appears as a flat, submissive character who is given no agency by either author or other characters. He simply responds in a predictable fashion to the whims of the more fully developed characters that are around him. In light of the panorama of feelings that causes the other characters in the chapter to behave in uncharacteristic ways, the Cushite is allowed only to do humbly as he is instructed.

In fact, the Cushite is not even granted the dignity of a name.[265] We are struck by the unequal valuation of his person-hood, seen most clearly in the contrast

---

"indicate the nature of the message" (n. 102). He suggests that the Cushite was chosen because he was an outsider. For a similar perspective, see Walter Brueggemann, *First and Second Samuel* (Louisville, Ky.: John Knox, 1990), 321. Hertzberg, perhaps betraying his own biases, points out that הַכּוּשִׁי was a "negro" sent to relay the bad news to the king; see Hans Wilhelm Hertzberg, *1 & 2 Samuel: A Commentary* (trans. J. S. Bowden; Philadelphia: Westminster, 1964), 360.

260.   Several commentators have pointed out the Cushite's familiarity with the "polite" and courtly language used to address King David. Cf. Peter R. Ackroyd, *The Second Book of Samuel* (London: Cambridge University Press, 1977), 172. Also see Adamo, "Africa," 130–31, and Hertzberg, *Samuel*, 361. Cushi appears to be a loyal subject with access to the king.

261.   For example, Num 25:2; Josh 23:16.

262.   For example, 1 Kgs 1:23; 2 Kgs 14:22, 33; 24:20.

263.   For example, 1 Kgs 2:15.

264.   For example, Gen 33; 46:2; Ruth 2:10.

265.   Adele Reinhartz, *"Why Ask My Name?" Anonymity and Identity in Biblical Narrative* (New York: Oxford University Press, 1998), 35–36, suggests that anonymous characters like this Cushite have their identity circumscribed solely by their occupational role. We are given the advantage of knowing his ethnicity, hence this was likely the aspect of the Cushite's identity that the author wanted us to focus our attention on as we read this narrative. If we interpret the Cushite's role as what Reinhartz calls the "Servants, Stewards and Armor Bearer" type of character, then we can conclude that the actions of this foreign courtier are intended to illustrate aspects of those deemed his "masters" (pp. 33–34). I suggest that his alien identity establishes the contrast between the loyal outsider and the compromised Judean officials in David's court. Further, that he is described as a Cushite may have implications for our understanding of his ability to run. I will return to this issue below.

between v. 21 where Joab does not call the Cushite by name or give him advice, and v. 22 where Joab calls Ahimaaz by name, advises him, and even affectionately refers to him as "my son." In all but one instance the Cushite is simply identified by the use of the gentilic, הַכּוּשִׁי. It is only in v. 21 that the term appears without the definite article.[266] It is unlikely that כוּשִׁי ("Cushi") represents his personal name, though it seems to function in lieu of one. This courtier is consistently identified only by the designation of the ethnic group to which he belonged, an act that further essentializes him, overshadowing his personal identity.

A final point to be made about this chapter is that the Cushite is described as a runner in the army. This emphasis on the athletic prowess of the Cushite may represent another stereotype also found in Isa 18:2, that of the fast Cushite.[267] Stereotypical swiftness is the aspect of the Cushite courtier's identity emphasized in 2 Sam 18:23, for the narrative conveys the otherwise irrelevant detail that Ahimaaz passed the Cushite. This event only merits attention if it would have been deemed unusual for an Israelite priest's son to surpass a Cushite running, particularly one with a head start.[268]

Though from a later period, an early seventh-century inscription designated the "Race Stela of Taharqa"[269] sheds light on the type of training Cushite soldiers may have engaged in to prepare themselves for military service. Malamat describes a rigorous training program that included daily 100 km runs that took perhaps 9 hours to run at a pace of 11 km per hour. The stela suggests that Taharqa (Tirhakah) himself actually participated in the event.[270] If such dedication to swift running was characteristic of Cushite soldiers in general, then Ahimaaz' feat in v. 23 did merit rehearsal.

In sum, this chapter presents a mixed perspective on the Judahite view of Cushites. Positively, Dtr has portrayed the Cushite as a loyal and faithful officer, a member of the army of Israel, and one who is not unfamiliar with politics of the royal court. Thus, the Cushite Other is depicted as behaving admirably. However, less positively Dtr has presented the Cushite as a depthless character who only does as he is told and no more, whose life is expendable to his commanding officer Joab and his colleague Amihaaz. Thus the same Cushite Other is denied full humanity. Yet, in the end, Dtr presents the Cushite as the sole uncompromised character in a narrative where the other characters each demonstrate deceit (Ahimaaz), cunning (Joab), callous indifference (Joab), or disloyalty (David).

---

266.   Conroy (*Absalom*, 154) suggests, reading against the tendency of the LXX to make Cushi a personal name, that the definite article should also be assumed for the single instance of Cushi without the definite article in v. 21. See also P. Kyle McCarter, *II Samuel: A New Translation with Introduction, Notes and Commentary* (AB 9; Garden City, N.Y.: Doubleday, 1984), 402 n. 21.

267.   See Section 2.2.3.2 on Isa 18. Also see Entine, *Taboo*.

268.   The traditional reading of this text suggests that Ahimaaz took a shorter (cf. Ackroyd, *Samuel*, 172) or less treacherous route (cf. Gordon, *Samuel*, 286). Here I agree with Alter (*David*, 308), who concludes, based on vv. 25–27, that the text implies that Ahimaaz ran faster than the Cushite.

269.   Cf. Ahmed M. Moussa, "A Stela of Taharqa for the Desert Road of Dahshur," *MDAIK* 37 (1981): 331–37.

270.   Abraham Malamat, "Foot-Runners in Israel and Egypt in the Third Intermediate Period," *Hommages a Jean Leclant* 4 (1994): 109–201 (200).

Finally, we must also consider the apparent stereotyping implied by the motif of the "swift Cushite" who is surpassed by the priest's son. Noting the emphasis on the stereotype of the "swift-Cushite," we classify the reference to הַכּוּשִׁי in 2 Sam 18 as a "swift-Cushite" text. Though we could legitimately deem this an essentialization, a constituent element of racialist thought similar to those associations of "race" and athletic prowess mentioned in Entine's text,[271] it certainly does not represent a negative assessment of the Cushites.

### 3.2.7.3. *2 Kings 19: Tirhakah King of Cush.*

The term כּוּשׁ occurs once in 2 Kgs 19:9 and is identified as the region over which King Tirhakah ruled. Though not explicitly mentioned, the Judean audience would have understood that Egypt could have been subsumed under the designation כּוּשׁ in this chapter. The ambiguities abound in the account of the Cushite involvement in Hezekiah's resistance to Sennacherib's invasion. The narrative in 2 Kgs 18–19 suggests that Sennacherib invaded Judah during the fourth year of Hezekiah's reign and laid siege to the fortified cites of Judah because of the Judean king's rebellion against his Assyrian overlord implicit in 18:14 and 20. Though not clear, in part Hezekiah's rebellion included an alliance with the king of Egypt (18:21–24). This alliance, deemed futile by Sennacherib's spokesperson, Rabshakeh, appears to be the source of the reference to Tirhakah as the Cushite king of Egypt in 19:9.[272]

The role that Tirhakah plays in this narrative is far from clear. Based upon 2 Kgs 19:6–7, Tirhakah may be the spoiler in Sennacherib's plans of Judean conquest. In 19:7, the prophet Isaiah, sought out by Hezekiah to pray for the people of Judah, prophesies that YHWH would "put a spirit in him, so that he will hear a report and return to his land." Two verses later in 2 Kgs 19:9 we learn that "then he heard about Tirhakah, king of Cush, saying 'Behold, he has gone out to war with you.'" Based solely upon a reading of the text, it appears that the "report" that Isaiah prophesied Sennacherib would hear was the report of the arrival of Tirhakah's advancing troops.[273] However, this has not been universally accepted as historical for a number of reasons.

Chief among these reasons is a matter of chronology. As a number of biblical scholars have noted, Sennacherib's invasion has been dated to ca. 701 B.C.E., which would have been roughly eleven years before Tirhakah ascended the throne in 690 B.C.E.[274] Several solutions have been suggested to resolve this dilemma. One solution is to see the events recorded in 2 Kgs 18–19 as largely literary

---

271.  Entine, *Taboo*.

272.  This story recurs in 2 Chr 32 and Isa 37:1–13. Though the Isaianic narrative is true to the details of 2 Kgs 19, in 2 Chronicles there is no reference to the contributions of the Cushites nor the Egyptians for that matter. There it is YHWH alone who produces the victory by slaughtering Sennacherib's forces and facilitating his retreat to Assyria. The decision to omit the reference to Tirhakah the Cushite king of Egypt runs contrary to the general pattern in Chronicles that emphasized the role played by Cushites in Judean history (cf. 2 Chr 12; 14; 16; 21).

273.  Cf. Richard D. Nelson, *First and Second Kings* (Atlanta: John Knox, 1987), 239; Donald J. Wiseman, *1 and 2 Kings*, vol. 2 (Leicester: Inter-Varsity, 1993), 279.

274.  So Adamo, "Africa," 182–87; Gwilym H. Jones, *1 and 2 Kings*, vol. 2 (Grand Rapids: Eerdmans, 1984), 575; Wiseman, *Kings*, 280.

fiction woven around a historical kernel.[275] Another solution has been to suggest that the essence of the report in 19:9 is correct, namely, that Tirhakah was instrumental in leading an army against Sennacherib in 701 not as king of Cush and Egypt, but as general during his brother Shebitku's reign.[276]

Still another possibility is that Sennacherib invaded Judah twice. The first time was the 701 B.C.E. invasion documented in the Assyrian Annals, which contains an account of Sennacherib's activities from 705–689 B.C.E. The second invasion occurred after 689 and, hence, is not contained in any known Assyrian documents. Sennacherib, returning from his successful campaign against Babylon, attempted to crush the opportunistic rebellions arising in the Judean region. Proponents of this position find evidence to support their contentions in the biblical text, which they argue is a conflation of both invasion stories.[277] However, in the absence of evidence about the outcome of this confrontation, supporters of the second-invasion theory generally viewed Tirhakah's campaign as unsuccessful,[278] following Herodotus (II:141).[279]

In a recent article, Shea has championed the second-invasion theory.[280] Though the theory has largely remained unchanged, Shea has clearly delimited the elements describing two invasions, supplementing the evidence with data from recent excavations and newly translated Egyptian documents. According to Shea, the first invasion in 701 was the one clearly referred to in the Assyrian Annals and highlighted in the reliefs in Sennacherib's throne-room in Nineveh. Hezekiah ended this siege by offering the gifts described in 2 Kgs 18:13–16 and in the Assyrian relief of the siege of Lachish to Sennacherib.[281] Shea points out that though the relief accurately depicts the double wall of the city, it does not depict

---

275.  John Gray, *1 and 2 Kings: A Commentary* (2d edn; Philadelphia: Westminster, 1970), 663–64. Gray comes to this conclusion following the lead of Brevard S. Childs and Georg Fohrer, who emphasized the literary character of these texts and found two different versions of the story (18:17–19:7, 36; and 19:9b–35).

276.  G. H. Jones, *Kings*, 575. Jones notes the theory that Sennacherib invaded Judah a second time, but favors the view that the royal title was retrojected onto this man known as a great and enduring pharaoh. See also, Wiseman, *Kings*, 279–80; Miller and Hayes, *History*, 361–62; Mordechai Cogan and Hayim Tadmor, *II Kings: A New Translation with Introduction and Commentary* (AB 11; Garden City, N.Y.: Doubleday, 1988), 234 n. 9, 249 n. 3.

277.  Bright, *History*, 285–88; Adamo, "Africa," 182–87.

278.  There is also evidence from Sennacherib's Prism that he defeated a Cushite/Egyptian army: "(Hezekiah) . . . had become afraid and had called (for help) upon the kings of Egypt (*Mus[u]ri*) (and) the bowmen, the chariot(-corps) and the cavalry of the king of Ethiopia (*Meluhha*), an army beyond counting—and they (actually) had come to their assistance. In the plain of Eltekeh (*Al-ta-qu-u*), their battle lines were drawn up against me and they sharpened their weapons. Upon a trust(-inspiring) oracle (given) by Ashur, my lord, I fought with them and inflicted a defeat upon them. In the melee of the battle, I personally captured alive the Egyptian charioteers with the(ir) princes and (also) the charioteers of the king of Ethiopia." Leo Oppenheim, "Sennacherib (704–681): The Seige of Jerusalem," in *The Ancient Near East*, vol. 1, *An Anthology of Texts and Pictures* (ed. James B. Pritchard; Princeton, N.J.: Princeton University Press, 1958), 199–200.

279.  Bright, *History*, 288.

280.  William H. Shea, "Jerusalem Under Siege: Did Sennacherib Attack Twice?," *BARev* 25 (1999): 36–44, 64. For a similar view, see A. Kirk Grayson, "Sennacherib," in *ABD* 5:1088–89.

281.  Oppenheim, "Sennacherib," 199–200.

the large earthen siege ramp known to have been erected by the Assyrians prior to the destruction of the Judean city, but two smaller wooden ramps.[282] Hence, he concludes that that these are all elements of the first invasion.[283]

Shea relates the second invasion to 2 Kgs 18:17–19:37, and uses several archaeological data in conjunction with documentary sources to support this proposition. For example, the earthen Assyrian siege ramp at Lachish must post-date the 701 siege based upon the Nineveh relief. Further, reading 2 Chr 32:2–5, he concludes that Jerusalem's outer wall and the two free-standing towers built over the Gihon spring and Hezekiah's tunnel[284] were built in anticipation of Sennacherib's invasion and could not have been constructed prior to the 701 siege. During that siege the Assyrian king suddenly shifted his attention from his efforts to pacify his eastern provinces to focus his attention on Palestine. Such a monumental building program could not have been completed during the interim between the time Hezekiah knew of Sennacherib's imminent arrival and when he laid siege to Judah's fortified cities.[285]

Finally, Shea employs a recently translated Egyptian document composed during Tirhakah's administration that describes a significant victory over an unnamed foreign foe, definitively dated to the years immediately prior to 685.[286] Though the text has many lacunae and is ambiguous at best, it does provide the context for an Egyptian military victory over a significant foreign foe at precisely the moment we would expect the second Assyrian invasion.[287] Hence, Shea concludes that 2 Kgs 18–19 describes two distinct incursions by Sennacherib into Judah, the first resolved by Hezekiah's tribute and the second as a result of a prophesied "rumor," likely that of Tirhakah's advancing armies.

Shea's contribution to the understanding of the historical events undergirding this narrative is significant. Not only has his investigation challenged our

282. Shea, "Jerusalem," 41.

283. Shea, "Jerusalem," 36–41.

284. So Ronny Reich and Eli Shukron, "Light at the End of the Tunnel—Warren's Shaft Theory of David's Conquest Shattered," *BARev* 1 (1999): 22–33, 72; Hershel Shanks, "Everything You Ever Knew about Jerusalem is Wrong," *BARev* 6 (1999): 20–29.

285. Shea, "Jerusalem," 43.

286. Donald B. Redford, "Taharqa in Western Asia and Libya," *ErIsr* 24 (1993): 188–91; William H. Shea, "The New Tirhakah Text and Sennacherib's Second Palestinian Campaign," *AUSS* 35 (1997): 181–87.

287. Cf. Redford, "Taharqa," 190. Here Redford provides a brief translation of the relevant portion of the stele, which is dated to the time of Tarhakah by the reference to the flood (line 14), with brief editorial notes: "'I [. . .] to this city in order to provide horses, char[iots and . . .] more than anything,' the enemy 'did all this in marching against me (7),' but the speaker set forth 'hastening to the place where they were (7),' 'they were destined for a severe and grievous blow, the work of my hands . . . I had no compassion on the least of them nor (10) [on the most influential of the (?). . .]'; and soon they were 'fleeing before me with fear pulsating through their limbs . . . (11). . . . I forced (?) his confederates to the ground all at once.' Next comes the settlement after the victory: (11) '[I placed the . . .] in quarters, I settled them in villages, and [their] cattle [in . . . (13) the . . . came their benevolences] in their hands; and I brought the mellifers of the levy [and I put them in the . . .] of the House of Amun and made them responsible for the divine income of honey.'" It is interesting to note that Redford does not make the connection between this text and the Assyrians since he views the reference to Tarhakah in 2 Kgs 19:9 as "an anachronism" (p. 191 n. 17). He also lacks the more recent data Shea used to support his hypothesis.

historical understanding of the early seventh century Palestine, but also it provides compelling evidence for a more active role for King Tirhakah in the unfolding history of the Levant.[288] Not only has he effectively posited Cushite involvement in the second instance of Assyrian aggression in Judah,[289] he has concluded that the Cushites may have prevailed against the considerable might of Sennacherib's forces.[290]

With this new understanding of the text, the Cushites take on a greater significance in the unfolding biblical narrative. The Cushites are represented as a fierce intimidating force whose arrival marks a significant turning point in the story. Tirhakah's forces represent the fulfillment of YHWH's word through Isaiah and facilitate the deliverance promised by Judah's deity. In this regard, the portrayal of the Cushites is brief but positive, as allies working to eliminate the dreaded northern menace.

Still, Dtr diminishes the role played by the Cushites. This is likely the result of Dtr's theological *Tendenz*, which was similar to that of the author of Isaiah[291] and not a deliberate attempt by the author to demean the Cushites. Noting that the author of Isaiah rejected reliance on Egyptian might as an act of infidelity toward YHWH (Isa 30:1–7), we could assume that a certain anti-ethnic sentiment also informed the Deuteronomistic writer's presentation. Because of the similarity in their theological perspectives, both of which emphasized total reliance on YHWH, the author of Isaiah may have decided to adopt Dtr's narratives about the siege of Judah with only minor editorial changes. Thus the Cushites' contribution to the fate of Jerusalem was not forgotten but subtly remembered by Dtr; and Tirhakah's actions to intervene on behalf of his ally Hezekiah were implicitly "recorded" between the lines of this passage. In fact, the passage presents these Cushites as the fulfillment of YHWH's word through Isaiah ensuring protection for King Hezekiah and Judah (2 Kgs 19:7).[292]

---

288.   Futher, Shea's conclusions clarify some other discrepancies in the biblical account. For instance, Assyrian records suggest that the defeat of the Cushites occurred prior to the siege of Jerusalem (see Sennacherib's annals). Further, we know that Sennacherib ruled for two decades following the 701 invasion of Palestine. Positing a later invasion helps to reconcile these dilemmas. Cf. Clements, *Isaiah*, 283–88.

289.   The first invasion by the Cushites (Isa 20, see Section 2.2.3.3) was evidently a failure as mentioned above. So Oppenhiem, "Sennacherib," 199–200. The second took place about twelve years later and was headed by then king Tirhakah. This suggests a continued Cushite involvement in assuring the welfare of Judah.

290.   Adamo also raised this as a possibility in his 1986 dissertation, citing an unnamed Egyptian legend of a defeat of Sennacherib by Egyptian forces following the suggestion of Norman H. Snaith ("2 Kings," *IB* 3:187-338 [303]), though without the benefit of the recently identified data Shea employed. See Adamo, "Africa," 186–87.

291.   See above (Section 2.2.3.4 on Isa 37) where I concluded that part of Isaiah's overall purpose was to present YHWH as the sole agent responsible for Judah's salvation. Openly acknowledging the Cushite contribution could compromise the author's vision of YHWH's sovereignty over Judah.

292.   This connection between Isaiah's prediction of a "report" and the report of the advancing Cushites is emphasized in the Hebrew text, which follows שְׁמוּעָה וְשָׁמַע in v. 7 immediately with: וַיִּשְׁמַע אֶל־תִּרְהָקָה מֶלֶךְ־כּוּשׁ in v. 9. The report is of the imminent arrival of the Cushites.

It is also relevant that the portrayal of the Cushites here is inconsistent with a racial presentation. Though their contributions to the unfolding of the history of Judah have been diminished, the Cushites are portrayed as an allied force; there is no enmity associated with Tirhakah or his army in this chapter. Further, the power differential described here is the reverse of what we would expect to see in a racialist presentation. Tirhakah and his armies are the powerful protectors of a vulnerable Judah; Cush is the dominant partner in this alliance, not the dependent one. In fact, any disparagement of Cush in this passage can be attributed to Rab-shakeh, Sennacherib's henchman (2 Kgs 18:21), and not to any Judean source. This mention of Tirhakah is consistent with what we would expect in a "mighty-Cush" type reference.

*3.2.7.4. Summary of Cush in the Works of the Deuteronomistic Historian.* As discussed above, Dtr represents Israelite/Judahite interaction with Cushites or Cush-related peoples during every pre-exilic historical period. The portrait presented by the Deuteronomistic historian,[293] however, is mixed. With the initial reference to Cushan, Dtr demonstrated that Cush-related terms do not always automatically receive deference or neutrality. Judges 3 actually represents one of the most troubling references to a Cush-related term in the Hebrew Bible because it associates the ethnic term "Cushan" with the concept of extreme wickedness. Because of this association, we must question whether the term Cushan, though likely not Cush, could have been negatively understood by Judean authors and audiences.

In 2 Sam 18, the Dtr provides us with a view inside the royal court of the United Monarchy. We should not be surprised to find a Cushite courtier there, savvy in the way to address the king and faithful in his service. However, Joab and the Cushite's colleague Ahimaaz reward his fidelity with deceit and betrayal. Even the author diminishes this character, making him flat amid changing characters, exploiting his otherness to make an allusion to the stereotype of the swift Cushite. In the end, the Cushite remains a positive stable character amid the morally compromised assembly found in 2 Sam 18.

The last time that we encounter Cushites in Dtr's work is in 2 Kgs 19. Here we have found evidence that Cushite-led forces may have intervened on behalf of Judah when the latter was besieged by Sennacherib's Assyrian hordes. After excavating the text, we have posited that though his brother Shebitku had failed at Eltekeh at the close of the eighth century B.C.E. to defeat the Assyrians, Tirhakah succeeded in thwarting the Assyrians in a second invasion of Judah in the early seventh century B.C.E. However, Dtr has almost completely erased the Cushites from the text and their contribution to the fate of Judah remains only peripheral in this narrative. This is most plausibly due to Dtr's theological intent to portray YHWH as the sole entity responsible for Judah's salvation and not because he bore ill will for this southern Other.

293. Eichrodt, *Ezekiel*, 519–22.

In the end, we leave Dtr with a mixed perspective on his view of Cushites. In two instances they are somewhat mitigated by the author and the other characters in the narrative, but they remain noble if flat characters. In the other instance, the reference to the Cush-related term "Cushan" demonstrates that the Other could be used in Judah to mock foreign foes.

### 3.3. *Summary: Cush in Seventh Century to Exilic Hebrew Literature*

#### 3.3.1. *General Statement of Findings*

Though we have noted a variety of portrayals of Cushites in this section, we should emphasize one point. Nahum seems to mark a significant moment in the history of the Cushites, the moment of their defeat at Thebes. Though descendants of the XXVth Dynasty continued to reign in Cush for centuries, they never again exercised the same sway in the Levant that they had when they were sovereign in Egypt. As a result, the myth of invulnerability that surrounds the Cushites and is referenced in Nah 3:9 is less prominent in subsequent literature. References to defeated Cushites in Zeph 2, Jer 46, and Ezek 29 and 30, unlike those of Isa 20 and even (Deutero-)Isaiah (43 and 45), likely reflect actual military losses. However, we must keep in mind that many of these defeats may have been experienced only by Cushite mercenaries in foreign armies and not by Cush itself.

The initial reference to a Cush-related term in the work of the Deuteronomistic Historian revives the notion of a Levantine Cushite community discussed above in the section on Amos 9 (see Section 2.2.2). In Judg 3 they are fodder for taunts against Israelite tribal enemies. Yet such a denigration does not transfer to the people of Cush proper, who admirably serve in the military and royal court of King David (2 Sam 18) and come to the rescue of Hezekiah's Jerusalem (2 Kgs 19). Further, the references to Cush-related terms in Zephaniah, Jeremiah, and Dtr often imply close contact between Cushites and Judeans.

#### 3.3.2. *The Reason Why Cush Is Employed in Hebrew Literature*

The Cushites play a number of different roles in Hebrew literature composed during the period between the seventh century and the Exile. The trope of the mighty Cushites appears in Nah 3, Zeph 2, Isa 43 and 45, Jer 46, Ezekiel, and 2 Kgs 19. This is clearly the most common understanding of Cushites.

Though the narrative in Jer 38 and 39 defies typification, we should consider its similarity to 2 Sam 18, where another Cushite has access to a Judean king. Jeremiah 36 and Zeph 1 may also fit this pattern; if Yehudi and Zephaniah are of Cushite stock, there are influential Cushites in key positions at the beginning and the end of the monarchy in Jerusalem.

Jeremiah 39 also shows that YHWH's favor can come to Cushites. This favor appears to be returned in the gifts-from-Cush type reference in Zeph 3. We have seen this type in Isa 18 and will again in Ps 68. God's dread can also come upon people associated with Cush, as is evident in the portrait of a fearful Cushan as it trembled before YHWH (Hab 3). This text is of the same type as is Amos 9, suggesting that there were descendants of Cushites who remained in the Levant.

The author of Ezekiel portrays the Cushites as a conquered people. However, it is likely that the destruction he predicts is suffered only by mercenaries who served in the Egyptian army and who shared the fate of their colleagues. For their hubris and idolatry, YHWH will vanquish them and their partners. Here the Cushites are symbols of military might that will fall, having been conquered and despoiled by YHWH via Nebuchadnezzar.

Cushite phenotypes play a small role in two passages discussed already in Chapter 2 (Num 12 implicitly, and Isa 18 explicitly), and these phenotypes receive less attention in the later literature. Only in one instance in the literature from this period is there a Cushite phenotypical trait inferred—namely, dark skin (Jer 13). Also, there is only one behavioral essentialism in this literature—the notion of athleticism demonstrated by swiftness (2 Sam 18). However, one of the most precarious uses of a Cush-related term in the Hebrew Bible occurs in literature from this period (Judg 3).

Chapter 4

A WORD STUDY OF THE HEBREW ROOT "CUSH" IN POST-EXILIC
HEBREW LITERATURE

### 4.1. *Introduction to the Exegesis of Cush*
*in Post-Exilic Hebrew Literature*

In this chapter we will review the references to Cush-related terms in post-exilic literature: 1 and 2 Chronicles, Psalms, Daniel, Esther, and Job. The most significant post-exilic texts are those in Chronicles, because they provide invaluable information regarding the Cushites' function in the Egyptian hegemony. The Cushite presence in Egyptian expeditionary forces may have been the genesis of Cushite military power in the Levant; and if the Chronicler's account is any indication, Cushites were active in the region south of Judah for several centuries. We will also see commodified Cushites (Dan 11) and a reference to Cush as the signpost of the end of the world (Esth 1 and 8).

### 4.2. *Analysis of the Term "Cush" in Post-Exilic Hebrew Literature*

#### 4.2.1. *Cush in Chronicles*
The Chronicler's portrayal of Israel/Judah's history essentially follows the same outline as the Deuteronomistic historian's, although it often differs in the details it presents. One such difference is the number of times Cushites occur in the Chronicler's narratives. The Cushites appear more frequently in the Chronicles than in Dtr's telling of the same stories. In fact, two significant additions to Dtr's account of the history of Judah are narratives describing Cushite activity in Palestine (2 Chr 14; 21 [2 Chr 12 contains additional material]).[1] The Chronicler also omits Cushites from narratives where they figure prominently in Dtr's works (2 Sam 18; 2 Kgs 19).

In all the references to the Cushites (except those in 1 Chr 1), the Chronicler presents Cushites as mighty warriors who serve as instruments of YHWH's judgment or the impetus for the people of Judah to rely completely upon YHWH. More specifically, the Chronicler understood the Cushites to be enduring fixtures in the

---

1. For an account of additions to the Chronicler's version of Israel's/Judah's history, see Sara Japhet, *The Ideology of the Book of Chronicles and its Place in Biblical Thought* (New York: Peter Lang, 1989), 438.

Levant exercising sway on behalf of the larger Egyptian empire and often administering an army consisting of Egyptians, Libyans, Arabians, and Philistines.

4.2.1.1. *1 Chronicles 1: The Table of Nations, Redacted.* The term כּוּשׁ occurs three times in 1 Chr 1. Here in the Chronicler's version of the Table of Nations it is clearer than in Genesis that the intent of the genealogy is to establish the background for the people of Israel. This supposition is most evident because the Chronicler fails to include the various narrative portions found in Genesis (10:5, 10–12, 18b–20, 30–31) and condenses other less significant patronymics in order to focus specifically on the story of Abraham's offspring.

This version of the Table of Nations is similar to that of Gen 10. The most significant difference between the two is the omission of the problem-laden Gen 10:9–14, the section that has led many scholars to posit the existence of a northern Cassite Cush.[2] These five verses were likely a portion of the adopted Genesis genealogy deemed unnecessary for the Chronicler's objectives and ones that did not concur with what was commonly known about the Cushites active in the history of the people of Judah. By omitting Gen 10:9–14 from his account, the Chronicler has produced a less problematic genealogy for Cush.

Whether or not the Chronicler consciously decided to omit the problematic five verses is unclear. However, the remaining text is consistent with the image of the Cushites portrayed in the rest of Chronicles. The Cushites are from the nation south of Egypt and participate in the Chronicler's narratives because of their political and military affiliation with their northern neighbor during the time of the XXIInd Dynasty. In fact, the Egyptian troops mentioned in Chronicles are largely composed of nations whose eponymous ancestors are identified as descendants of Ham in 1 Chr 1.

As I concluded above in my discussion of Gen 10,[3] the Chronicler neither disparages the Cushites nor denigrates their land. In fact, they are presented as part of the human continuum; they are members of the same family as the Judahites' own ancestors. Further, the Cushites were perceived negatively in this chapter. On the contrary, Cush is recognized as the father of a certain Nimrod, who, though dislocated from his northern descendants, is not disassociated from his glory. Indeed, 1 Chr 1:10 notes, "Cush became the father of Nimrod; he was the first to be a mighty one on the earth."

4.2.1.2. *2 Chronicles 12: Shishak Invades.* The term וְכוּשִׁים occurs once in 2 Chr 12, in v. 3. This account begins in the fifth year (ca. 925) of the reign of King Rehoboam of Judah (ca. 930–913), when Shishak (Sheshonq I), the Libyan founder of the XXIInd Egyptian Dynasty, invades the land of Judah. Shishak, an interesting character in his own right, was heir to the chiefdom of the Libyan Meshwesh tribe.[4] He was raised in the court of Psusenes II, the last pharaoh of

---

2. Cf. Hidal, "Land," 99–103.

3. See Section 2.2.1.3.

4. However, Japhet seems to think otherwise in her recent commentary. In her words, "the fact that Shishak himself was a Nubian ('Cushite' in the Bible) gives added credibility to this information."

the XXIst Dynasty. Psusenes, impressed with the charisma of Shishak,[5] designated him his heir, and upon Psusenes' death, Shishak sat upon the throne of Egypt. The connections between Shishak and the XXIst Dynasty continued after his reign, as evidenced by the marriage of his son and heir, Orsokon I, to Psusenes II's daughter Makarere.

When during Shishak's rule the invasion of Judah occurred is a matter of contention, as are a number of other factors related to Shishak's relationship with his neighbors to the north. Kenneth Kitchen, following Albright, theorizes that this invasion was the work of a firmly entrenched ruler, twenty or so years into his reign. According to Kitchen, Shishak had been successful in a prior campaign to pacify the Cushites on Egypt's southern border and then turned his attention to Palestine, in disarray following the split of the United Kingdom of Israel.[6] He notes that it was Shishak who initially gave asylum to the exiled Jeroboam (1 Kgs 11.40), which would imply an alliance with his subsequent Northern Kingdom, Israel. However, Kitchen does not explain why Shishak invaded Israel and why he seemed concerned more with devastating Israel[7] than Judah.[8]

In contrast, Donald Redford suggests that the invasion of Judah occurred fairly soon after Shishak began to rule Egypt, citing an inscription from Karnak that calls his foray into Palestine his first great victory.[9] Redford also suggests that the Bible may not have accurately portrayed the reason for the invasion. He notes that the Egyptian role in Palestine prior to the rise the Assyrians was that of overlord. He thus suggests that the Egyptian king may have entered Palestine at the behest of Rehoboam, son of Egyptian ally Solomon, to eliminate the threat the rebellious northern kingdom posed to the stability in the region.[10] Shishak, thus, does not raid Jerusalem; and he takes the Solomonic golden shields (v. 9) as payment for services rendered to Rehoboam rather than as booty. Such a view is

Here she argues against her sources, Williamson and Dillard's commentaries, which identify Shishak as Sheshonq I the Libyan. See Japhet, *1 & 2 Chronicles*, 667; Raymond B. Dillard, *2 Chronicles* (WBC; Waco, Tex.: Word Books, 1987), 99–100; Hugh G. M. Williamson, *1 & 2 Chronicles* (NCBC; Grand Rapids: Eerdmans, 1982), 246–47.

5.   So Donald B. Redford, "Relations between Palestine and Egypt," *Journal of the American Oriental Society* 93 (1973): 3–17 (8).

6.   Kitchen, *Third Intermediate Period*, 72–76.

7.   So Kitchen, *Third Intermediate Period*, 296–300.

8.   2 Chronicles 12:4 describes the devastation of Shishak's invasion on the fortified cities of Judah. However, the archaeological record and Shishak's topographical inscription at Karnak suggest that the majority of the cities destroyed were unfortified cities in the Negev, save Aijalon. So Kitchen, *Third Intermediate Period*, 432–47.

9.   Redford, "Relations," 10.

10.   See also Redford, "Relations," 3–11. In Redford's paradigm, Egypt looked favorably on the United Monarchy, particularly during the time of David and Solomon, because Israel kept the Philistines and Transjordanians pacified, had cordial relations with Egypt's Phoenician allies, and were allied through Solomon's marriage to either Siamun or Psusennes II's daughter. In addition, Redford links the invasion of Palestine to other factors, including the void of strong charismatic leadership in the region following Solomon's death and the absence of a political alliance between the XXIInd Dynasty and Palestine. In a later article, he speculates that Shishak may have come as Jeroboam's champion; see Donald B. Redford, "Shishak," in *ABD* 5:1221–22.

not inconsistent with 2 Chr 12:8, where Judah's enduring service to Egypt is implied.[11]

This discussion of the historical background of the Chronicler's narrative is not peripheral to the matter at hand; it is necessary to understand the context. For it is Shishak who is the raison d'être for the reference to the Cushites in 2 Chr 12:3, and it is because of the general instability in the region that his army enters Palestine.

Shishak's army is notable for its ethnic composition. The Chronicler reports that the Egyptian king invaded Judah with a horde of Libyans, Sukkites, and Cushites. The first two groups need little explanation, for Shishak was the chief of the Meshwesh, a powerful tribe of Libyan warriors (Sukkites are thought to have been another Libyan group and are obvious allies for their fellow national in his present powerful position).[12] The Cushites, however, were likely included in this larger army as a result of Shishak's campaign into Cush, about which little is actually known.[13] However, their presence in this narrative is consistent with what we know about the composition of the Egyptian army: historically they were an integral component of the Egyptian military.[14]

Cushites likely remained in the general region as a military occupying force and as emissaries of the XXIInd Dynasty in the Levant, as evidenced by their occasional recurrence in the Chronicler's account (chs. 14; 16; 21).[15] The Chronicler's description of Judah in Egypt's "service" (12.8) implies that Egypt placed forces in the Levant to ensure their vassal Judah's loyalty. Here it is Judah that is subjugated by Shishak's forces, which include the Cushites. The same Cushites become the principal agents enforcing Egyptian supremacy in subsequent periods (see the discussion of chs. 14 and 21 below, Sections 4.2.1.3 and 4.2.1.5).

---

11. Cf. Redford, "Shishak"; the argument that Judean temple objects were exchanged for Egyptian military assistance is largely absent from this later Redford article.

12. Kitchen, *Third Intermediate Period*, 295 n. 291; Martin J. Selman, *2 Chronicles* (Leicester: Inter-Varsity, 1994), 373.

13. Kitchen, *Third Intermediate Period*, 293–300. Kitchen presumes that Shishak's campaign into lower Cush was intended to secure resources from the rich region and/or to resolve a border dispute. After this campaign, he thus enlisted the Cushite troops into the host mentioned in 2 Chr 12.

14. See Kitchen, *Third Intermediate Period*, 293–300; Williamson, *Chronicles*, 247. For an historical assessment of the role Cushites played in the Egyptian army, we should consider the words of Albright, who stated that "from the Sixth Dynasty on down through the Eleventh, Eighteenth, Nineteenth, and later dynasties we find that [Cushite] troops formed the backbone of the Egyptian army, however ambitious their princes may have been"; see W. F. Albright, "Egypt and the Early History of the Negeb," *JPOS* 47 (1924): 131–61 (133).

15. Redford argues against this position, stating that there is "no evidence that [Shishak] made any real attempt to secure the territory he ravaged"; Redford, "Relations," 11. However, the literary evidence of the recurring appearance of the Cushites in the Chroniclers narratives suggests that the Egyptians may have stationed them there, especially since they are known to have arrived as military agents of Egypt. This would not be unprecedented, as Albright noted: "(Cushite) garrisons placed (in the western Negeb) by the Pharaohs of the Twelfth Dynasty"; see Albright, "Egypt," 133. The persistence of a garrison of Cushites in the Negeb may represent an enduring Egyptian strategy for securing their interests in Canaan.

The Chronicler's depiction of the Cushites in 2 Chr 12 is not what we would expect if they were racially othered. They are not impotent or dominated by the Judahite community that was responsible for recording the narrative.[16] The Chronicler portrays them as part of a group having superior power and influence. Such an image of their power becomes more pronounced in the subsequent narratives, where they are not masked by their Egyptian allies, but rather participate in the narratives as the primary impetus for the stories.

*4.2.1.3. 2 Chronicles 14: Zerah's Myriads.* The term הַכּוּשִׁים occurs twice (v. 11) and the terms הַכּוּשִׁי (v. 8) and מִכּוּשִׁים (v. 12) each once in 2 Chr 14, a chapter in which Zerah serves as the commander of an awesome force with a myriad of soldiers (literally אֶלֶף אֲלָפִים, "a million") who represent a significant threat to the people of Judah. The Chronicler portrays the threat of Zerah's invading force as a cause for concern significant enough to drive King Asa to rely completely upon YHWH. The resulting narrative, recounting Asa's victory over Zerah's superior forces, reminds the audience that no matter how ferocious the foreign threat may be, YHWH is more powerful.

Zerah is unique among the Cushites in Chronicles; he alone has a name and is endowed with agency, however limited, in events unfolding in the narrative.[17] His name appears to be Hebrew, from the root זרח, meaning "to rise" or "to come forth." Knauf suggests that the name occurs in Arabian contexts, as in Hab 3:7 and Num 12:1. Zerah, he concludes, is a member of an Arabian Cushan tribe, not a Cushite from Cush proper, while the narrative was likely ahistorical.[18] Though Japhet similarly notes fictional elements in the narrative, she claims that the story reflects an historical event despite its absence from Dtr's work, which often lacks concern about military details. She concludes that the present narrative refers to a minor conflict with a local, southern foe.[19]

What does seem likely for several reasons is that the Chronicler viewed Zerah as an actual Cushite rather than a Bedouin initiating a local border dispute with Judah. First, 1 Chr 16:8 mentions the Cushites working in conjunction with the Libyans, a combination that occurs in Gen 10:13, 1 Chr 1:11, 2 Chr 12:3, and Dan 11:43. The larger literary contexts of these verses mention Egypt; the former two refer to them all as בְּנֵי חָם, an association that has political overtones,[20] and the latter two imply that Libya and Cush were subject to Egyptian hegemony. It is unlikely that Libyans unaffiliated with Egypt would have been found in southern Judah, distant from their native land. The presence of Libyans in this narrative

16. One could suggest that Shishak who led their Egyptian overlords dominated the Cushites. However, the narrative is silent on the nature of the subjugation of the Cushites by the Egyptians. Further, Judah is not portrayed as exercising any sway over these Cushites.

17. See the introduction of Reinhartz, *"Why Ask My Name?"*, 3–15, for the importance of names in biblical narratives.

18. See Ernst A. Knauf, *Midian Midian: Untersuchungen zur Geschichte Palästinas und Nordarabiens am Ende des 2. Jahrtausends v. Chr.* (Wiesbaden: Otto Harrassowitz, 1988), as well as his "Zerah," in *ABD* 6:1080–81.

19. Japhet, *1 & 2 Chronicles*, 709–10. See also Hidal, "Cush," 104–5.

20. See Section 2.2.1.3 on Gen 10.

betrays Zerah's affiliation with Egypt's XXIInd (Libyan) Dynasty. Thus, the Cushites mentioned here were likely part of a detachment of Egyptian soldiers who served alongside the Libyans.[21]

The story thus represents a reversal of the earlier account of Shishak's victory over Judah, complete with a description of the booty the Judean army takes from the conquered foe (2 Chr 12:9). A Judean victory over Egyptian forces gives theological importance to the narrative: when the Judeans trust in Y$HWH$, despite the odds, their victory over even the most powerful adversaries is assured.

Asa's conflict with Zerah should be considered in conjunction with the narrative of Shishak's invasion of Judah in the tenth century, for the events pertain to similar historical periods. Zerah's battle with Asa (ca. 897 B.C.E.)[22] would have followed Shishak's invasion too closely, implying obvious connections. Further, even if the Chronicler exaggerated the size of the invading force when he describes Zerah's 300 chariots and 1,000,000 troops, the audience would hardly have conceived of a bordering Arab band having such vast military resources, particularly chariots. Thus Zerah is likely a general serving under Shishak's son, Orsokon I.[23]

Based on this conclusion and 2 Chr 14:13–15, Albright's theory that there was a Cushite fortress near Gerar should be revisited, for a Cushite stronghold in southern Judah is implied in the Chronicler's account.[24] Despite the lack of evidence of a fortress *at* Gerar,[25] the reference to the Judeans' raid on inhabitants of the town and region סְבִיבוֹת גְּרָר (*"surrounding Gerar"*) implies that they were allied with Zerah's forces. Further, because of the explicit reference to tents in v. 15, there may have been a temporary staging ground for Zerah's attack *in the environs of Gerar*. The Philistines, who are associated with the Cushites in 2 Chr 21:16, populated the region near Gerar; this adds to the evidence for an Egyptian encampment, if not a fortress, close to Gerar.

The ability of Judah to stand up against Cushites, who represent Egyptian might, is a symbol of Y$HWH$'s fidelity to Judah. Were the Cushites not perceived as a legitimate threat or the victory not considered a miraculous occurrence over a superior foe, the event would not merit mention in the Chronicler's theologically based account.

---

21. Kitchen, *Third Intermediate Period*, 309, speculates that an elderly Orsokon sent his general Zerah to attack King Asa and return spoils to Egypt as his father Shishak (Sheshonq I) had done. This was not recorded in Egyptian annals, perhaps because of Zerah's defeat. See also Jacob M. Myers, *II Chronicles: Translation and Notes* (AB 13; Garden City, N.Y.: Doubleday, 1965), 85.

22. Selman, *2 Chronicles*, 389.

23. Selman, *2 Chronicles*, 388–89; William Johnstone, *1 & 2 Chronicles*, vol. 2, *2 Chronicles 10–36 Guilt and Atonement* (JSOTSup 253; Sheffield: Sheffield Academic Press, 1997), 62–64.

24. Albright, "Egypt," 146–47.

25. Hidal, "Cush," 100–101. Hidal correctly notes that the text does not say that Zerah began his raid from Gerar or that there was actually a fortress there. However, against his position is the observation that the inhabitants of the region are treated as enemies by the Judean forces who sack them as they did the Cushites. Though a fortress at Gerar may be speculative, an alliance with the local inhabitants and a staging ground for Zerah's attack near Gerar are implied in the narrative. See also Williamson, *1 & 2 Chronicles*, 263–65.

The one named "Cushite" in Chronicles is all but forgotten by the Chronicler; as Japhet notes, his fate is even omitted from the narrative's conclusion.[26] It is not certain that he is an historical character whose role in the narrative the Chronicler received from tradition. However, a Cushite-led force as described in this chapter is not inconsistent with what we know about the XXIInd Egyptian Dynasty and its armies. Still, it is plausible that Zerah's Cushite identity and the size of his army were emphasized in v. 8 because the "mighty-Cushite" trope was familiar to the audience. Zerah's sole role is to propel the narrative forward, demonstrating the benefits of reliance (cf. 2 Chr 14:10, נִשְׁעַנּוּ, "we have relied") on YHWH, who helps the weak against the mighty. Again, contrary to what we would expect in a racialist paradigm, it is Judah who is vulnerable and the Cushite-led forces who are mighty. Hence, Asa's victory is only possible because of YHWH's favor.

In 2 Chr 14, the Cushites are not denigrated or derided in any way. On the contrary, Zerah and his forces represent the significant military might of Egypt and are conquered not because of any defect they possess but because of YHWH's fidelity toward King Asa and the people of Judah. In fact, the Chronicler was able to perceive of Zerah, a Cushite officer, as the commander of Egypt's armies in the Levant.

### 4.2.1.4. *2 Chronicles 16: YHWH's Victory Revisited.* The term הַכּוּשִׁים occurs

once in 2 Chr 16, in v. 8. In this chapter, the Chronicler's generally favorable gaze on the life of King Asa shifts. The Chronicler relates two instances in which the reforming king Asa (2 Chr 15), previously zealous for YHWH, is now relying on humans instead of YHWH. The first offense occurs in 16:3–4, when he forms an alliance with King Ben-hadad of Aram when threatened by Israel's King Basha; the second offense, in 16:12, occurs when he relies on healers instead of YHWH to cure him of a disease in his feet. The reference to the Cushites occurs between these reversals of fortunes.

No Cushite characters are mentioned in these passages; rather, there is a reference to the victory YHWH won for Asa over the hoards of Zerah. This recollection of YHWH's victory over הַכּוּשִׁים וְהַלּוּבִים ("the Cushites and the Libyans") stands in contrast to ch. 14, where the host that attacked Judah in Asa's early years is identified simply as הַכּוּשִׁים ("the Cushites"). The inclusion of the Libyans is not inconsequential,[27] for it confirms that the Chronicler views Zerah's attack as part of an Egyptian expedition. The Libyans are the unmistakable fingerprints of the XXIInd Dynasty.[28]

This connection with the Egyptians offers firm evidence for the identity of the Cushites in both 2 Chr 14 and this chapter; they are natives of the region south of Egypt and are serving in an Egyptian expeditionary force. The Chronicler leaves little doubt that ch. 14 does not refer to Bedouin raiders from an Arabic Cushan. This conclusion is not meant to dismiss Hidal's argument that there was an

---

26. Japhet, *1 & 2 Chronicles*, 713.
27. See Section 4.2.1.3.
28. Williamson, *1 and 2 Chronicles*, 274; Myers, *II Chronicles*, 85.

Arabian Cush, for such a view does have merit in light of Hab 3:7.[29] In fact, the 2 Chr 14 account may depend on an earlier tradition regarding a border dispute with a Bedouin group. But ch. 16 indicates that a small band of local Bedouin border raiders are not Judah's antagonists. As in ch. 14, the Cushites here demonstrate YHWH's fidelity by recalling Asa's victory over a mighty army. The audience is reminded that YHWH is great precisely because only Judah's God could conquer the mighty myriad Cushite troops.

*4.2.1.5. 2 Chronicles 21: Under Cushite Authority.* The term כּוּשִׁים occurs once in 2 Chr 21, in v. 16, in a narrative that describes an encounter between a southern coalition and Jehoram, king of Judah. Because Jehoram's reign was short (848–841 B.C.E.), the confrontation can be dated to a decade in the mid-ninth century.

A close examination of this passage shows its relevance to this study. In v. 16, the coalition is said to consist of הַפְּלִשְׁתִּים וְהָעַרְבִים אֲשֶׁר עַל־יַד כּוּשִׁים. The typical translation of this phrase is "the Philistines and the Arabs who are near the (Cushites)."[30] This translation understands the prepositional construction עַל־יַד to mean "near" and sees a reference to an Arabian Cushan, following Hidal's conclusion that there was a Cush-related group in the Arabian Peninsula.[31] This is a plausible interpretation based on the probability of Cushites living in the Levant.[32]

The construction עַל־יַד also can be understood as "under the authority of" (cf. 1 Chr 25:2; 29:8; 2 Chr 26:11; 34:10, 17).[33] When the Chronicler employs the prepositional construction עַל־יַד, it is generally to demonstrate the authority of the entity that immediately follows over the entity or entities that immediately precedes it. Accepting this reading of עַל־יַד, v. 16b would read "the Philistines and the Arabs who are under the authority of the Cushites."[34]

This reading is important for understanding 2 Chr 21. First, the military coalition, often understood to consist only of Philistines and Arabs, would have consisted of Philistines, Arabs, and Cushites, with the Cushites in control of the hosts. Second, the similarity between 2 Chr 21:16 and 2 Chr 14, where Zerah the Cushite is identified as the leader of the Egyptian forces and a similar power hierarchy is in effect, is noteworthy. Third, the theological parallel to 2 Chr 12,

29. See Section 3.2.3 above.

30. See Japhet, *1 and 2 Chronicles*, 814–15; Selman, *2 Chronicles*, 436; Williamson, *1 and 2 Chronicles*, 308; Myers, *II Chronicles*, 123.

31. Hidal, "Land," 100–103. However, Selman posits a group of Arabs from far South Arabia; see Selman, *2 Chronicles*, 436. Though I do not understand this passage as a reference to an Arabic Cushan, I do argue for an Arabic Cushan in Amos 9:7; Judg 3; and Hab 3:7.

32. In addition to the sections on 2 Chronicles (Sections 4.2.1.2–4), also consider the discussion of Amos 9:7 (Section 2.2.2); Judg 3 (Section 3.2.7.1); and Hab 3:7 (Section 3.2.3).

33. See also Jer 5:31 and 33:13.

34. Johnstone (*1 and 2 Chronicles*, 113) arrives at a similar conclusion: "Others take the phrase to mean, 'who are beside the Nubians' (cf. NRSV), but a mere geographical sense seems too weak. For the meaning, 'at the direction of', see, for example 2 Chr 26:18." This is consistent with his general perception of Cushites as the "ultimate terrifying menace from the furthest extremity of Egypt, both geographically and psychologically speaking".

where the Egyptian army served as agents of YHWH's wrath against an unfaithful Judean king, is also significant. In ch. 12 YHWH punishes Rehoboam for his infidelity and in 2 Chr 21 Jehoram is likewise chastised by an Egyptian coalition. Hence, the Chronicler employs the powerful Cushites as the conduit of YHWH's wrath.

Our reading of 2 Chr 21 places it in line with other biblical passages alluding to "mighty Cushites." In fact, the account in ch. 21 is the last appearance of the powerful Egyptian league in the Chronicler's larger work.[35] In light of this, we see an *inclusio*; the first (ch. 12) and last (ch. 21) stories referencing the Egyptian league in Chronicles describe both the coalition's victory over an unfaithful Judean king and its sacking of the royal Judean coffers (12:9; 21:17). Thus, the Chronicler uses the Cushites and their allies as tropes not just of military might but also of the metaphoric sword wielded to remind YHWH's people of their responsibility to be faithful to the covenant with their God.

Furthermore, we can discern no disparagement of the Cushites in 2 Chr 21. On the contrary, they appear as leaders, not just members, of a force mightier than that of Judah. The Chronicler, however, does not provide members of this othered group with a voice or with any depth as characters. Rather, they are an undifferentiated mass that attacks the people of Judah and that is essentialized under a common ethnic tag. Still, it is not uncommon for the Chronicler to limit the voice, agency, and depth of character of Israel/Judah's enemies.

### 4.2.1.6. *Summary of Cush in Chronicles.*

Prior to the advent of Shishak, Cush is only mentioned in 1 Chr 1, an abbreviated and revised version of the Table of Nations of Gen 10. The Chronicler omits precisely the portion of the text (Gen 10:9–12) that is difficult to reconcile with the known power south of Egypt, which Hidal postulates was one of only two possible references in the Hebrew Bible to a northern Cassite Cush.[36] The Chronicler here understood the Cushites to have come from the nation to the south of Egypt, and other ocurrences of Cushites in 2 Chronicles support this hypothesis.

In 2 Chr 12, Shishak becomes a significant figure in the history of Judah, setting the stage for several centuries of subsequent Judahite reliance upon and conflict with Egypt. It is in this context that the Cushites arrive with the Libyan king of Egypt and his ethnically diverse invading army, they appear to persist in the region as an occupying presence. Their continued presence represents their enduring participation in the administration of the Egyptian Empire. Truly, they remained the "backbone of the Egyptian army."[37]

Whether or not the Cushite forces actually remained in the region as emissaries for the Egyptians is historically unclear; however, the Chronicler's version of history implies that they did. In fact, he employs them as agents of YHWH's wrath in a manner that is historically plausible, considering what is known about Egypt under the XXIInd Dynasty. The Cushites appear to be a mighty and

---

35. Save possibly 2 Chr 26:6–7, if "Gur-baal" is understood as a scribal error for "Gerar."

36. Hidal, "Cush," 97–106. The other is Gen 2:13, though this is far from certain.

37. Albright, "Egypt," 133.

dominant Egyptian warrior class, with the function in Chronicles of demonstrating the power of YHWH either to punish or to rescue Judah. The Cushites played an increasingly significant role in later periods, twice identified as agents of aggression in their own right (2 Chr 14; 21), though they were apparently linked to Egypt[38] even when the Egyptians were not explicitly named. Perhaps the XXIInd Dynasty's reliance on Cushites to oversee their interest in the Levant stems from the threat of betrayal from indigenous Egyptian troops. Despite the favor Shishak initially enjoyed in Egypt, there is evidence that there was some resentment toward the XXIInd Dynasty among native Egyptians.[39]

Though Chronicles has several references to Cushites, remarkably there is no mention of the XXVth Cushite Egyptian Dynasty. In fact, after 2 Chr 21:16, Egypt does not seem to play any role in the Chronicler's history again until Pharoah Neco is mentioned in 2 Chr 35:20, which refers to a period subsequent to the XXVth Dynasty (in the late seventh century). Why the Chronicler chose not to allude to the Cushites during the most significant period of their involvement in the affairs of the Levant remains enigmatic, particularly in the parallel narrative to 2 Kgs 19 (2 Chr 32), where Tirhakah's involvement is omitted.

Nowhere in 1 or 2 Chronicles is there a reference to any phenotypical traits of the Cushite people; the Chronicler is noticeably silent about this aspect of Cushite identity. Indeed, the author produces a relatively neutral portrayal of this Other, portraying them without disdain even though the Cushites are at all times adversaries of Judah. While Cush-related terms are mentioned eleven times in Chronicles, only one Cushite is given a personal name—and even then the Chronicler does not allow him a voice. Though they lack the agency and voice granted to the Assyrians (e.g. 2 Chr 32), they are clearly not viewed with intense acrimony and instead represented in a manner not unlike Judah's other foes. Despite the limited role Cushites play in Chronicles, they are always consequential to the unfolding of the overall narrative, either falling prey to YHWH or chastising a rebellious Judah on YHWH's behalf. The Chronicler mentions Cushites for historical reasons, and he also uses them to demonstrate YHWH's faithfulness to deliver the faithful and punish the infidel.

Ultimately, in the Chronicler's account, it is YHWH who uses the Cushites to punish Judah (ch. 12), YHWH who rescues Judah from them (ch. 14), YHWH who recalls that act of deliverance (ch. 16), and then finally YHWH who uses forces under Cushite authority to punish a wayward Judah. The Cushites, though they remain unaffected, silent, and faceless characters, are not in any manner racialized or disparaged by the Chronicler. On the contrary, they are portrayed as fierce and mighty warriors who are in command of the Egyptian expeditionary forces in Palestine and who are defeated only by the intervention of YHWH.

38. Note the presence of Libyans in the reference to the 2 Chr 14 conflict in 16:8. The Libyan presence implies the ongoing involvement of the larger Libyan Dynasty in Egypt, though Zerah, an apparent Cushite military leader, figures most prominently in the present narratives.

39. Cf. Redford, "Relations," 9. Redford notes the contempt for this foreign king felt by some native Egyptians, particularly Thebans. Hence, it may have been shrewd to employ foreign enforcers since they would be less likely to care if their Egyptian overlord was native or not.

### 4.2.2. *Cush in the Psalms*

Cush-related terms occur three times in the Psalter, in Pss 7:1, 68:32, and 87:4. In Ps 7 the term "Cush" is used as a personal name for a Benjaminite adversary of King David. In Ps 68 Cush performs a symbolic gesture of submission to YHWH. And Ps 87 is a brief but corrupt text about YHWH's involvement in the origins of several nations.

Our discussion of Psalms passages is included with post-exilic literature because of the nature of this collection. The psalms are an assortment of liturgical songs that originate in various *Sitz-im-Leben* and periods. Weiser suggests that the majority of the psalms are pre-exilic; but he also concedes that one must date them individually.[40] Sabourin, after a thorough review of the periods to which individual psalms have been assigned, determined that the majority of psalms are post-exilic.[41] Kraus suggests that there are many pre-exilic elements in the psalms but that there was considerable post-exilic redaction to individual psalms before the Psalter was canonized, ca. 300 B.C.E.[42] Thus, in light of the lack of consensus about dating individual psalms and the relatively late crystalization of the Psalter, I assign a late date to this collection of texts. Further, at least two of the texts that we consider in this section are post-exilic (Pss 68 and 87).

### 4.2.2.1. *Psalm 7: Cush the Bejaminite.* 

The term כּוּשׁ occurs once in the apparently pre-exilic[43] Ps 7, in the superscription (v. 1), within a reference to a character called כּוּשׁ בֶּן־יְמִינִי ("Cush a Benjaminite"). Except for the reference to the eponymous ancestor of the Cushites mentioned in the Table of Nations (Gen 10 and 1 Chr 1), this the only place that כּוּשׁ appears as a personal name in the Hebrew Bible. The superscription to Ps 7 is problematic for exegetes because it assumes the reader knows of an historical moment in King David's life when he interacted with an unknown character, "Cush." This event, however, is not mentioned in Dtr's or the Chronicler's histories. Scholars have sought to resolve the problem posed by the superscription in a variety of ways. Kraus, for example, suggests 7:1 refers to a tradition known by the original audience but which has been lost to us because it was not included elsewhere in the Bible.[44] Rogerson and McKay suppose that the story originated in one of the many instances when David fled from Saul's Benjaminite troops.[45] Weiser holds a more conservative

---

40. Artur Weiser, *The Psalms: A Commentary* (trans. Herbert Hartwell; Philadelphia: Westminster, 1962), 91–95.

41. Leopold Sabourin, *The Psalms: Their Origin and Meaning* (Staten Island, N.Y.: Alba House, 1969), 23–24.

42. Hans-Joachim Kraus, *Psalms 1–59: A Commentary* (trans. Hilton C. Oswald; Minneapolis: Augsburg, 1988), 68.

43. So Kraus, *Psalms 1–59*, 169; Sabourin, *Psalms*, 23. Weiser could not date this psalm based upon its content; see Weiser, *Psalms*, 130.

44. Kraus, *1–59*, 169.

45. John W. Rogerson and John W. McKay, *Psalms 1–50* (Cambridge: Cambridge University Press, 1977), 37.

position, claiming that though the incident may have been recorded in the texts, it is now impossible to associate it definitively with any known event.[46]

That this Cush could be perceived as a Bejaminite raises a few questions: (1) Was כוש used as a personal name in Judah? If so, why would a name that referred to a distinct ethnic group be given to a Judahite? (2) Does the name imply an association of the bearer with the people of Cush? (3) If not, was this appellation, known to be a secondary color term[47] employed because it described a phenotypical trait of the bearer or a quality he possessed (might, wealth, status)? (4) Does the use of the name in this context, in a psalm about an enemy, suggest that the bearer was disparaged?

One way of resolving the first question would be to posit that כוש בֶּן־יְמִינִי does not refer to a Benjaminite at all, but to a Cushite. Taken literally, this phrase means "Cush, a son of the south." The term יָמִין alludes to a southern region several times in the Hebrew Bible (e.g. 1 Sam 23:19, 24; 2 Kgs 23:13). In fact, יָמִין in Ps 89:13 can be so understood. Yet, in order to interpret v. 1 as a reference to "Cush, a son of the south," the text should be emended to read כוש בֶּן־יָמִין.

With this understanding of v. 1, two elements in the psalm merit our attention. The first is found in v. 3: פֶּן־יִטְרֹף כְּאַרְיֵה נַפְשִׁי פֹּרֵק וְאֵין מַצִּיל ("lest he rend me as a lion, dividing [me] and there is no rescuer"). This image of a lion may be a simile for a Cushite, for Cush was the supplier of exotic fauna to the ancient Near Eastern world.[48] Hence, associating the ferocity and might of the lion to a Cushite would be fitting.

The second element is the reference in v. 13 to warrior imagery—יִלְטוֹשׁ קַשְׁתּוֹ דָּרַךְ ("he has bent his bow")—and the subsequent allusion to חִצָּיו ("his arrows") in v. 14. Cushites were associated with bows by the Egyptians and were considered fierce warriors in part because of their military prowess with this weapon. As a result, the Egyptians called the region of Cush, "the Land of Bow."[49] If Cush in the context of Ps 7 is identified as a "son of the south," then these references suggest that the author was familiar with the reputation of Cush as a source of exotic fauna and as a region known for its skillful archers. Though the emendation of the text to read, "Cush, a son of the south," provides us with promising interpretive options for this psalm, there may be better ways to understand it.

Hutton proposes an interpretation of this psalm based on his understanding of the phrase עַל־דִּבְרֵי־כוּשׁ בֶּן־יְמִינִי, meaning "concerning the words of Cush a Benjaminite." He views this as an allusion to the story in 2 Sam 18 (cf. Section 3.2.7.2) about הַכּוּשִׁי ("the Cushite"), the courtier who informed King David

---

46. Weiser, *Psalms*, 134.

47. Brenner, *Colour Terms*, 42.

48. Cf. Peter L. Shinnie, "Trade Routes of the Ancient Sudan 3,000 BC–AD 350," in *Egypt and Africa: Nubia from Prehistory to Islam* (ed. Winifred V. Davies; London: British Museum, 1991), 49–50; Jean Leclant, "Egypt in Sudan: The New Kingdom," in *Sudan: Ancient Kingdoms of the Nile* (ed. Dietrich Wildung; Paris: Flammarion, 1997), 119–27 (124).

49. Hays, "Cushites . . . History," 270–71; Derek A. Welsby, *The Kingdom of Kush: The Napatan and Meroitic Empires* (Princeton, N.J.: Markus Wiener, 1998), 7.

about Absalom's demise. His reading is consistent with the LXX, which offers Χουσι for the Hebrew כּוּשׁ. Focusing on the term דִּבְרֵי ("words"), Hutton proposes that the "words" of the הַכּוּשִׁי ("Cushite"), reporting to King David concerning the death of his heir apparent Absalom, inspired this psalm.[50]

Hutton's hypothesis poses more problems than it solves. Identifying this character "Cush" with another who had no name and who is identified only by a gentilic, "Cushi," meaning "the national from Cush,"[51] is only one dilemma. Further, Hutton's hypothesis ignores the tension caused by the man being both called a Cushite and Benjaminite. Also, information in the superscription to Ps 7 bears little resemblance to David's crisis in 2 Sam 18. The psalmist does not appear to be lamenting the loss of a beloved though disloyal son, but rather seeks to escape a persistent enemy. In the end, Hutton's hypothesis is unconvincing.

One relevant aspect of his argument, however, is that Hutton sees Cush as a member of the tribe of Benjamin. If "Cush" is a signifier of ethnicity, it would mean that a Cushite lived among the people of Israel.[52] However, Hays, who acknowledges that the initial audience of this psalm would have been familiar with Cushites, argues that if the bearer of the name was neither ethnically Cushite nor of mixed Cushite-Judean heritage, the name was likely given to him because of the "positive reputation of that nation."[53]

To understand this "Cush" we must consider some details of the psalm. As Weiser reminds us, the petitioner in this psalm is "shaken by a mortal terror" because of an enemy likened to a "ravening beast of prey."[54] This image is one that dehumanizes the opponent. Still, the dehumanization does not necessarily imply a racialist perspective. Such tactics are not uncommon in descriptions of enemies (e.g. Cushan-rishathaim in Judg 3:8–10; Eglon in Judg 3:12–30; Ish-bosheth in 2 Sam 2–4). In fact, by defining this "Cush" as a Benjaminite, the psalmist does not question his humanity: he is identified as an Israelite and his personhood is reaffirmed. David's enmity towards Cush the Benjaminite is likely based solely on the fact that they found themselves on opposing sides in a political struggle for power between David and Saul, not because of any other aspect of his identity.

So who was this Cush? The superscription of Zephaniah (see Zeph 1:1 and Section 3.2.2.1) and the mention of Yehudi in Jeremiah (see Jer 36:14 and

---

50. Hutton, "Cush," 123–37.

51. Save in 2 Sam 18:21, where he may be called simply כּוּשִׁי, meaning "Cushite." However, the courtier here is identified not by a name, but only by a gentilic designation in each instance. See Section 3.2.7.2.

52. George A. F. Knight, *Psalms*, vol. 1 (Philadelphia: Westminster, 1982). Knight notes on p. 39 that "the name *Cush* may refer to someone from the Sudan, and so, perhaps, to a black man. If this is correct, then he was evidently accepted quite happily as one of the tribe of Benjamin. The Hebrews seem to have been completely free of all colour-consciousness." Though I would point out Knight's uncritical acceptance of modern "racial" typologies and the perhaps overly optimistic supposition that Cushites were accepted "quite happily" based on the anguished appeal of the petitioner in this psalm, I would concur with his general assessment of Hebrew color-consciousness.

53. Hays, "Cushites . . . Bible," 407.

54. Weiser, *Psalms*, 136.

Section 3.2.5.2), supply other Israelite/Judean characters whose names include Cush-related terms. In light of Lipiński's conclusion[55] that the name "Cushi" gained prominence in eighth- and seventh-century Palestine, at the precise moment when Cush was most prominent in Levantine politics, we could conclude that Cush-related names were not uncommon in Israel/Judah. Such names likely came into popular use as terms of honor that defined the character of the person who bore the name, suggesting that the individual was mighty, or merited respect.[56] Whether the phenomena of Cush-related naming was widely practiced as early as the tenth century is not clear. Nor can we preclude the possibility that this "Cush" was an ethnic Cushite while also being an ethnic Israelite from the Tribe of Benjamin. What is clear is that in the imagination of Israelite/Judahite authors and audiences, a man from the tribe of Benjamin could have a name that recalled the glory of the southern Other, Cush.

4.2.2.2. *Psalm 68: Yahwists from Cush.* The term כוּשׁ occurs once in this Ps 68 in v. 32. Psalm 68 is a Psalm of Praise[57] that extols the mighty acts of אֱלֹהִים ("God"),[58] principally for his victories during the exodus, but also for God's continued sustenance of Israel. Although there is no consensus about the date of Ps 68, most exegetes acknowledge that it contains very ancient traditions.[59] Kraus presents the most nuanced dating, suggesting that the majority of the verses are pre-exilic and northern, but that v. 29 is later because it refers to Jerusalem and vv. 30 and following are definitely post-exilic[60] because of their concern for nations praising Israel's God.

There is a considerable amount of corruption in Ps 68, especially in v. 32, part of a section that Knight deems the "most notorious in the whole Bible."[61] The phrase יֶאֱתָיוּ חַשְׁמַנִּים מִנִּי מִצְרָיִם כּוּשׁ תָּרִיץ יָדָיו לֵאלֹהִים, which the NRSV translates "Let bronze be brought from Egypt; let Ethiopia hasten to stretch out its hands to God," is particularly difficult. The first portion of this verse is problematic for a variety of reasons: the word יֶאֱתָיוּ ("they will come") is relatively rare; and the *hapax legomenon* חַשְׁמַנִּים has perplexed translators. The latter has been translated as "bronze"[62] (NRSV) or "princes" (KJV), concepts that are unrelated.

---

55. Lipiński, Review of Kapelrud, 689.

56. Cf. Reinhartz, *"Why Ask My Name?"*, 6–7.

57. Actually, Ps 68 likely represents a number of very early selections from a variety of different psalms that were later redacted into a single psalm; so Knight, *Psalms* 1:305–6. Weiser even suggests that it may be a collection of the first lines of a variety of ancient psalms; see Weiser, *Psalms*, 481–83.

58. Elohim is the general designation for God in Ps 68, though the name יָהּ ("Yah") is used once, in v. 5.

59. Weiser, *Psalms*, 481–83, notes that this psalm contains ancient cultic traditions; others suggest that it is likely pre-exilic. See Arnold A. Anderson, *The Book of Psalms*, vol. 1, *1–72* (Paulton: Purnell & Sons, 1972), 482; Sabourin, *Psalms*, 23.

60. Hans-Joachim Kraus, *Psalms 60–150: A Commentary* (Minneapolis: Augsburg, 1989), 51.

61. Knight, *Psalms* 1:315. Also Kraus, *Psalms 60–150*, 47; Rogerson and McKay, *Psalms 51–100*, 82.

62. LePeau suggests that the term חַשְׁמַנִּים is an Egyptian loan-word from *hsmn*. He argues that the word was transliterated in Hebrew with the meaning "bronze"; see John Philip LePeau, "Psalm 68:

Emendations might resolve the problem posed by חַשְׁמַנִּים. The initial consonant could be changed to ה, yielding הַשְׁמֹנִים ("the eighty"), but this does not provide any more clarity. Or, the initial ח could be dropped, yielding שְׁמָנִים, implying either "fatness" suggesting "richness" (cf. Isa 25:6; 28:1, 4), or special oils (cf. Amos 6:6). Dahood suggest that the term is an Egyptian transliteration of the Akkadian *hasmanu* meaning "blue cloth."[63]

Perhaps the most satisfactory emendation would be to suppose the intended term to be חָשִׁים ("swift ones"), related to the root חוּשׁ.[64] "Swift ones" in this context would refer to speedy emissaries sent forth from Egypt with messages for Jerusalem, like the designation for emissaries in Isa 18, where they are called מַלְאָכִים קַלִּים ("swift messengers").[65] Such a reconstruction fits with the LXX, which has πρέσβεις, the typical plural from of πρέσβευτης, meaning "ambassadors." Hence, the text might read "let ambassadors come from Egypt."

This particular solution has merit because it links thematically the first and second stichoi of v. 32. The second stichos, that which refers to Cush, also has a reference to haste. It reads כּוּשׁ תָּרִיץ יָדָיו לֵאלֹהִים ("O Cush, let his hands hasten to God").[66] The outstretched Cushite arms likely are a symbol of Cushite submission to Yнwн, but this does not preclude the idea that the Cushites' arms are outstretched bearing gifts.[67] In this scenario both these "great" southern powers are depicted making haste to the Temple in Jerusalem to "bring their offerings peacefully and willingly" to Yнwн, the sovereign of the world.[68] As Copher aptly remarks, "true universalism will have been achieved when these two nations come to accept Yahweh as their deity."[69] Reverent people from Cush appear in Isa 18:7 (see Section 2.2.3.2) and Zeph 3:10 (see Section 3.2.2.3).

This passage has important implications. One is that people from Cush were perceived within the scope of Yahwism. This psalm calls on kings of various nations (vv. 30 and 33) to recognize the greatness of Judah's deity and make pilgrimages to Jerusalem to worship Yнwн. Of all the nations that the psalmist could have chosen to represent this burgeoning Yahwism, only two are identified; and Cush is one of them.

The Cushites are also employed in this psalm to emphasize Yнwн's greatness by having these mighty southern powers, who have been the sovereigns of great lands, submit themselves in reverent posture, with arms extended, before Judah's

---

An Exegetical and Theological Study" (Ph.D. diss., Graduate College of the University of Iowa, 1981), 214.

63. Mitchell Dahood, *Psalms*, vol. 2, *51–100: Introduction, Translation, and Notes* (AB 17; Garden City, N.Y.: Doubleday, 1968), 150.

64. The editor of *BHS* suggests this reading.

65. See Section 2.2.3.2.

66. LePeau suggests that there is a gender agreement problem in the phrase כּוּשׁ תָּרִיץ יָדָיו לֵאלֹהִים, since he claims that Cush is feminine in this construction and that the suffix on יָדָיו ("his hands") is masculine; see LePeau, "Psalm 68," 214–15. However, I suggest that Cush is masculine, as is attested by its use in the patronymics in Gen 10 and 1 Chr 1, and that the feminine subject of the verb is likely the "hands." Hence we could translate the phrase: "Cush; let his hands hasten to God."

67. Copher, "Africans," 174–75.

68. Knight, *Psalms* 1:315.

69. Copher, "Africans," 177–78.

God. Far from denigrating Cush, this passage implicitly confirms its prominence. The psalmist does not prohibit Cushites from entering into the most intimate act of the Judahites, Yahwism. Were Egypt and Cush nations of no account, it would not be remarkable that they would be submitting to Judah's God. However, because of their history of dominance and might, the image of great nations bowing before the God of a vassal state has great rhetorical power. Again, we can infer the commonplace understanding of Cush as a mighty and potent nation from this biblical passage.

**4.2.2.3. *Psalm 87: Cush was Born There.*** The term כּוּשׁ occurs once in Ps 87, in v. 4. This enigmatic text is also fraught with structural problems, which obscure the message.[70] The psalm, which apparently emphasizes Jerusalem as the legitimate birthplace for Judeans throughout the Diaspora,[71] appears to be post-exilic because of the dispersal pattern of exiled Judeans in such far away places as Babylon and Cush.[72] The eschatological emphasis on the universal worship of YHWH by these nations in toto or proselytes from their midst also supports a post-exilic date.[73]

Psalm 68 has a number of other difficulties besides the structural ones. The mention of רַהַב ("Rahab") in v. 4 poses problems. This may be a reference to the ferocious and oppressive dragon of Canaanite mythology: YHWH slaughters Rahab as a creative act in Job 26:12 and Ps 89:11. Rahab could be a metaphor for Egypt, as in Isa 30:7 and 51:9. The latter interpretation is more plausible because v. 4 mentions Rahab in conjunction with other nations, including Cush,[74] which is frequently mentioned with Egypt. The absence of Egypt in this verse would be remarkable because of its pivotal role in the history of Israel/Judah.[75]

---

70. Many have suggested that the order of this chapter in the MT complicates the interpretive process. Knight recognized that the MT begins with a pronoun with no antecedent, implying that there must have been an alteration in the original order; see George A. F. Knight, *Psalms*, vol. 2 (Philadelphia: Westminster, 1983), 182. Kraus addresses the structural problems by reorganizing the psalm in the following order: vv. 1a, 2, 1b, 5b, 7, 3, 6a, 4b/6b, 4a, and 5a; see Kraus, *Psalms 60–150*, 185. Weiser took a more conservative approach to his reorganization of the psalm, critiquing those who have transformed it into a "jigsaw puzzle." He proposes reading in this order: vv. 1, 2, 3, 6, 4, 5, 7; see Weiser, *Psalm 60–150*, 579. Anderson suggests that this is one of the most problematic of the psalms, though he retains the order of the MT; see Arnold A. Anderson, *The Book of Psalms*, vol. 2, *73–150* (Paulton: Purnell & Sons, 1972), 618.

71. In fact, Anderson suggests that it belongs to a group of psalms deemed Hymns of Zion, including Pss 46, 48, 76, 84, 122, 137; see A. Anderson, *Psalms* 2:618–19.

72. So Kraus, *Psalms 60–150*, 188. Anderson suggests that the reference in v. 2 to the "dwelling places of Jacob" may be a reference to the Samaritan schism; see A. Anderson, *Psalms* 2:619.

73. For an earlier date, see Dahood, *Psalms*, vol. 2, *51–100*, 298. Dahood suggests that the psalm may be seventh or sixth century B.C.E., during or after the period of XXVth Egyptian Dynasty, because of the psalmist's knowledge of Cushites and the absence of Assyrians from the nation list.

74. See the discussion of Amos 9:7 (Section 2.2.2). Though a Cush-related people who have migrated to Canaan appear to be the subject of that verse, such a reading is unlikely for the Cush term in this instance because: (1) the term used is כּוּשׁ, a term which is not a derivative or differentiated term as in Amos 9:7 or Hab. 3:7; (2) people are described in relation to God and God's mountain, not to the disparate places whence nations came.

75. John Day, "Rahab (Dragon)," in *ABD* 4:610–11.

What is the point of this psalm? One possibility is that all the nations of the world trace their origin to Jerusalem. As Knight points out, "the straightforward meaning of the text suggests nations, and not Jews exiled among nations" are its subjects.[76] This emphasizes the universal worship of YHWH by all the nations of the world, here represented by host of former enemies who have become יֹדְעָי ("acquaintances", v. 4) or even "friends" of YHWH. But the relationship is more intimate than friendship, for YHWH, in symbolic adoption, declares that they are each born in Zion. According to Dahood, though they were "born abroad, these converts to Yahwism will become citizens of the spiritual metropolis Zion."[77] No longer do the nations owe their allegiance to their homelands; they are citizens of Jerusalem.

Other interpretations are also possible. If the subjects are Diaspora Judeans, then the psalm reminds them that Zion is their actual birthplace, the place that demands their ultimate loyalty.[78] Psalm 87 thus reminds Judean Yahwists who dwell in other nations that they owe their allegiance to Jerusalem.

Another interpretation, offered by Weiser, posits that the subjects of this psalm are foreign proselytes who have come to the Temple for worship, perhaps for a pilgrimage festival. The psalm is uttered by one of the pilgrims at the gathering of Yahwists from many nations.[79]

Kraus and Weiser's positions are both plausible. In either case, the psalmist does not belittle Cush. If Weiser is correct and this psalm refers to proselytes, then the representation of Cush in this passage is similar to his representation of other Others. The people of Judah, not unlike the people of various nations, even Cush, have a place of origin. Cush and the rest of this assembly know YHWH, another badge of respect or recognition of their extensive history of conflict with Judah's God. In this way the psalm would resemble Amos 9:7 (Section 2.2.2), for YHWH is associated with the founding and establishing of various nations.

According to Kraus' interpretation, the text may indicate that the exile extended as far as Cush. Judean exiles found a home there and could be identified simply as "Cush," indicating that there was no stigma associated with this term. Not only could Cushites integrate into Judah,[80] but also Judeans could find a home among Cushites and be identified as Cushites.

4.2.2.4. *Summary of Cush in the Psalms.* Although we cannot detect a common thread that connects the Psalms references to Cush, Pss 68 and 87 appear to assert YHWH's lordship over all nations, including the Cushites, Ps 87 suggests YHWH's sovereignty over the origins of citizens of other nations, and Ps 68 predicts YHWH's future sovereignty over their end. Foreigners will come bearing

---

76. Knight, *Psalms* 2:183.

77. Dahood, *Psalms*, vol. 2, *51–100*, 300.

78. Kraus, *Psalms 60–150*, 188. However, Anderson cautions us against excluding proselytes from this assembly of dispersed Yahwists. A. Anderson, *Psalms* 2:619.

79. Cf. Knight, *Psalms* 2:71–74; see Weiser, *Psalms*, 580–81.

80. See Num 12; 2 Sam 18; and Jer 38–39 for explicit references to Cushites dwelling among the people of Israel/Judah.

fine gifts for Judah's God. Psalm 7 acknowledges YHWH's lordship and uses Cush as a personal name for a Benjaminite. The superscription of this psalm suggests that Israelites may have employed a name that honored Cushites, or that there were Cushites who had integrated into the tribe of Benjamin as early as the tenth century B.C.E.

### 4.2.3. *Daniel 11: Egypt's Assets*

The term וְכֻשִׁים occurs once in Dan 11, in v. 43. Daniel 11 contains one of the many complex narratives in the book that combine historical accounts with material that is inconsistent with historical records. As Towner notes, the "scenario described in 11:40–45 simply never transpired."[81] In fact, contemporary scholars even consider Daniel to be a legendary retrojection, composed between the exile and the early Hasmonean period. However, they also concede that many of the narratives are dependent on earlier traditions and sources, such as the document concerning Nabonidus found at Qumran (4QPrNab).[82] Lacocque has found in the details of the apocalyptic prophecy in Dan 11 an assortment of themes borrowed from Isa 10:5–34, 31:8–9, and Ezek 38–39, forming a collage of recycled eschatological imagery.[83]

The occasion for the reference to "Cushites" is a discussion of the end of time, when a mythic king will come and wreak havoc among the southern nations. Scholars generally agree, based upon a correlation of events in the prophecy with the historical record, that the king represented in this text is Antiochus IV, also known as Antiochus Epiphanes.[84] This brutal Seleucid ruler (175–164 B.C.E.), who attacked Jerusalem in 169 and 167 B.C.E., exterminated much of the male population, and sought to destroy all vestiges of the Jewish cult.[85] He is described in v. 43 as one who will rule לֻבִים וְכֻשִׁים בְּמִצְעָדָיו ("Libyans and Cushites in his wake/steps"). That is, he will conquer Egypt, take possession of the wealth of the land, and then the Libyans and the Cushites will follow in his "steps." The NRSV translates the passage "he shall become ruler of the treasures of gold and of silver, and all the riches of Egypt; and the Libyans and the Ethiopians shall follow in his train." Note here the addition of the verbal quality, perhaps implied

---

81. W. Sibley Towner, *Daniel* (Atlanta: John Knox, 1984), 164.

82. John J. Collins, "Daniel, Book of," in *ABD* 2:29–37 (30).

83. André Lacocque, *The Book of Daniel* (trans. David Pellauer; Atlanta: John Knox, 1979), 232.

84. Bright, *History*, 417–27; Paul M. Lederach, *Daniel* (Scottdale, Pa.: Herald Press, 1994), 251; Norman W. Porteous, *Daniel: A Commentary* (Philadelphia: Westminster, 1965), 165–71. Proposing a modified version of this hypothesis, Van Henten, following Jürgen C. H. Lebram, suggests that though the focal character is Antiochus IV, much of his description in Daniel is derived from "older representations of typical figures derived from different sources"; see Jan W. Van Henten, "Antiochus IV as a Typhonic Figure in Daniel 7," in *The Book of Daniel in Light of New Findings* (ed. Adam S. Van Der Woude; Leuven: Leuven University Press, 1993), 223–43 (233).

85. John Whitehorne, "Antiochus," in *ABD* 1:269–72 (270). See also Otto Morkholm, *Antiochus IV of Syria* (Copenhagen: Gyldendal, 1966); David S. Russell, *Jews from Alexander to Herod* (London: Oxford University Press, 1967); Avigdor Tcherikover, *Hellenistic Civilization and the Jews* (trans. S. Applebaum; Philadelphia: Jewish Publication Society of America, 1959).

by the use of the noun with affixed preposition and pronoun, בְּמִצְעָדָיו, that literally means, "in (by or with) his steps."[86]

There is no evidence that Antiochus ever conquered Egypt or Cush.[87] So why were Cush and Libya incorporated into this prophecy about Egypt? Keil suggests that the Cushites and Libyans represented all of the allies of the Egyptians, which may also be the case in Ezek 30:5 and Nah 3:9.[88] Heaton suggests that they are included to describe the furthest limits of Egypt on the south and west.[89] Lacocque speculates that they were mentioned as those under Egypt's yoke and that Antiochus would be a liberator to them.[90] While the former two suggestions are plausible, the latter is historically inaccurate. Cush and Libya appear in other oracles against Egypt.[91] Their continued presence in the armies of the Egyptians predates the XXIInd Egyptian Dynasty and likely indicates the composition of the Egyptian armies known by Judean authors. If Egypt were to be attacked, they would be expected to participate in its defense.

Daniel 11:43 speaks of Antiochus' subjugation of the Cushites and the Libyans. They are included in this text because of their close association with the Egyptians. But in this text, they appear to function less as conquered soldiers do, inasmuch as they are associated with the Egyptians' gold, silver, and desirable goods. I suggest that they are in v. 43 listed among Egypt's assets. Such an assessment has both favorable and unpleasant consequences. Positively, this passage demonstrates the significance of Cush, whether as allies or as mercenaries to Egypt's success.

However, the commodification of Cush and Libya effaces their humanity, making them akin to other items of great worth.[92] Unlike other instances where Cushites were to be enslaved or placed in chains and led away (Isa 43; 45), this passage is ambiguous, perhaps suggesting that they may become soldiers in Antiochus' army. Still, the Cushites are not treated as human beings, but as war booty from a campaign into Egypt destined for failure. In some ways this passage is reminiscent of Isa 43:1–7 (Section 3.2.4.1) and Isa 45:14 (cf. Section 3.2.4.2), where the prophet assigns to Cush and several of its allies a similar fate. However, it was ultimately YHWH who was the agent seeking obeisance in those Deutero-Isaianic passages. In this instance, the commodification of Cush and Libya is unmitigated by an appeal to YHWH's sovereignty, for the Cushites and

86. The only verb in this verse is וּמָשַׁל ("and he will rule"), which is found in the first stichos. Though the first and second stichoi are separated by an *athnach*, the force of the verb מָשַׁל seems to govern to Lybia and Cush.

87. Lacocque, *Daniel*, 232; Porteous, *Daniel*, 169.

88. Carl F. Keil, *The Book of the Prophet Daniel* (trans. Matthew G. Easton; Edinburgh: T. & T. Clark, 1891), 472.

89. Eric W. Heaton, *The Book of Daniel: Introduction and Commentary* (London: SCM Press, 1956), 239.

90. However, this perspective was historically inaccurate since Cush was an independent nation during the second century B.C.E.; see Lacocque, *Daniel*, 233.

91. See Isa 43:3; 45:14; Jer 46:9; Ezek 29:10; 30:4, 5, 9.

92. Perhaps such a notion of commidification inspired Lacocque's hypothesis that Cush and Libya would look to Antiochus Epiphanes as their liberator from Egyptian hegemony; see Lacocque, *Daniel*, 233.

Libyans are treated as property that will pass from the hand of the Egyptians to Antiochus.

Two propositions might qualify this understanding of the role the Cushites and Libyans play in this text. First, perhaps the Cushites and Libyans in this passage are not meant to denote the entire nation, especially because Antiochus never conquered Cush; rather, they may be a group of Cushites closely associated with the Egyptians. Second, this passage refers to the fate of Cushite and Libyan mercenaries serving in the Egyptian army. In this view the commodification of the Cushites and Libyans is slightly more palatable, for Antiochus' acquisition of these soldiers may represent a change in their employers rather than a forfeiture of their humanity.[93]

However, this view does not completely sanitize this text, which remains one of the most difficult and problematic in this study. Though we can confidently argue against a system of racialist ideology informing the author of Daniel, we still recognize an implied hierarchy of humanity in this passage, whereby Cushites and Libyans can be treated as property to be acquired as spoils of war. However, this constituent element of racialist thought does not appear to be connected with any larger schema based upon phenotype or peculiar behavioral traits; and it does not single out Cushites for special abuse. Here the Cushites, Libyans, and Egyptians, though a powerful trio of nations, are once again portrayed enduring defeat together.

### 4.2.4. *Esther 1 and 8: The End of the World*

The phrase וְעַד־כּוּשׁ ("and unto Cush") occurs once in Esth 1:1 and once in 8:9. Scholars generally agree that Esther was composed in the post-exilic period, and usually date it as early as the fifth century or as late as the second. For example, Stiehl suggests that the book is very late (165–140 B.C.E.) because of similarities to Daniel and Judith and because it contains Elamite vocabulary.[94] Baldwin concludes that it is late fifth to early fourth century because of its use of Persian words and its knowledge of Artaxerxes.[95] White claims that it was composed as late as the early fourth century because it lacks accurate details of Persian history and that it was written prior to the Hellenistic period because it has a positive view of a foreign king.[96] However, Moore makes the most compelling argument. Taking into consideration many of the factors noted in the works of other scholars, Moore proposes that Esther was probably composed in phases, with the first edition in the late fourth century and the final edition early in the Hellenistic period.[97]

---

93. Pertaining to the capture of soldier from opposing armies, note Sennacherib's statement after his victory at Eltekeh, that he "personally captured alive the Egyptian charioteers with the(ir) princes and (also) the charioteers of the king of Ethiopia"; see Oppenheim, "Sennacherib," 200.

94. Ruth Stiehl, "Das Buch Esther," in *Studies in the Book of Esther* (ed. Carey A. Moore; New York: Ktav, 1982), 249–67.

95. Joyce G. Baldwin, *Esther: An Introduction and Commentary* (Leicester: Inter-Varsity, 1984), 48–49.

96. Sidnie Ann White, "Esther," in *The Women's Bible Commentary* (Carol A. Newsome and Sharon H. Ringe, eds.; Louisville, Ky.: Westminster John Knox, 1992), 124–29 (124–25).

97. Carey A. Moore, "Esther, Book of," in *ABD* 2:633–43 (641).

Cush is used in Esther to convey the extent of the empire of King Ahasuerus of Persia. The two references provide a glimpse of the perceived geography of the ancient world, which was understood to extend from the region of Cush in the southwestern extreme to as far away as הֹדּו ("India") in the northeast.[98]

These brief references are significant. They indicate that the region of Cush was understood to refer to the land south of Egypt. Any of the other proposed regions for Cush's location, that is, a northern Cush or an Arabian Cush, would preclude significant regions of the known world. The former would exclude the Levant itself and all regions south of it from King Ahasuerus' purview, and the latter would exclude Egypt. Significant portions of the known world would be beyond Ahasuerus' dominion, a notion contrary to the author's intent.

The author of Esther located Cush at the outer limit of the world;[99] the region beyond was either an utter mystery, or it played such a limited role in international politics that it did not merit mention. Cush functions in Esther as it does in Gen 2:13 (cf. Section 2.2.1.1) and Zeph 3:10 (cf. Section 3.2.2.3).

If Cush symbolized the extreme end of the world, it is surprising that the people were not more definitively othered. After all, coming from the end of the earth and having an appearance and culture that differ from the Judeans would supply ample opportunity for ethnographic comparisons between the two groups. Also, the distance and differences would alienate this people living at the edge of the world. Yet, as with phenotypical differences, the Judeans never seemed to emphasize the differences between the Cushites and themselves.[100] Perhaps Cushites were in close enough proximity to and had an extensive history of affiliation with Judah to preclude such a perspective of distant, hence strange, Other from developing.

### 4.2.5. *Job 28: The Chrysolite of Cush*

The term כּוּשׁ occurs once in Job, in v. 19 of ch. 28. This book has been notoriously difficult to date principally because it contains no references to historical events. Tur-Sinai suggests, based on linguistic evidence, that the text was originally composed in Aramaic during the exile and latter translated into Hebrew during the period when Ezra–Nehemiah was composed.[101] Good and Habel both suggest that some elements of the book are pre-exilic, while the complete text is

---

98. Cf. Baldwin, "Esther," 55–56. Baldwin suggests that the region identified as "India" should actually be understood as modern Pakistan and that the southern extent of Egypt was the end of Persia's domain, at the border of Cush.

99. Baldwin, "Esther," 55–56. Also note George Lawson, "Discourses on the Whole Book of Esther," in *Expositions of Ruth and Esther* (ed. George Lawson and Alexander Carson; Evansville, Ind.: Sovereign Grace Publishers, 1960), 1–331 (153). In this text Carson describes the vast portion of the earth encompassed by the boundary markers "India" and "Cush."

100. Again, see Jer 13:23 (Section 3.2.5.1). Note that even when we would expect Hebrew authors to attend to the differences in phenotype between Judeans and Cushites, such differences are virtually ignored.

101. Naphtali H. Tur-Sinai, *The Book of Job: A New Commentary* (Jerusalem: Kiryath Sepher, 1967), XXXVII–XXXVIII.

post-exilic.[102] Crenshaw agrees with Rowley that the text should be dated to the fifth century.[103]

The mention of Cush comes in a metaphorical comparison in ch. 28 showing that wisdom is a priceless asset that is difficult to acquire. Mines for precious metals and gems are hidden from animals but can be searched out by human beings and their wealth can be exploited. But no mine can be found for wisdom, and human beings can neither identify its source nor match its worth. The source of wisdom remains the purview of God alone.

Verses 15–19 feature a rhetorical strategy in which a list of precious commodities is compared to wisdom. Gold, silver, jewels, coral, and pearls are all far less valuable than wisdom. In v. 19, Cush is said to be the source of פִּטְדַת ("chrysolite")[104] and possibly כֶּתֶם טָהוֹר ("pure gold").

Cush is one of two place-names mentioned in this list as a source of a luxury item. The other is Ophir, a region thought to have been either in eastern Africa or on the opposite shore of the Red Sea on the Arabian Peninsula.[105] In the Hebrew Bible Ophir is the source of many exotic and costly items, including fine wood, a distinctive pure gold, and precious stones.[106] It is also mentioned on an eighth-century ostracon from Tell Qasile,[107] which appears to be a list of goods and reads, "gold of Ophir to Beth-horon. 30 shekels."[108] That Cush is one of two sources of luxury items in this list indicates that the name, "Cush," like Ophir, was associated with high quality precious goods.

Cush as the source of valuable "gifts" appears in Isa 18:7 (Section 2.2.3.2), Zeph 3:10 (Section 3.2.2.3), and probably Ps 68:32 (Section 4.2.2.2). The nature of these "gifts" is not provided in the Hebrew Bible. However, we do know that Cush supplied Egypt and the larger Near Eastern world with many exotic commodities, including "wood, ivory, perfumes, ostrich feathers, leopard skins and precious stones."[109] Cush was also known for its fine and abundant supplies of gold,[110] sub-Saharan African goods,[111] and horses.[112] Thus the people of the

---

102. Edwin M. Good, *In Turns of Tempest: A Reading of Job with a Translation* (Stanford, Calif.: Stanford University Press, 1990), 4–5; Norman C. Habel, *The Book of Job: A Commentary* (Philadelphia: Westminster, 1985), 40–42.

103. James C. Crenshaw, "Job, Book of," in *ABD* 3:858–68; H. H. Rowley, *Job* (Grand Rapids: Eerdmans, 1980), 21–23. Rowley also suggests that Job may even be late fifth century.

104. The NRSV favors "chrysolite" to translate the Hebrew term פִּטְדַת. Others choose to translate פִּטְדַת as "topaz", following the LXX's τοπάζιον, found in Job 28:19 as well as in Exod 28:17 and Ezek 28:13. Both interpretations affirm that the word פִּטְדַת refers to an exotic precious stone valued in the ancient Near East. See Habel, *Job*, 391; Rowley, *Job*, 183. Hidal suggests, following Ludwig Kohler, that פִּטְדַת is actually a loan-word from the Sanskrit word for "yellow," *pita*; see Hidal, "Cush," 99.

105. Cf. David W. Baker, "Ophir," in *ABD* 6:26–27; Robert North, "Ophir/Parvaim and Petra/ Joktheel," *Proceedings of the World Congress of Jewish Studies* 4 (1967): 197–202.

106. 1 Kings 9:28; 10:11; 22:49; 2 Chr 8:18; 9:10; Job 22:24; Ps 45:10; and Isa 13:12.

107. Benjamin Maisler, "Two Hebrew Ostraca from Tell Qasile," *JNES* 10 (1951): 265–67.

108. Maisler, "Ostraca," 266.

109. Hays, "Black . . . History," 276; Shinnie, "Trade," 49.

110. Hays, "Black . . . History," 275; Shinnie, "Trade," 51.

111. Shinnie, "Trade," 51.

ancient world likely considered Cush to be a bounteous land, rich with rare goods. Hence, when Cush is mentioned in Job 28:19, it qualifies the "chrysolite" as the finest of its kind.

Though the nature of a nation's goods does not necessarily reflect the status of the people who live there, clearly no attempt is made to diminish the importance of Cush. Rather, like the others of this type, Cush is represented as a wealthy nation that provided extravagant "gifts" to the larger world.

### 4.3. *Summary: Cush in Post-Exilic Hebrew Literature*

#### 4.3.1. *General Statement of Findings*

The latest literary strata of the Hebrew Bible provide the most comprehensive portrait of Cushite involvement in the Levant. The Chronicler describes Cushites active in maintaining Egyptian hegemony in the region south of Judah for a period of several hundred years. Though it is likely that Cushites fulfilled this role prior to the advent of the XXIInd Dynasty, for the Chronicler that was the moment when Judah first encounters them on the battlefield (2 Chr 12). Throughout the unfolding narratives, they appear to gain increasing autonomy and are said to have initiated later skirmishes without direct Egyptian oversight (2 Chr 14; 21). Perhaps the most perplexing aspect of the Chronicler's representation of the Cushites is that he does not record Judean encounters with them during their zenith in the eighth and seventh centuries. For the duration of the XXVth Dynasty, the Chronicler was noticeably silent on any Egyptian activity in the Levant.

Daniel 11 includes Cushites in a list of booty to be taken by Antiochus IV. Though it is likely that these events are as fanciful as the prophesied ascension of Gog in Ezek 38, they represent a disturbing trend toward envisioning Cushites as a conquered and subjugated people, reminiscent of Isa 43:3 and 45:14.

In the Psalms, a man named "Cush" (Ps 7) shares enmity with David and demonstrates that the reputation of mighty Other was perceived favorably in Judah and possibly even in Israel.[113] Psalms 68 and 87 contain strong evidence that the people of Cush were birthed by YHWH and welcomed to worship Judah's God.

The final two post-exilic references indicate how Cush functioned ideologically in Late Biblical Hebrew literature. In both the earliest (Gen 2:7)[114] and in the latest literary strata of the Hebrew Bible (Esth 1:1; 8:9), Cush functions as a geographical marker for the furthest southern point in the world known to Judean authors. Further, Job 28 confirms that biblical authors could employ Cush to denote a region from which fine luxury objects originated.

---

112. Heidorn, "Horses," 105–14.

113. Note that, as a "Benjaminite," this character would be associated with an Israelite, not a Judean tribe.

114. See the conclusion of the discussion of Gen 2:7 in Section 2.2.1.1: in an effort to produce a creation narrative that was universal in its scope, Judean authors included Cush as one of the distant points on their compass.

*4.3.2. The Reason Why Cush Is Employed in Hebrew Literature*

Late Hebrew literature uses Cushites as tropes for human might in every instance in which Cushites appear: in 2 Chronicles as well as in Ezekiel and Daniel. Cush-related terms in Pss 68 and 87 suggest that Cushites will participate in the worship of YHWH. Psalm 68 presents an image of Cushites bringing gifts to Judah's God. What are these gifts? Job 28 suggests that the Cushites' gifts could be fine luxury items, valued in the ancient Near Eastern marketplace; Cush was apparently known for its rare and costly goods. Also, the author of Esther depicts the rim of the world by using the term "Cush" in geographical contexts (chs. 1 and 8).

# Chapter 5

## CONCLUSIONS

As we reflect on what we have learned about biblical use of Cush-related terms, we are able to answer several questions: Who were the Cushites known to the Judean authors? How did the Judean authors represent the Cushite Other? What are the implications of this study for discussions about race? What remains to be done?

### 5.1. *Who Were the Cushites Known to the Judean Authors? A Brief Ethnography*

The Cushites were known to have been a tall, smooth (Isa 18), dark-skinned (Num 12; Jer 13:23) people from the farthest extent of the known world. They were born in a riparian land of mythic renown (Isa 18), rich and arable, full of luxuriant commodities (Job 28). Their economy, which likely depended on trade with Egypt and the people to the north, was facilitated by papyrus-sailing vessels that traversed the Nile (Isa 18). In the land of Cush they grew powerful, and from this land they came as warriors. The biblical authors knew the Cushites principally as soldiers participating in the Judean army (2 Sam 18), in their own Cushite-led forces (2 Kgs 19; Isa 37), or in larger Egyptian military coalitions (e.g. 2 Chronicles; Isa 20; 43; 45). Because they appear in Egyptian expeditionary forces in every biblical period, it is no wonder that whenever Judeans thought of Egypt's armies, they thought of Cushites.

Because Cushites were so frequently seen in these roles, the "Cushite" became a trope representing military might and the false pride that resulted from trusting in human strength (e.g. Isa 20:3-5; Nah 3:9). As such, Cushites served both to enact YHWH's will (2 Kgs 19; 2 Chr 12; 21:16-17; Isa 37) and to oppose it (Isa 20:3-5). Their service as the "strength" of the Egyptian expeditionary forces (Nah 3:9) over the centuries was likely the reason for their *entrée* into the Levant (2 Chr 12; 14; 16; 21).

The literary evidence presented in this study suggests that there were other groups with Cush-related names living in the Levant. One such group was the people of Cushan (Hab 3:7), who inhabited a region synonymous or closely affiliated with Midian. The historical hint of animosity between the people of Cushan and Israelite/Judahites (Hab 3:7) provides insight into the brief Judg 3:8-10 narrative about the foe, Cushan-rishathaim, set in the pre-state period. The novel construction "sons [or offspring] of the Cushites", which occurs in Amos 9:7, indicates a group of Levantine Cushites brought to the region by YHWH. Hence, throughout the biblical period there was likely contact with descendants of Cushites dwelling near Judah's southern border.

But Levantine Cushites were not relegated solely to the lands south of Judah; they found their way into Judah and even lived with, married (Num 12), and worked among the people of Jerusalem. The earliest hint of Cushites sojourning among the Israelites is in Num 12, in the narrative about Moses, one of the most significant characters in biblical history, and his Cushite wife. Though Miriam's complaint about this union suggests that there was some resistance to such marriages within the Judean community, YHWH's response confirms that there was no divine prohibition against Israelite–Cushite unions.

A Cushite courtier who served as a loyal agent for King David appears in a story set in the early monarchic period. This character, known only by his ethnicity, had direct access to another of the most significant figures in biblical history and was not alone in Judah's royal courts. Centuries later, other figures appear: Ebed-melech (Jer 38–39), who convinced King Zedekiah to rescue Jeremiah; Yehudi (Jer 36), who possessed the ability to read the words of Baruch's scroll to King Jehoiakim; and the prophet Zephaniah (Zeph 1:1), a member of the Judean royal house who proclaimed YHWH's word. Each of these characters are somehow related to Cushite identity and function in the inner-circle of Judean power.

Though one could argue against a Cushite heritage for Yehudi (Jer 36:14) and Zephaniah (Zeph 1:1), suggesting that the names "Cushi" in their patronymics are simply personal names devoid of ethnic content, one would still have to acknowledge that such names, among lists replete with others having Yahwistic elements, were acceptable in Judean society. Also, the use of the name "Cushi" suggests the esteem prominent Judean (perhaps even Israelite, as "Cush the Benjaminite" in Ps 7:1) families had for Cushites.

From the ends of the earth, Cushites had infiltrated the mainstream of Judean society, integrated with the Judean population, and influenced the naming of their children. People from the region of Cush are found in Hebrew literature that dates to or describes every biblical period and are often associated with prominent biblical characters, indicating their persistent presence in Judean minds. Even at the end of time, on YHWH's day of reckoning Cushites will be there. Though the Cushites were likely idolaters (Isa 45:20) in their indigenous land, they too could be the recipients of YHWH's favor (Jer 39). On the last day, they will come with outstretched arms (Ps 68:32) full of gifts (Isa 18:7; Zeph 3:10), and they will bow before YHWH in full submission, acknowledging that "God is with [Judah] alone, and there is no other; there is no god beside [YHWH]" (Isa 45:14, NRSV).

## 5.2. *How Did the Judean Authors Represent the Cushite Other?*

Judean authors employed Cush-related terms in their works in several ways. Examining these usage-types reveals the commonplace value Cush would have had for the intended audience. Several "types" of uses[1] can be identified for Cush-related terms in the Hebrew Bible:

---

1.   Consider also the assessment made by Bailey, "Africans," 178.

- As tropes for military might: 2 Sam 18; 2 Kgs 19; 2 Chr 12; 14; 16; 21;
  Zeph 2; Isa 20; 37; 43; 45; Jer 46; Ezek 29; 30; 38; Nah 3; Dan 11.
- As tropes for stereotyped swiftness: 2 Sam 18; Isa 18.
- As tropes for dark color: Num 12; Jer 13.
- As tropes for foreign gift-bearers and worshippers: Ps 68; 87; Isa 11;
  18; Zeph 3.
- As tropes for the end of the world: Gen 2; Esth 1; 8.
- As a trope for wealth: Job 28.

Cush-related terms are also employed:
- For inhabitants of the Levant: Judg 3; 2 Sam 18; Jer 38–39; Amos 9;
  Hab 3.
- In genealogies and patronymics: Gen 10; 1 Chr 1; Jer 36; Zeph 1.

The instances where constituent elements of racialist thought occur tend to be relatively few, though there are on occasion isolated instances where the othering could be deemed suspect. Generally, it appears that the people of Cush were regarded not unlike the other ethnic groups with whom the Israelite/Judahites interacted. Indeed, often when they are ostracized most in biblical texts, the context includes Egypt and/or its other allies. The Cushites under Egypt assaulted Judah. When reigning in Egypt, they formed alliances with Judah (Isa 18). Apparently they even welcomed Judean exiles into their nation (Ps 87; Isa 11; Zeph 3).

Though phenotypical differences are occasionally noted (Num 12; Isa 18; Jer 13), these texts are in no way preoccupied with this aspect of the Cushite persona, nor does it circumscribe the way the Cushites were perceived. The Hebrew Bible alone yields very limited information about Cushite appearance: they are dark (Num 12:1), their skin could not change (likely to "white" Jer 13:23), and they are tall with hairless faces (Isa 18:2, 7). Such descriptions were given no valuation by the Judean authors, except for Isa 18 where we discern the tenor to be decidedly positive.

Negative portrayals of Cushites can often be linked to particular historical events and not to a persistent ideology of behavioral defects or character flaws indicative of racialist thought. Such portrayals are employed to elicit a particular response from the intended audience. For instance, when Isaiah of Jerusalem debases the Cushites in his uncloaked prophetic performance (Isa 20), he seeks to thwart Judean complicity in an anti-Assyrian plot. Similarly, Deutero-Isaiah's denigration and subjugation of Cushites in Isa 43 and 45 may not reflect historical reality; rather, it elevates the faltering esteem of a nation recovering from the historical trauma of the exile. These instances reveal less about how the Cushites were perceived, and more about the historical contingencies of the prophets. Though these portrayals may be disturbing in today's world, replete with racialist imagery, for the Judean populace they were not meant to ground an enduring ideology of Cushite subjugation.

Further, in instances where differences in power are emphasized, Cush is usually the more powerful entity. When Cushites are said to have been conquered by Judean forces (e.g. 2 Chr 14, 16) or submitted to Judean authority (e.g. Isa 43:3; 45:14), it is only because of YHWH's intervention.

The portrayal of the Cushites is remarkably consistent throughout the Hebrew Bible. For example, both early and late texts contain references to "mighty-Cushites" and their participation in Egyptian military coalitions. There are, however, modest changes in the way biblical authors portrayed Cushites related to differing historical contexts.

For example, Gen 2 is consistent with what we would expect from the earliest strata of biblical texts, for it provides limited information about Cush as a nation by a river. The image of Cush in that verse contrasts with Isa 18—a fuller, more informed portrait of Cush in a later prophetic work. Isaiah of Jerusalem tends to portray the Cushites in a fairly positive manner (Isa 11; 18; 37). The single exception is Isa 20, which warns the people against joining the anti-Assyrian plot inspired by the king of Ashdod. The positive, more informed portrayal of the Cushites during this period coincides with the reign of the XXVth Dynasty in Egypt, the zenith of Cushite power.

Late monarchic to exilic texts such as Jeremiah present an intimate portrayal of Cushites consistent with the situation in the late monarchy. Cush-related terms in Jeremiah tend to refer to people within the community. Characters like Ebed-melech (Jer 38–39) and probably Jehudi (Jer 36) may represent the remnants of a Cushite community that had become integrated into Judah following the mid-seventh-century fall of Thebes. Other portrayals from this period, such as the two in Deutero-Isaiah's texts (Isa 43; 45), present a defeated, subdued Cush that may commingle the memory of their historic defeat at Thebes with the expectation that they would not be able to withstand a Persian assault. Similarly Ezek 29, 30, and 38, and Dan 11 consistently represent the Cushites less intimately—as commodities or as mercenaries who will suffer defeat. These depictions reflect the political situation in the exilic and post-exilic periods, when Cush had retreated to Napata, then Meroë,[2] and the Cushites mentioned in Ezekiel and Daniel most likely were hired soldiers. Although the portrayal of the Cushites in the Hebrew Bible does not change markedly, changing historical factors affecting the relationship between Judah and Cush are discernible.

### 5.3. *What Are the Implications of this Study for Discussions about Race?*

Despite the potential for racialist representation of this group, the Hebrew Bible presents Cushites in a manner not unlike other Others. Although in a number of instances biblical texts have employed constituent elements of racialist thought and even stereotypes of Cushites, there does not appear to be a convergence of such elements into a system of racialist ideology in the Hebrew Bible.

---

2. David O'Connor, *Ancient Nubia: Egypt's Rival in Africa* (Philadelphia: University of Pennsylvania Press, 1993), 70–84.

Wherever Cushite phenotypes are mentioned, they are represented in a neutral to a noble manner. Likewise, the few references to Cushite phenotypes describe superficial differences in somatic type and never address other differences such as the appearance of faces, hair, or body-types. While one could plausibly argue that the authors of the Hebrew Bible had a racial taxonomy, one that is not fully represented in biblical literature, I would suggest that there was no taxonomy because there was no burgeoning concept of race among the ancient Hebrews. By "no concept of race," I mean that prejudices based on the appearance of Cushites did not foster notions of inherent Cushite inferiority, negative behavioral traits, ontological differences, or a legitimating ideology to support their subjugation. Whatever the differences in phenotype and culture may have been, they did not inspire a racialist type of othering in biblical thought.

Instead, the literary evidence in this study suggests that throughout the biblical period the Levant was home to a diverse assortment of ethnic groups. Members of these groups traversed the region for reasons of trade and conquest; and some of them settled there and even intermarried with the Judean population. As a result, there were likely people of various somatic types, complexions, and hues fully participating in each stratum of Judean society.

Biblical narratives that are utilized in contemporary contexts to promote the notion of a biblically endorsed racialist ideology are void of any racial content. For example, the "curse of Ham" was never actually a curse on "Ham" but on "Canaan," intended to legitimate and sanction the local *status quo* in post-settlement Canaan. The inclusion of Ham in that biblical narrative represents a later redactor's attempt to universalize the local narrative, and not the author's attempt ideologically to subjugate Ham.

Further, because the Table of Nations likely represents political alliances and geographic continuity more than kinship and descent, it is implausible that the Judean authors, redactors, and audience could have conceived that the curse of Canaan applied to the other "descendants" of Ham. That Cush and Egypt historically were much mightier, more prosperous than, and never subject to Judah, as were the Canaanites, serves to emphasize that point.

Finally, inasmuch as we have found no evidence for a systematized racialist classification of the Cushites in ancient Judean society, we should be careful not to read modern biases into biblical texts. Too often exegetes present a jaded and erroneous portrait of the biblical Cushites because they have allowed their own racialist assumptions to obscure the biblical record. Nowhere has this been more obvious than in contemporary interpretation of and commentary on Amos 9.7. For modern scholars blind to the racialist ideology in which we Westerns are steeped, the comparison of the sons of Israel with a people deemed racially "black" immediately conjures otherwise latent negative thoughts about "blackness." Though at the time when Amos prophesied they were ruling the most powerful empire in the ancient world, Cushites when read through the lenses of centuries of denigration and disparagement of "black" figures ahistorically become slaves, primitives, social degenerates, or worst. Racialist thinking, when anachronistically applied to the ancient Judean contexts, precludes us from knowing that world, forcing it to assume our prejudices. Further, since the object of inquiry is Scripture, venerated by many as sacrosanct, racialism itself takes on religious dimensions; it becomes sacralized.[3] Thus, even a verse that speaks of God's universal concern for all people, including some of Judah's most bitter enemies, can be transformed into a venomous curse when our vision is obscured by systemic racism.

And the problem is systemic racism. By this I do not mean to suggest that certain scholars did not intend to present the Cushites in a negative light; there will always be racists, even among biblical scholars. However, the interpretive problem is much larger than just exegetes with malicious intentions. As long as the normative gaze and the attendant stereotypes of race are uncritically accepted in the larger society, tainted scholarship is inevitable. As long as racialist thought, the concept that because of our physical appearance we are fundamentally different in qualitative ways, persists, the biblical world will be subject to the prejudices of the modern world. As long as the well is poisoned, all the water that is drawn from it will be toxic too.

Consequently, readers who depend on biblical scholars to depict the world of holy writ accurately have been and will continue to be bombarded with uncritical and historically inaccurate portrayals of the Cushites and the role they have played in the unfolding history of the ancient Near East. In addition to perverting the historical record, such portrayals serve only to perpetuate damaging stereotypes, reinforce modern racialist ideology, and reify systemic racism.

Systemic racism is certainly a formidable opponent. Yet, its influence will be lessened as individual scholars begin to question the impact of racialist thinking, the assumption that racial categories define valid human difference on an ontological level, and become self-critical as they examine Cushites and other Others on the pages of the biblical texts. Subsequently they could examine the impact of racialism on the theoretical framework of post-Enlightenment thought and evaluate its continued impact on modern biblical scholarship. Only then it is possible for Scripture to be freed from the yoke of humanity's most dangerous myth, void of the imposition of detrimental contemporary ideology, and constrained from fostering perilous theology. I hope that this study has in some way mitigated the potential damage caused by eisegeting modern racialist ideology into biblical narratives and has reminded us all to be more critical in our analysis of Others in the Bible.

## 5.4. *What Remains to be Done?*

There are several projects that might stem from this study. The first is an examination of post-biblical Jewish literature to gain a formal understanding of how images of Cush and Cushites changed over time. Though I have noted some change in the biblical period in the portrayal of Cushites, I have found a generally consistent portrait of the Cushites. The introduction of new variables into Jewish life, such as Hellenism and the experience of the Diaspora, likely modified

---

3. Felder, *Troubling*, 38. Felder defines sacralization as, "The transposing of an ideological concept into a tenet of religious faith in order to serve the vested interests of a particular ethnic group."

biblical understandings of Others in general and Cushites in particular. This is already evident in the LXX, where the Greek translational equivalent for "Cushite" becomes "Ethiopian," meaning "burnt face." The introduction of a phenotypically descriptive and less ethnically precise term for this southern Other undoubtedly had ramifications for the Jewish perception of Cushites in the late Second Temple period and beyond.

In addition to this, I would suggest to all biblical scholars and exegetes the urgent need to revisit their assumptions about the Cushites. Too often in the course of this study we have encountered instances where modern racial biases have perverted otherwise sound exegetical insight. I would suggest that such a phenomenon has less to do with an individual exegete's intention and more to do with his or her uncritical acceptance of racialist assumptions. It is only by using such clouded lenses that a powerful and wealthy people at the zenith of their national development can be described as an "uncivilized" and subservient people.

I would also urge that we modify our understanding of the Egyptian armies. Because of the prevalence of Cushites in biblical narratives describing Egypt's military forces, it is likely that there were Cushites stationed at Egyptian strongholds throughout the ancient Near East in the biblical period. Perhaps, therefore, we should look for evidence of Cushite presence in the Levant precisely in those places where and when Egypt was known to have established fortresses and trading outposts. Further, inasmuch as Cushite kings ruled Egypt from the mid-eighth until the mid-seventh centuries, references to Egypt in texts either composed during or describing events during this period may actually be references to Cush.[4]

In addition to these tasks, future literary scholars will need to consider the following questions: Though we have begun to develop an understanding of the way that Judean authors othered the Cushites in the Hebrew Bible, does the nature of their othering change significantly in the Septuagint?[5] Though the Cushites were never explicitly associated with "blackness," how were images of "blackness" and "darkness" valued in the Hebrew Bible and later post-biblical literature? Now that we have discerned literary and epigraphic evidence that suggests that there were Cushites in the Levant throughout the biblical period, could we employ additional archaeological data that would indicate the extent to which they were present in ancient Palestine?

As a result of this study, I hope that biblical scholars will no longer view Cushites through a narrow lens and understand that their impact on the "people of the book" has been far greater than it has been portrayed in surveys of the ancient Near East and in biblical commentaries. This Other from a distant land played an important role in the thought and theology of biblical authors and in the lives of the people of ancient Judah. By explicating this role, I hope that students of the Hebrew Bible will begin to understand the significance of Cush in the biblical world.

---

4. For example, the reference to Thebes in Nah 3:9.

5. Consider the LXX version of Isa 18, where there is a markedly more negative tone in the portrayal of the Cushites.

# BIBLIOGRAPHY

"AAA Statement on Race." *American Anthropologist* 100 (1999): 712–13.

"AAPA Statement on Biological Aspects of Race." *American Journal of Physical Anthropology* 101 (1996): 569–70.

Aaron, David H. "Early Rabbinic Exegesis on Noah's Son Ham and the So-Called 'Hamitic Myth.'" *Journal of the American Academy of Religion.* 63 (1996): 721–59.

Achtemeier, Elizabeth. *Nahum–Malachi.* Atlanta: John Knox, 1986.

Ackroyd, Peter R. *The Second Book of Samuel.* London: Cambridge University Press, 1977.

Adamo, David T. "The Place of Africa and Africans in the Old Testament and its Environment." Ph.D. diss., Baylor University, 1986.

Adams, William Y. "The Kingdom and Civilization of Kush in Northeast Africa." Pages 775–89 in *Civilizations of the Ancient Near East: Volume 2.* Edited by Jack M. Sasson. New York: Simon & Schuster MacMillan, 1995.

—"Post-Pharonic Nubia in the Light of Archaeology." *Journal of Egyptian Archaeology* 50 (1964): 102–20.

Adams, William Y. et. al. *Africa in Antiquity: The Art of Ancient Nubia and the Sudan.* 2 vols. New York: Brooklyn Museum Division of Publication and Marketing Services, 1978.

Albright, William F. "Egypt and the Early History of the Negeb." *Journal of the Palestinian Oriental Society* 47 (1924): 131–61.

—"The Psalm of Habakkuk." in *Studies in Old Testament Prophecy.* Edited by Harold H. Rowley. Edinburgh, Scotland: T. & T. Clark, 1950.

Allport, Gordon. *The Nature of Prejudice.* Reading, Mass.: Addison-Wesley Publishing Company, 1979.

Alter, Robert. *The Art of Biblical Poetry.* New York: Basic Books, 1985.

Amit, Yairah. *The Book of Judges: The Art of Editing.* Translated by Jonathan Chipman; Leiden: Brill, 1999.

Andersen, Francis I., and David Noel Freedman. *Amos: A New Translation with Introduction and Commentary.* Anchor Bible 24A. Garden City, N.Y.: Doubleday, 1989.

Anderson, Arnold A. *The Book of Psalms.* Vol. 1, *1–72.* Paulton: Purnell, 1972.

—*The Book of Psalms.* Vol. 2, *73–150.* Paulton: Purnell, 1972.

Anderson, Bernhard W. *Understanding the Old Testament.* 4th ed.; Englewood Cliffs, N.J.: Prentice–Hall, 1986.

Anderson, Hugh. *The Gospel of Mark.* London: Oliphants, 1976.

Anderson, Roger W. "Zephaniah ben Cushi and Cush of Benjamin: Traces of Cushite Presence in Syria–Palestine." Pages 45–70 in *The Pitcher is Broken: Memorial Essays for Gosta W. Ahlström.* Edited by Steven W. Holloway and Lowell K. Handy. Journal for the Study of the Old Testament Supplement Series 190. Sheffield: Sheffield Academic Press, 1995.

Appiah, Kwame Anthony. "Racisms," Pages 3–17 in *Anatomy of Racism.* Edited by David Theo Goldberg. Minneapolis: University of Minnesota Press, 1990.

—"Race: An Interpretation." Pages 1575–80 in *African: The Encyclopedia of the African and African American Experience.* Edited by Kwame Anthony Appiah and Henry Louis Gates, Jr.; New York: Civitas Books, 1999.

Arkell, Anthony J. *A History and Religion of Israel.* Oxford: Oxford University Press, 1961.

Ashley, Timothy R. *The Book of Numbers.* Grand Rapids: Eerdmans, 1993.

Avigad, Nahman. *Hebrew Bullae from the Time of Jeremiah: Remnants of a Burnt Archive.* Jerusalem: Israel Exploration Society, 1986.

—"Six Ancient Hebrew Seals." Pages 305–6 in *A Book for Shemuel Levin.* Edited by Shmuel Abramski and Yohanan Aharoni. Jerusalem: Kiryat-Sepher, 1970 (Hebrew).

Bailey, Randall. "Beyond Identification: The Use of Africans in Old Testament Poetry and Narratives." Pages 165–86 in *Stony the Road We Trod.* Edited by Cain Hope Felder. Minneapolis: Fortress, 1991.

Baker, Donald G. *Race, Ethnicity and Power.* London: Routledge & Kegan Paul, 1983.

Baker, David W. "Cushan." Pages 1219–20 in vol. 1 of *The Anchor Bible Dictionary.* Edited by D. N. Freedman. New York: Doubleday, 1992.

—"Ophir." Pages 26–27 in vol. 6 of *The Anchor Bible Dictionary.* Edited by D. N. Freedman. New York: Doubleday, 1992.

Baker, Lee D. *From Savage to Negro: Anthropology and the Construction of Race, 11896–1954.* Berkeley, California: University of California Press, 1998.

Baldwin, Joyce G. *Esther: An Introduction and Commentary.* Leicester: InterVarsity, 1984.

Baltsam, Hayim, ed. *Webster's New World Hebrew Dictionary.* New York: Prentice–Hall, 1992.

Banks, Marcus. *Ethnicity: Anthropological Constructions.* London: Routledge, 1996.

Barth, Frederick. *Ethnic Groups and Boundaries: The Social Organization of Culture Difference.* London: Allen & Unwin, 1969.

Bellis, Alice Ogden. *Helpmates, Harlots, Heroes: Women's Stories in the Hebrew Bible.* Louisville, Ky.: Westminster John Knox, 1994.

—"Zipporah: Issues of Race, Religion, Gender and Power." An unpublished Paper presented at the Duke Hebrew Bible Fall Seminar. Durham, N.C. October 12, 2000.

Ben Zvi, Ehud. *A Historical-Critical Study of the Book of Zephaniah.* Berlin: de Gruyter, 1991.

Berlin, Adele. "Parallelism." Pages 155–62 in vol. 5 of *The Anchor Bible Dictionary.* Edited by D. N. Freedman. New York: Doubleday, 1992.

—*Zephaniah: A New Translation with Introduction and Commentary.* Anchor Bible 25A. Garden City, N.Y.: Doubleday, 1994.

Berridge, John M. "Zephaniah." Page 1075 in vol. 6 of *The Anchor Bible Dictionary.* Edited by D. N. Freedman. New York: Doubleday, 1992.

Birch, Bruce C. *Hosea, Joel, and Amos.* Louisville, Ky.: Westminster John Knox, 1997.

Blackwood, Jr., Andrew W. *Commentary on Jeremiah.* Waco, Tex.: Word Books, 1977.

Blenkinsopp, Joseph. *Ezekiel.* Louisville, Ky.: John Knox, 1990.

Block, Daniel I. *The Book of Ezekiel: Chapters 25–48.* Grand Rapids: Eerdmans, 1997.

Boice, James Montgomery. *The Minor Prophets: An Expositonal Commentary.* Vol. 1, *Hosea–Jonah.* Grand Rapids: Zondervan, 1983.

Boling, Robert G. *Judges: Introduction, Translation, and Commentary.* Anchor Bible 6A. Garden City, N.Y.: Doubleday, 1975.

Brantlinger, Patrick. "Victorians and Africans: The Genealogy of the Myth of the Dark Continent." Pages 185–222 in *"Race," Writing, and Difference.* Edited by Henry Louis Gates, Jr. Chicago: University of Chicago Press, 1986.

Braude, Benjamin. "The Sons of Noah and the Construction of Ethnic and Geographical Identities in the Medieval and Early Modern Periods." *William and Mary Quarterly* 54 (1997): 103–142.

Brenner, Athalya. *Colour Terms in the Old Testament.* Journal for the Study of the Old Testament Supplement Series 21. Sheffield: JSOT Press, 1982.

Bright, John. *A History of Israel.* Philadelphia: Westminster, 1981.

Brooks, Lester. *Great Civilization of Ancient Africa.* New York: Four Winds, 1972.

Brown, William P. *Obadiah through Malachi.* Louisville, Ky.: Westminster John Knox, 1996.

Brueggemann, Walter. *First and Second Samuel.* Louisville: John Knox, 1990.

Budge, Ernest A. W. *Egyptian Sudan.* 2 vols. New York: Arno, 1976.

Burney, Charles Fox. *The Book of Judges*. New York: Ktav, 1970.

Burstein, Stanley. *Graeco-Africana: Studies in the History of Greek Relations with Egypt and Nubia*. New Rochelle, N.Y.: Aristide D. Caratzas, 1995.

Carroll, Robert P. *Jeremiah: A Commentary*. Philadelphia: Westminster, 1986.

Carson, Cottrel R. "Do You Understand What you are Reading?' A Reading of the Ethiopian Eunuch Story (Acts 8.26–40) from a Site of Cultural Marronage." Ph.D. diss., Union Theological Seminary, 1999.

Cathcart, Kevin J. "Nahum, Book of." *Anchor Bible Dictionary* 4:998–1000.

Childs, Brevard S. *Isaiah*. Louisville, Ky.: Westminster John Knox, 2001.

Clark, John D. "A Re-examination of the Evidence for Agricultural Origins in the Nile Valley." in *Proceedings of the Prehistoric Society*. 39 (1971): 34–79.

Clark, John D. and A. Stemler. "Early Domesticated Sorghum from Central Sudan." *Nature* 254 (1975): 588–91.

Clement, Ronald E. *Isaiah 1–39*. Grand Rapids: Eerdmans, 1987.

Clifford, James and George E. Marcus. *Writing Culture: The Poetics and Politics of Ethnography*. Berkeley: University of California Press, 1986.

Coats, George W. *African Empires and Civilizations*. New York: African Heritage Studies, 1974.

—*Genesis: With an Introduction to Narrative Literature*. Grand Rapids: Eerdmans, 1983.

Cogan, Mordechai and Hayim Tadmor. *II Kings: A New Translation with Introduction and Commentary*. Anchor Bible 11. Garden City, N.Y.: Doubleday, 1988.

Coggins, Richard J. *Israel among the Nations*. Grand Rapids: Eerdmans, 1985.

Cohen, Ronald. "Ethnicity: Problem and Focus in Anthropology." *Annual Review of Anthropology* 7 (1978): 379–403.

Collins, John J. "Artapanus." in *OTP* 2:889–904.

—"Daniel, Book of." Pages 29–37 in vol. 2 of *The Anchor Bible Dictionary*. Edited by D. N. Freedman. New York: Doubleday, 1992..

Conroy, Charles. *Absalom, Absalom: Narrative and Language in 2 Sam 13–20*. Rome: Biblical Institute, 1978.

Copher, Charles B. *Black Biblical Studies: An Anthology of Charles B. Copher*. Chicago: Black Light Fellowship, 1993.

—"The Black Man in the Biblical World." *Journal of the Interdenominational Theological Center* 1 (1974): 7–16.

—"The Black Presence in the Old Testament." Pages 146–65 in *Stony the Road We Trod: African American Biblical Interpretation*. Edited by Cain Hope Felder; Minneapolis: Fortress, 1991.

—"Three Thousand Years of Biblical Interpretation with Reference to Black Peoples." *Journal of the Interdenominational Theological Center* 13 (1986): 225–46.

Craigie, Peter C. *The Twelve Prophets*. Vol. 1, *Hosea, Joel, Amos, Obadiah, and Jonah*. Philadelphia: Westminster, 1984.

— *The Twelve Prophets*. Vol. 2, *Micah, Nahum, Habakkuk, Zephaniah, Haggai, Zechariah, and Malachi*. Philadelphia: Westminster, 1985.

Cranfield, Charles E. B. *The Gospel according to Saint Mark*. Cambridge: Cambridge University Press, 1985.

Crenshaw, James C. *Education in Ancient Israel: Across the Deadening Silence*. New York: Doubleday, 1998.

—"Job, Book of." Pages 858–68 in vol. 3 of *The Anchor Bible Dictionary*. Edited by D. N. Freedman. New York: Doubleday, 1992.

Dahood, Mitchell. *Psalms*. Vol. 2, *51–100: Introduction, Translation, and Notes*. Anchor Bible 17. Garden City, N.Y.: Doubleday, 1968.

Davidson, Robert. *Jeremiah*, Vol. 1. Philadelphia: Westminster, 1983.

—*Jeremiah, Vol. 2, and Lamentations*. Philadelphia: Westminster, 1985.

Davies, Eryl W. *Numbers*, Grand Rapids: Eerdmans, 1995.

Davies, Philip. *In Search of "Ancient Israel"*. Journal for the Study of the Old Testament Supplement Series 148. Sheffield: JSOT Press, 1992.

Day, John. "Rahab (Dragon)." Pages 610–11 in vol. 4 of *The Anchor Bible Dictionary*. Edited by D. N. Freedman. New York: Doubleday, 1992.

Desnoyers, Louis. "Le prophète Amos," *Revue Biblique* 26 (1917): 218–46.

Dever, William G. "Archaeology, Ideology, and the Quest for 'Ancient' or 'Biblical Israel.'" *Near Eastern Archaeology* 61 (1998): 39–52.

—"Histories and Non-histories of Ancient Israel." *Bulletin of the American Schools of Oriental Research* 316 (1999): 89–105.

Dillard, Raymond B. *2 Chronicles*. WBC. Waco, Tex. Word Books, 1987.

Diop, Anta Cheikh. *African Origin of Civilization: Myth or Reality?* Translated by Mercer Cook. Westport: Lawrence Hill, 1974.

Dixon, D. M. "The Origin of the Kingdom of Kush (Napata-Meroe)." *Journal of Egyptian Archaeology* 50 (1904): 121–32.

Drake, St. Clair. *Black Folk Here and There*, Vol. 2. Los Angeles: Center for Afro-American Studies, University of California, 1990.

Driver, George R. "Isaiah 1–39: Textual and Linguistic Problems." *Journal of Semitic Studies* 13 (1968): 36–57.

Driver, Samuel R. *The Book of Genesis*. London: Methuen, 1907.

—*The Minor Prophets: Nahum, Habakkuk, Zephaniah, Haggai, Zechariah, Malachi*. New York: Oxford University Press, 1919.

Dunham, Dows, and Miles F. L. MacAdam. "Names and Relationships of the Royal Family of Napata." *Journal of Egyptian Archaeology* 35 (1949): 139–49.

Dunston, Alfred G. *The Black Man in the Old Testament and Its World*. Philadelphia: Dorrance, 1974.

Edelman, Diana. "Ethnicity and Early Israel," Pages 25–55 in *Ethnicity and the Bible*. Edited by Mark G. Brett; Leiden: E. J. Brill, 1996.

Edghill, Ernest Arthur. *The Book of Amos*. London: Methuen, 1926.

Edwards, David N. *Archaeology and Settlement in Upper Nubia in the 1st Millennium A.D.* 1989. BAR International Series 537. Oxford: British Archaeological Reports.

Eichrodt, Walther. *Ezekiel: A Commentary*. Translated by Cosslett Quin. Philadelphia: Westminster, 1970.

Emery, Walter B. *Egypt in Nubia*. London: Hutchinson, 1965.

English, Donald. *The Message of Mark: The Mystery of Faith*. Leicester: Inter-Varsity, 1992.

Entine, Jon Entine. *Taboo: Why Black Athletes Dominate Sports and Why we are Afraid to Talk about It*. New York: Public Affairs, 2000.

Erman, Adolf. *The Literature of Ancient Egyptians*. Translated by Aylward M. Blackman. London: Methuen, 1927.

Fairbairn, Patrick. *Ezekiel, and the Book of his Prophecy: An Exposition*. Edinburgh: T. & T. Clark, 1863.

Faulkner, Raymond O. *A Concise Dictionary of Middle Egyptian*. Oxford: Griffith Institute, 1981.

Felder, Cain Hope. "Race, Racism and the Biblical Narratives." Pages 127–45 in *Stony the Road We Trod: African American Biblical Interpretation*. Edited by Cain Hope Felder. Minneapolis: Fortress, 1991.

—*Troubling Biblical Waters: Race, Class, and Family*. Maryknoll, N.Y.: Orbis, 1989.

Feldman, Louis H. "Josephus' Portrait of Moses," *The Jewish Quarterly Review* 83 (1993): 301–30.

Fohrer, Georg. *Introduction to the Old Testament*. Nashville: Abingdon, 1978.

Frick, Frank S. *A Journey through the Hebrew Scriptures*. Forth Worth, Tex.: Harcourt Brace, 1995.

Friedman, Richard Elliott. *Who Wrote the Bible?* New York: Harper & Row, 1989.

Gardiner, Alan H. "Piankhi's Instructions to His Army." *Journal of Egyptian Archaeology* 21 (1939): 219–23.

—*The Tomb of Huy: Viceroy of Nubia in the Reign of Tutankhamen*. London: The Egypt Exploration Society, 1926.

Gates, Henry Louis. *"Race," Writing and Difference*. Chicago: University of Chicago Press, 1986.

Gemser, Berend. "The Instructions of `Onchsheshonqy and Biblical Wisdom Literature," Pages 102–28 in *Congress Volume: Oxford, 1959*. Leiden: Brill, 1960.

George, Katherine. "The Civilized West Looks at Primitive Africa, 1400–1800." *Isis* 49 (1958): 56–72.

Good, Edwin M. *In Turns of Tempest: A Reading of Job with a Translation*. Stanford, Calif.: Stanford University Press, 1990.

Gordon, Robert P. *1 & 2 Samuel: A Commentary*. Grand Rapids: Regency, 1986.

Gorg, Manfred. "Gihon." Pages 1018–19 in vol. 2 of *The Anchor Bible Dictionary*. Edited by D. N. Freedman. New York: Doubleday, 1992.

Gossett, Thomas. *Race: The History of an Idea in America*. New York: Oxford University Press, 1997.

Gray, John. *1 & 2 Kings: A Commentary*. 2nd ed. Philadelphia: Westminster, 1970.

Grayson, A. Kirk. "Sennacherib." Pages 1088–89 in vol. 5 of *The Anchor Bible Dictionary*. Edited by D. N. Freedman. New York: Doubleday, 1992.

Greenberg, Moshe. *Ezekiel 21–37: A New Translation with Introduction and Commentary*. Anchor Bible 22A. Garden City, N.Y.: Doubleday, 1997.

—*Introduction to Hebrew*. Englewood Cliffs, N.J.: Prentice–Hall, 1965.

Greenstein, Edward L. "Wordplay, Hebrew," Pages 968–71 in vol. 6 of *The Anchor Bible Dictionary*. Edited by D. N. Freedman. New York: Doubleday, 1992.

Haak, Robert D. "'Cush' in Zephaniah,"Pages 238-51 in *The Pitcher is Broken*. Edited by Lowell K. Handy and Steven W. Holloway. Sheffield: Sheffield Academic Press, 1995.

Habel, Norman C. *The Book of Job: A Commentary*. Philadelphia: Westminster, 1985.

Hagg, Tomas. *Nubian Culture Past and Present*. Stockholm: Almqvist & Wiksell International, 1987.

Haldar, Alfred. *Studies in the Book of Nahum*. Upsala: A. B. Lundequistska Bokhandeln, 1947.

Halpern, Baruch. "Kenites." Pages 17–22 in vol. 4 of *The Anchor Bible Dictionary*. Edited by D. N. Freedman. New York: Doubleday, 1992.

Hamilton, Jeffries M. "Paran." Page 162 in vol. 5 of *The Anchor Bible Dictionary*. Edited by D. N. Freedman. New York: Doubleday, 1992.

Hamilton, Victor P. "Marriage (Old Testament and ANE)." Page 559–68 in vol. 4 of *The Anchor Bible Dictionary*. Edited by D. N. Freedman. New York: Doubleday, 1992.

Hammershaimb, Erling. *The Book of Amos: A Commentary*. Oxford: Basil Blackwell, 1970.

Hansberry, William Leo. *Africa and Africans as Seen by the Classical Writers*. Washington, D.C.: Howard University Press, 1977.

Hanson, James "Demetrius the Chronographer." Pages 843–54 in vol. 2 of *The Old Testament Pseudepigrapha*. Edited by J. H. Charlesworth. 2 vols. New York: Doubleday, 1983.

Harris, Joseph E., ed. *Africa and Africans as Seen by Classical Writers*. Washington, D.C.: Howard University Press, 1977.

Harrison, Faye V. "Introduction: Expanding the Discourse on 'Race.'" *American Anthropologist* 100 (1998): 609–31.

Hays, J. Daniel. "The Cushites: A Black Nation in the Bible." *Bibliotheca Sacra* 153 (1996): 396–409.

—"The Cushites: A Black Nation in Ancient History." *Bibliotheca Sacra* 153 (1996): 270–80.

Heaton, Eric W. *The Book of Daniel: Introduction and Commentary*. London: SCM Press, 1956.

Heflin, J. N. Boo. *Nahum, Habakkuk, Zephaniah, and Haggai*. Grand Rapids: Zondervan Books, 1985.

Heidorn, Lisa A. "The Horses of Kush." *Journal of Near Eastern Studies* 56 (1997): 105–14.

Herbert, Arthur S. *The Book of the Prophet Isaiah Chapters 1–39*. Cambridge: Cambridge University Press, 1973.

—*The Book of the Prophet Isaiah Chapters 40–66*. Cambridge: Cambridge University Press, 1975.

Herrnstein, Richard J., and Charles A. Murray, *The Bell Curve: Intelligence and Class Structure in American Life*. New York: Free Press, 1989.

Hertzberg, Hans Wilhelm. *1 & 2 Samuel: A Commentary*. Translated by John Bowden. Philadelphia: Westminster, 1964.

Hidal, Sten. "The Land of Cush in the Old Testament." *Svensk Exegetisk åsbok* 41 (1977): 97–106.

Hiebert, Theodore. "Theophany in the Old Testament." Pages 505–11 in vol. 5 of *The Anchor Bible Dictionary*. Edited by D. N. Freedman. New York: Doubleday, 1992.

Hoch, James E. *Middle Egyptian Grammar*. Mississauga, Ont.: Benben Publications, 1997.

Hood, Robert E. *Begrimed and Black: Christian Traditions on Blacks and Blackness*. Minneapolis: Fortress, 1994.

Holladay, William L. *Jeremiah: A Commentary on the Book of the Prophet Jeremiah Chapters 1–25*. Philadelphia: Fortress, 1986.

Holter, Knut. *Tropical Africa and the Old Testament: A Select and Annotated Bibliography*. Oslo: University of Oslo, 1996.

—*Yahweh in Africa: Essays on Africa and the Old Testament*. New York: Peter Lang, 2000.

Horton, Robert F. *The Minor Prophets*. Vol. 1. Edinburgh, Scotland: Oxford, 1904.

Hulse, E. V. "The Nature of Biblical 'Leprosy' and the Use of Alternative Medical Terms in Modern Translations of the Bible." *Palestine Exploration Quarterly* 107 (1975): 87–105.

Hutton, Rodney R. "Cush the Benjaminite and Psalm Midrash." *Hebrew Annual Review* 10 (1986): 123–37.

Isaac, Ephraim. "Ethiopia." Pages 273–78 in vol. 2 of *The Oxford Encyclopedia of Archaeology in the Near East*. Edited by E. M. Meyers. 5 vols. Oxford: Oxford University Press, 1997.

—"Genesis, Judaism, and the Sons of Ham." in *Slaves and Slavery in Muslim Africa*. Edited by J. R. Willis. London: Frank Cass, 1985.

—"Ham." Pages 31–32 in vol. 3 of *The Anchor Bible Dictionary*. Edited by D. N. Freedman. New York: Doubleday, 1992.

Jackson, John G. *Ethiopia and the Origin of Civilization*. Baltimore: Black Classic Press, 1982.

Japhet, Sara. *I and II Chronicles: A Commentary*. Louisville, Ky.: Westminster John Knox, 1993.

—*The Ideology of the Book of Chronicles and Its Place in Biblcial Thought*. New York: Peter Lang, 1989.

Johnstone, William. *1 and 2 Chronicles*. Vol. 2, *2 Chronicles 10–36: Guilt and Atonement*. Journal for the Study of the Old Testament Supplement Series 253. Sheffield: Sheffield Academic Press, 1997.

Jones, Douglas Rawlinson. *Jeremiah*. Grand Rapids: Eerdmans, 1992.

Jones, Gwilym H. *1 and 2 Kings*, Vol. 2. Grand Rapids: Eerdmans, 1984.

Jünker, Hermann. "The First Appearance of the Negroes in History." *Journal of Egyptian Archaeology* 7 (1921): 121–32.

Kaiser, Otto. *Isaiah 1–12: A Commentary*. Translated by John Bowden; Philadelphia: Westminster, 1983.

—*Isaiah 13–39: A Commentary*. Translated by R. A. Wilson. Philadelphia: Westminster, 1974.

Kaiser, Werner. "Elephantine." Pages 234–36 in vol. 2 of *The Oxford Encyclopedia of Archaeology in the Near East*. Edited by E. M. Meyers. 5 vols. Oxford: Oxford University Press, 1997.

Kapelrud, Arvid S. *The Message of the Prophet Zephaniah*. Oslo: Universitetsforlaget, 1975.

Kaplan, Steven. *The Beta Israel (Falasha) in Ethiopia: From Earliest Times to the Twentieth Century*. New York: New York University Press, 1992.

Keil, Carl F. *The Book of the Prophet Daniel*. Translated by Matthew G. Easton. Edinburgh: T. & .T Clark, 1891.

Kendall, Timothy. "Kings of the Sacred Mountan: Napata and the Kushite Twenty-Fifth Dynasty of Egypt." Pages 160–204 in *Sudan:Ancient Kingdoms of the Nile*. Edited by Dietrich Wildung. Paris: Flammarion, 1997.

Kessler, David. *The Falashas: A Short History of the Ethiopian Jews*. London: Frank Cass, 1996.

Kissane, Edward J. *The Book of Isaiah*, Vol. 1. Dublin: Browne & Nolan, 1960.

Kitchen, Kenneth A. *The Third Intermediate Period in Egypt (1100–650 B.C.)*. Warminster: Aris & Phillips, 1973.

Kormyschewa, Eleonora. "Local Gods of Egypt in Cush and Problems of Egyptian Settlers." *Meroitica* 12: 195–223.

Knauf, Ernst A. *Midian Midian : Untersuchungen zur Geschichte Palästinas und Nordarabiens am Ende des 2. Jahrtausends v. Chr.* Wiesbaden, Germany: Otto Harrassowitz, 1988.

—"Teman." *Anchor Bible Dictionary*. Pages 347–48 in vol. 6 of *The Anchor Bible Dictionary*. Edited by D. N. Freedman. New York: Doubleday, 1992.

—"Zerah." Pages 1080–81 in vol. 6 of *The Anchor Bible Dictionary*. Edited by D. N. Freedman. New York: Doubleday, 1992.

Knight, George A. F. *Psalms*, Vol. 1. Philadelphia, Westminster, 1982.

—*Psalms*, Vol. 2. Philadelphia, Westminster, 1983.

Kraus, Hans-Joachim. *Psalms 1–59: A Commentary*. Translated by Hilton C. Oswald. Minneapolis: Augsburg, 1988.

—*Psalms 60–150: A Commentary*. Translated by Hilton C. Oswald. Minneapolis: Augsburg, 1989.

Kselman, John S. "Zephaniah, Book of." Pages 1077–80 in vol. 6 of *The Anchor Bible Dictionary*. Edited by D. N. Freedman. New York: Doubleday, 1992.

Lacocque, André. *The Book of Daniel*. Translated by David Pellauer. Atlanta: John Knox, 1979.

Larue, Gerald A. *Old Testament Life and Literature*. Boston: Allyn & Bacon, 1968.

Lawson, George. "Discourses on the Whole Book of Esther." Pages 1–331 in *Expositions of Ruth and Esther*. Edited by George Lawson. Evansville, Ind.: Sovereign Grace Publishers, 1960.

Leclant, Jean. "Egypt in Sudan: The New Kingdom." Pages 119–27 in *Sudan: Ancient Kingdoms of the Nile*. Edited by Dietrich Wildung; Paris: Flammarion, 1997.

Lederach, Paul M. *Daniel*. Scottdale, Pa.: Herald Press, 1994.

LePeau, John Philip. "Psalm 68: An Exegetical and Theological Study." Ph.D. diss., Graduate College of the University of Iowa, 1981.

Lemche, Niels Peter. *The Israelites in History and Tradition*. Louisville, Ky.: Westminster John Knox, 1998.

Leslie, Elmer. *Jeremiah: Chronologically Arranged, Translated, and Interpreted*. New York: Abingdon, 1954.

Lind, Millard C. *Ezekiel*. Scottdale, Pa.: Herald Press, 1996.

Lindars, Barnabas. *Judges 1–5: A New Translation and Commentary*. Edinburgh: T. & T. Clark, 1995.

Lipiński, Eduard. Review of Arvid S. Kapelrud, *The Message of the Prophet Zephaniah: Morphology and Ideas*. *Vetus Testamentum* 25 (1975): 688–91.

Luzzatto, Samuel D. *The Book of Genesis: A Commentary by ShaDaL*. Northvale, N.J.: Jason Aronson, 1998.

Maier, Walter A. *The Book of Nahum: A Commentary.* St. Louis: Concordia Publishing House, 1959.

Maisler, Benjamin. "Two Hebrew Ostraca from Tell Qasile." *Journal of Near Eastern Studies* 10 (1951): 265–67.

Malamat, Abraham. "Foot-Runners in Israel and Egypt in the Third Intermediate Period." *Hommages à Jean Leclant* 4 (1994): 199–201.

Marbury, Edward. *Obadiah and Habakkuk.* Ann Arbor: Sovereign Grace Publishers, 1960.

Marcus, George E., and Michael M. J. Fischer. *Anthropology as Cultural Critique: An Experiment in the Human Sciences.* Chicago: University of Chicago Press, 1986.

Martin, Clarice. "The *Haustafeln* (Household Codes) in African American Biblical Interpretation: 'Free Slaves' and 'Subordinate Women.'" Pages 206–31 in *Stony the Road We Trod: African American Biblical Interpretation*, Edited by Cain Hope Felder; Minneapolis: Fortress, 1991.

Martin, James D. *The Book of Judges.* Cambridge: Cambridge University Press, 1975.

Martin-Achard, Robert. *Amos: L'homme, le Message, l'influence.* Geneva: Labor et Fides, 1984.

Matthews, Isaac G. *Ezekiel.* Philadelphia: Judson, 1939.

May, Herbert G. *Oxford Bible Atlas.* New York: Oxford University Press, 1989.

Mays, James Luther. *Amos: A Commentary.* Philadelphia: Westminster, 1969.

McCarter, P. Kyle. *II Samuel: A New Translation with Introduction, Notes and Commentary.* Anchor Bible 9. Garden City, N.Y.: Doubleday, 1984.

McFall, Ernest A. *Approaching the Nuer of Africa through the Old Testament.* South Pasadena, Calif.: William Carey Library, 1970.

McKenzie, John L. *Second Isaiah: Introduction, Translation, and Notes.* Anchor Bible 20. Garden City, N.Y.: Doubleday, 1968.

Mendenhall, George E. "Midian." Pages 815–18 in vol. 4 of *The Anchor Bible Dictionary.* Edited by D. N. Freedman. New York: Doubleday, 1992.

Meshel, Zeev. "Did Yahweh Have a Consort?" *Biblical Archaeology Review* 5 (1979): 24–34.

Meyers, Carol, and Eric Meyers. *Haggai, Zechariah 1–8: A New Translation with Introduction and Commentary.* Anchor Bible 25b; Garden City, N.Y.: Doubleday, 1987.

—*Zechariah 9–14: A New Translation with Introduction and Commentary.* Anchor Bible 25c; Garden City, N.Y.: Doubleday, 1993.

Millard, Alan R. "Literacy (Israel)." Pages 337–40 in vol. 4 of *The Anchor Bible Dictionary.* Edited by D. N. Freedman. New York: Doubleday, 1992.

Miller, J. Maxwell, and John H. Hayes. *A History of Ancient Israel and Judah.* Philadelphia: Westminster, 1986.

Mitten, David G. "The Synagogue and the 'Byzantine Shops.'" *Bulletin of the American Schools of Oriental Research* 177 (1965): 17–37.

Monges, Miriam Ma'at-Ka-Re. *Kush: An Afrocentric Perspective (Sudan).* Ph.D. diss., Temple University, 1995.

Montagu, Ashley. *Man's Most Dangerous Myth: The Fallacy of Race.* New York: Columbia University Press, 1945.

Moore, Carey A. "Esther, Book of." Pages 633–43 in vol. 2 of *The Anchor Bible Dictionary.* Edited by D. N. Freedman. New York: Doubleday, 1992.

Morkhol, Otto. *Antiochus IV of Syria.* Copenhagen: Gyldendal, 1966.

Moussa, Ahmed M. "A Stela of Taharqa for the Desert Road of Dahshur." *Mitteilungen des Deutschen archaologischen Instituts.* 37 (1981): 331–37.

Müller, Walter W. "Havilah." Pages 82–83 in vol. 3 of *The Anchor Bible Dictionary.* Edited by D. N. Freedman. New York: Doubleday, 1992.

— "Pishon." Page 374 in vol. 5 of *The Anchor Bible Dictionary.* Edited by D. N. Freedman. New York: Doubleday, 1992.

—"Seba." Page 1064 in vol. 5 of *The Anchor Bible Dictionary*. Edited by D. N. Freedman. New York: Doubleday, 1992.

Myers, Jacob M. *II Chronicles: Translation and Notes*. Anchor Bible 13. Garden City, N.Y.: Doubleday, 1965.

Neher, André. *Amos: Contribution à l'etude du Prophetisme*. Paris: J. Vrin, 1981.

Nelson, Richard D. *First and Second Kings*. Atlanta: John Knox, 1987.

Nicholson, Ernest W. *The Book of the Prophet Jeremiah Chapters 26–52*. New York: Cambridge University Press, 1975.

North, Robert "Ophir/ Parvaim and Petra/ Joktheel." *Proceedings of the World Congress of Jewish Studies* 4 (1967): 197–202.

Noth, Martin. *Numbers: A Commentary*. Philadelphia: Westminster, 1968.

—*The Old Testament World*. Translated by Victor I. Gruhn. Philadelphia: Fortress, 1966.

O'Connor, David. *Ancient Nubia: Egypt's Rival in Africa*. Philadelphia: University of Pennsylvania, 1993.

Oduyoye, Modupe. *The Sons of Gods and the Daughters of Men: An Afro-Asiatic Interpretation of Genesis 1–11*. Maryknoll, N.Y.: Orbis Books, 1974.

Oliver, Roland, and Fagan B. *Africa in the Iron Age*. Cambridge: Cambridge University Press, 1975.

Oppenheim, A. Leo. "Sargon II (721–705): The Fall of Samaria." Pages 195–98 in *The Ancient Near East: An Anthology of Texts and Pictures*, Vol.1. Edited by James B. Pritchard. Princeton, N.J.: Princeton University Press, 1973.

—"Sennacherib (704–681): The Seige of Jerusalem." Pages 199–200 in *The Ancient Near East: An Anthology of Text and Pictures*, Vol. 1. Edited by James B. Pritchard. Princeton, N.J.: Princeton University Press, 1973.

Oswalt, John. *The Book of Isaiah: Chapters 1–39*. Grand Rapids: Eerdmans, 1986.

Overholt, Thomas W. *Cultural Anthropology and the Old Testament*. Minneapolis: Fortress, 1996.

Painter, John. *Mark's Gospel: Worlds in Conflict*. London: Routledge, 1997.

Peterson, Thomas. *Ham and Japheth: The Mythic World of Whites in the Antebellum South*. Metuchen, N.J.: Scarecrow, 1978.

Plumley, J. Martin. *Nubian Studies: Proceedings of the Symposium for Nubian Studies*. Warminster: Aris & Phillips, 1982.

Porteous, Norman W. *Daniel: A Commentary*. Philadelphia: Westminster, 1965.

Pritchard, James B., ed. *The Ancient Near East : An Anthology of Texts and Pictures*. Vol.1 Princeton, N.J.: Princeton University Press, 1973.

—*Solomon and Sheba*. London: Phaidon, 1974.

Rad, Gerhard von. *Genesis: A Commentary*. Philadelphia: Westminster, 1961.

Redford, Donald B. *Egypt, Canaan and Israel in Ancient Times*. Princeton, N.J.: Princeton University Press, 1992.

—"Relations between Palestine and Egypt." *Journal of the American Oriental Society* 93 (1973): 3–17.

—"Shishak." Pages 1221–22 in vol. 5 of *The Anchor Bible Dictionary*. Edited by D. N. Freedman. New York: Doubleday, 1992.

—"Taharqa in Western Asia and Libya," *Eretz Israel* 24 (1993): 188–91.

—"Thebes." Pages 442–43 in vol. 6 of *The Anchor Bible Dictionary*. Edited by D. N. Freedman. New York: Doubleday, 1992.

Reich, Ronny and Eli Shukron, "Light at the End of the Tunnel—Warren's Shaft Theory of David's Conquest Shattered." *Biblical Archaeology Review* 25 (Jan–Feb 1999): 22–33, 72.

Reinhartz, Adele. *"Why Ask My Name?" Anonymity and Identity in Biblical Narrative*. New York: Oxford University Press, 1998.

Reisner, George A. "The Viceroys of Ethiopia." *Journal of Egyptian Archaeology* 6 (1920): 28–55, 74–85.

Rice, Gene. "African Roots of the Prophet Zephaniah." *Journal of Religious Thought* 36 (1979): 21–31.

—"The Curse that Never Was (Genesis 9:18–27)," *The Journal of Religious Thought* 29 (1972): 5–27.

—"Two Contemporaries of Jeremiah." *Journal of Religious Thought* 32 (1975): 95–109.

—"Was Amos a Racist?" *The Journal of Religious Thought* 35 (1978): 35–44.

Rigby, Peter. *African Images: Racism and the End of Anthropology*. Oxford: Berg, 1996.

Robertson, Robert G. "Ezekiel the Tragedian." Pages 803–20 in vol. 2 of *The Old Testament Pseudepigrapha*. Edited by J. H. Charlesworth. 2 vols. New York: Doubleday, 1983.

Rogerson, John W. "Anthropology and the Old Testament." Pages 17–38 in *The World of Ancient Israel: Sociological, Anthropological and Political Perspectives*. Edited by Ronald E. Clements. Cambridge: Cambridge University Press, 1991.

Rogerson, John W., and John W. McKay. *Psalms 1–50*. Cambridge: Cambridge University Press, 1977.

Routtenberg, Hyman J. *Amos of Tekoa: A Study in Interpretation*. New York: Vantage, 1971.

Rowley, Harold H. *Job*. Grand Rapids: Eerdmans, 1980.

Rowley-Conway, P. "The Camel in the Nile Valley: New Radiocarbon Accelerator (AMS) Dates for Qasr Ibrim.'" in *Journal of Egyptian Archaeology* 74 (1988): 245–48.

Rushton, J. Philippe. *Race, Evolution, and Behavior*. New Brunswick, N.J.: Transaction, 1994.

—*Race, Evolution, and Behaviour*. Special Abridged ed. New Brunswick, N.J.: Transaction, 1999.

Russell, David S. *Jews from Alexander to Herod*. London: Oxford University Press, 1967.

Ryou, Daniel Hojoon. *Zephaniah's Oracles against the Nations: A Synchronic and Diachronic Study of Zephaniah 2:1–3:8*. Leiden: Brill, 1995.

Sabourin, Leopold. *The Psalms: Their Origin and Meaning*. Staten Island, N.Y.: Alba House, 1969.

Scharfstein, Ben-Ami, Raphael Sappan, and Zevi Scharfstein, eds. *English–Hebrew Dictionary*. Tel Aviv: Dvir Publishing Company, 1961.

Scullion, John J. "The Narrative of Genesis." Page 948 in vol. 2 of *The Anchor Bible Dictionary*. Edited by D. N. Freedman. New York: Doubleday, 1992.

Seebass, Horst. *Genesis I: Urgeschichte (1,1–11, 26)*. Neukirchen–Vluyn: Neukirchener, 1996.

Selman, Martin J. *2 Chronicles*. Leicester: Inter-Varsity, 1994.

Sertima, Ivan van. *Nile Valley Civilizations*. New Brunswick: Transaction Periodical Consortium, 1985.

Shanks, Hershel. "Everything You Ever Knew about Jerusalem is Wrong." *Biblical Archaeology Review* 6 (1999): 20–29.

Shea, William H. "Jerusalem Under Siege: Did Sennacherib Attack Twice?" *Biblical Archaeology Review* 25 (1999): 36–44, 64.

—"The New Tirhakah Text and Sennacherib's Second Palestinian Campaign." *Andrews University Seminary Studies* 35 (1997): 181–87.

Shinnie, Peter L. *Ancient Nubia*. London: Kegan Paul, 1996.

—"Trade Routes of the Ancient Sudan 3,000 BC–AD 350," Pages 49–53 in *Egypt and Africa: Nubia from Prehistory to Islam*. Edited by Winifred V. Davies; London: British Museum, 1993.

Simons, Jan "The 'Table of Nations' (Genesis 10): Its General Structure and Meaning." Pages 234–53 in *I Studied Inscriptions from before the Flood: Ancient Near Eastern, Literary, and Linguistic Approaches to Genesis 1–11*. Edited by Richard S. Hess and David Toshio Tsumura. Winona Lake, Ind.: Eisenbrauns, 1994.

Sivan, Reuben and Edward A. Levenston, eds. *The Megiddo Modern Dictionary Hebrew–English*. Tel Aviv: Megiddo, 1965.

Smedley, Audrey. *Race in North America: Origin and Evolution of a Worldview.* Boulder: Westview, 1993.

Smith, Gary V. *Amos: A Commentary.* Grand Rapids: Zondervan, 1989.

Smith, George Adam. *The Book of Isaiah.* Vol. 1, *Isaiah 1–39.* New York: Armstrong & Son, 1890.

Smith, Mark S. *The Early History of God: Yahweh and the Other Deities in Ancient Israel.* San Francisco: HarperSanFrancisco, 1990.

Smith, Regina. "A New Perspective on Amos 9.7a 'To Me, O Israel, You are Just Like the Kushites.'" *The Journal of the Interdenominational Theological Center* 22 (1994): 36–47.

Smith, Shelton H. *In His Image, But....* Durham, N.C.: Duke University Press, 1972.

Smith, Stuart Tyson. "A Model for Egyptian Imperialism in Nubia." *GM* 122 (1991): 77–122.

Snaith, Norman H. "2 Kings," *IB* 3:187-338.

Snowden, Jr., Frank M. *Before Color Prejudice: Ancient View of the Blacks.* Cambridge, Mass.: Harvard University Press, 1983.

—*Blacks in Anitiquity: Ethiopians in the Greco-Roman Experience.* Cambridge, Mass.: Harvard University Press, 1970.

Soggin, J. Alberto. *Introduction to the Old Testament: From its Origins to the Closing of the Alexandrian Canon.* Translated by John Bowden. Louisville, Ky.: Westminster John Knox, 1989.

—*Judges: A Commentary.* Philadelphia: Westminster, 1981.

—*The Prophet Amos: A Translation and Commentary.* Translated by John Bowden. London: SCM Press, 1987.

Sollors, Werner. *Beyond Ethnicity: Consent and Descent in American Culture.* New York: Oxford University Press, 1986.

—*The Invention of Ethnicity.* New York: Oxford University Press, 1989.

Speiser, Ephraim A. "In Search of Nimrod." Pages 270–77 in *I Studied Inscriptions from before the Flood: Ancient Near Eastern, Literary, and Linguistic Approaches to Genesis 1–11.* Edited by Richard S. Hess and David Toshio Tsumura. Winona Lake, Ind.: Eisenbrauns, 1994.

Stalker, David Muir Gibson. *Ezekiel: Introduction and Commentary.* London: SCM Press, 1968.

Stiehl, Ruth. "Das Buch Esther." Pages 249–67 in *Studies in the Book of Esther.* Edited by Carey A. Moore. New York: Ktav, 1982.

Stonehouse, George G. V. *The Books of the Prophets Zephaniah and Nahum.* London: Methuen, 1929.

*Sudan: Ancient Kingdoms of the Nile.* Paris: Institut du Monde Arab and Munich: Kunsthalle der Hypo-Kulturstiftung, 1997.

Szeles, Maria Eszenyei. *Wrath and Mercy: A Commentary on the Books of Habakkuk and Zephaniah.* Grand Rapids: Eerdmans, 1987.

Tcherikover, Avigdor. *Hellenistic Civilization and the Jews.* Translated by S. Applebaum. Philadelphia: Jewish Publication Society of America, 1959.

Templeton, Alan. "Human Races: A Genetic and Evolutionary Perspective." *American Anthropologist* 100 (1998): 632–50.

Thompson, Henry O. "Kir. 2," Pages 83–84 in vol. 4 of *The Anchor Bible Dictionary.* Edited by D. N. Freedman. New York: Doubleday, 1992.

Thompson, John A. *The Book of Jeremiah.* Grand Rapids: Eerdmans, 1980.

Thompson, Lloyd A. *Romans and Blacks.* London: Oklahoma: Routledge/Oklahoma University Press, 1989.

Thompson, Thomas L. *The Mythic Past: Biblical Archeology and the Myth of Israel.* New York: Basic Books, 1999.

Toivanen, Aarne. "A Bible Translation as the Communicator of Alien Culture." *Temenos: Studies in Comparative Religion* 26 (1990): 129–37.

Torok, Lazslo. "Iconography and Mentality: Three Remarks on the Kushite Way of Thinking." Pages 195–204 in *Egypt and Africa: Nubia from Prehistory to Islam*. Edited by William V. Davies. London: British Museum, 1993.

Tov, Emanuel. "The Book of Jeremiah: A Work in Progress." *Bible Review* 15 (2000): 32–38, 45.

Towner, W. Sibley. *Daniel*. Atlanta: John Knox, 1984.

Trigger, Bruce. *Nubia Under the Pharaohs*. London: Thames & Hudson, 1976.

Tur-Sinai, Naphtali H. *The Book of Job: A New Commentary*. Jerusalem: Kiryath Sepher, 1967.

Ullendorff, Edward. *Ethiopia and the Bible*. Oxford: Oxford University Press, 1968.

Van Henten, Jan W. "Antiochus IV as a Typhonic Figure in Daniel 7." Pages 223–43 in *The Book of Daniel in Light of New Findings*. Edited by Adam S. Van Der Woude. Leuven: Leuven University Press, 1993.

Wade, G. W. *The Book of the Prophet Isaiah: With Introduction and Notes*. London: Methuen, 1929.

Waters, John W. "Who was Hagar?" Pages 187–205 in *Stony the Road We Trod: African American Biblical Interpretation*. Edited by Cain Hope Felder. Minneapolis: Fortress, 1991.

Watts, John D. *The Books of Joel, Obadiah, Jonah, Nahum, Habakkuk and Zephaniah*. Cambridge: Cambridge University Press, 1975.

Webb, B. G. *The Book of Judges: An Integrated Reading*. Journal for the Study of the Old Testament Supplement Series 46; Sheffield: Sheffield Academic Press, 1987.

Weber, Max. "Ethnic Groups." Pages 301–9 in *Theories of Society*. Edited by Talcott Parsons, Edward Shils, K. D. Naegele, and J. Pitts. New York: Free Press, 1961.

Webster, Noah, and Jean L. McKechnie, eds. *Websters New Universal Unabridged Dictionary*. New York: Dorset & Baber, 1983.

Weiser, Artur. *The Psalms: A Commentary*. Translated by Herbert Hartwell. Philadelphia: Westminster, 1962.

Welsby, Derek A. *The Kingdom of Kush: The Napatan and Meroitic Empires*. Princeton, N.J.: Markus Wiener, 1998.

Wenham, Gordon J. *Numbers: An Introduction and Commentary*. Leicester: Inter-Varsity, 1981.

—*Numbers*. Old Testament Guides 5. Sheffield: Sheffield Academic Press, 1997.

West, Cornel. *Prophesy Deliverance:Afro-American Revolutionary Christianity*. Philadelphia: Westminster, 1982.

Westermann, Claus. *Genesis 1–11: A Commentary*. Minneapolis: Augsburg, 1984.

—*Isaiah 40–66*. Philadelphia: Westminster, 1969.

Wevers, John W. *Ezekiel*. London: Thomas Nelson, 1969.

White, Sidnie Ann. "Esther." Pages 124–29 in *The Women's Bible Commentary*, Edited by Carol A. Newsome and Sharon H. Ringe. Louisville, Ky.: Westminster John Knox, 1992.

Whitehorne, John. "Antiochus." Pages 269–72 in vol. 1 of *The Anchor Bible Dictionary*. Edited by D. N. Freedman. New York: Doubleday, 1992.

Whitney, Glayed. "On Possible Genetic Bases of Race Differences in Criminality." Pages 134–49 in *Crime in Biological, Social, and Moral Contests*. Edited by Lee Ellis and Harry Hoffman. New York: Prager, 1990.

Whybray, Roger N. *Isaiah 40–66*. Grand Rapids: Eerdmans, 1981.

Wildberger, Hans. *Isaiah 1–12: A Commentary*. Translated by Thomas H. Trapp. Minneapolis: Fortress, 1991.

Williams, Chancellor. *The Destruction of African Civilization*. Chicago: Third World Press, 1974.

Williamson, Hugh G. M. *1 and 2 Chronicles*. New Century Bible Commentary. Grand Rapids: Eerdmans, 1982.

Willoughby, Bruce E. "Amos, Book of." Pages 203–12 in vol. 1 of *The Anchor Bible Dictionary*. Edited by D. N. Freedman. New York: Doubleday, 1992.

Wilson, Andrew. *The Nations in Deutero-Isaiah: A Study on Composition and Structure.* Lewiston, New York: Edwin Mellen, 1986.

Wilson, Robert R. "Genealogy, Genealogies." Pages 929–32 in vol. 2 of *The Anchor Bible Dictionary*. Edited by D. N. Freedman. New York: Doubleday, 1992.

—*Prophecy and Society in Ancient Israel*. Philadelphia: Fortress Press, 1980.

Wiseman, Donald J. *1 and 2 Kings*, Vol. 2 (Leicester: Inter-Varsity, 1993)

—"Genesis 10: Some Archaeological Considerations." Pages 254–65 in *I Studied Inscriptions from before the Flood: Ancient Near Eastern, Literary, and Linguistic Approaches to Genesis 1–11*. Edited by Richard S. Hess and David Toshio Tsumura. Winona Lake, Ind.: Eisenbrauns, 1994.

Wolff, Hans Walter. *Joel and Amos: A Commentary on the Books of the Prophets Joel and Amos*. Philadelphia: Fortress, 1977.

Young, Edward J. *The Book of Isaiah: The English Text, with Introduction, Exposition and Notes*. Grand Rapids: Eerdmans, 1965.

Zimmerli, Walther. *Ezekiel 2*. Translated by James D. Martin. Philadelphia, Fortress, 1983.


*Websites:*

<http://www.pbs.org/wgbh/nova/israel/familylemba.html>

<http://www.pbs.org/wgbh/nova/israel/parfitt.html>

<http://www.pbs.org/wgbh/nova/israel/parfitt2.html>

# Index of Authors